TRINITY AND TRUTH
ooooooooooo

SPIRITUALITY AND THEOLOGY

First published in 1998 by
Darton, Longman and Todd Ltd
1 Spencer Court
140–2 Wandsworth High Street
London SW18 4JJ

ISBN 0–232–52188–3

A catalogue record for this book is available from the British Library.

Thanks are due to the following for permission to quote copyright
material: Macmillan General Books for 'Via negativa' by R.S. Thomas
taken from *Later Poems*; Paulist Press for *Julian of Norwich: Showings*
edited by Edmund Colledge and James Walsh.

Phototypeset by Intype London Ltd
Printed and bound in Great Britain by
Page Bros, Norwich

Spirituality and Theolog

Christian Living and the Doctrine of God

ⵊⵊⵊⵊⵊⵊ

PHILIP SHELDRAKE

DΛRTON·LONGMAN + TODD

CONTENTS

∞∞∞∞∞∞∞

FOREWORD

◇◇◇◇◇◇◇◇◇◇

Trinity and Truth is a series of theological books written by authors convinced that there is truth to be spoken about God, and that such truth is best explored when we speak about God as Father, Son and Holy Spirit.

Such a claim for truth has always been controversial. In the fourth Gospel's account of his trial before Pilate, Jesus said, 'All who are not deaf to truth listen to my voice.' Pilate's famous reply, 'What is truth?' was neither jest nor invitation to philosophical debate. It was an expression of impatient dissent. He intended to be understood as the sole arbiter of truth, because his was (he believed) the dominant ideology. And to illustrate how feeble were the claims of the 'king of the Jews', whose invisible 'kingdom' seemed to be on the point of collapse, Pilate had Jesus flogged.

Pilate's question has a postmodern ring about it. The truth for him was the extent to which he could impose his power over Jesus, and everyone else within range of his voice. But, said the writer of the fourth Gospel, this mockery of a judicial process contained the reversal of appearances. It is the judge who is judged. The prince of this world turns out to be powerless. There is another truth, which is a way, which leads to life.

In the long and turbulent history of Christian theology it has often been forgotten that belief in the Trinity entails a way of life. To many the doctrine of the Trinity has seemed too erudite to be relevant; and in truth theologians have not always avoided a self-defeating level of detailed pseudo-precision. But the fearsome complexities of the classic disputes of the early centuries are not the main concern of this series. The authors intend, instead, to demonstrate Trinitarian theology at work in the exploration and elucidation of modern questions.

Augustine of Hippo once pointed out that merely to utter the names, Father, Son and Holy Spirit, is physically to separate the sounds in time, and so to be misleading about the unity of 'substance' or 'being' of the three; for there is an irreplaceable history of narrative attaching to each of these names. And so what we signify when we utter the simple word 'God', is rich, complex and full of resource.

It is the purpose of this series to draw upon the continuing resourcefulness of Trinitarian theology. The books will not be restricted to expositions of classic doctrines, but will concern every aspect of Christian life, worship and spirituality. Ancient orthodoxy was never intended to be a static, backward-looking set of intellectual constraints. It is the belief of the authors of this series that the Trinitarian traditions of the Church are subversive and liberating convictions founded upon a willingness to listen freshly to the voice of truth.

STEPHEN SYKES
Bishop of Ely

PREFACE

∞∞∞∞∞∞∞∞

I am grateful for the opportunity to attempt a book on the relationship between spirituality and theology. It is a subject which has preoccupied me for some years. The invitation to write has forced me to gather my thoughts and some scattered material into some kind of provisional order.

Many people have contributed to the book in a variety of ways. Its origins lie partly in teaching spirituality. Much of the material has been used, refined and revised as the result of classes with students at London University, in Cambridge and at the University of Notre Dame as well as with participants in adult education and ministry formation courses. I am also grateful to former colleagues at Heythrop College, London, *The Way* journal and in the Cambridge Theological Federation for many stimulating conversations and thoughtful questions. In particular, I want to thank Michael Barnes for dialogue and friendship over many years. The Society for the Study of Christian Spirituality has offered me numerous opportunities for exchanges with American colleagues. In terms of this book, I am especially grateful for helpful conversations with Douglas Burton-Christie, Arthur Holder and Sandra Schneiders.

I could not have completed the book without study leave. I want to thank colleagues and friends at Westcott House, Cambridge for enabling me to take a sabbatical in

1996 and for a travel grant supplemented by a further award from the Divinity Faculty. My appointment as Visiting Scholar at The Church Divinity School of the Pacific, Berkeley, California enabled me to benefit from an excellent library and opportunities to contribute to seminars as well as to make new friends in the Graduate Theological Union. I also have affectionate memories of the warm hospitality of Ray Bucher and all the members of San Damiano Retreat, Danville. I was able to put the final touches to the book in the autumn of 1997 with the help of a temporary research post at The Queen's Foundation, Birmingham. As editor of the series, Bishop Sykes offered wise advice on aspects of the final draft. In the end, however, no one apart from myself is responsible for the foibles and imperfections of the book.

Finally, I want to acknowledge a very special debt to Susie without whose partnership, love and encouragement this book, along with so much else, would never have come to fruition.

Philip Sheldrake
Spring 1998

INTRODUCTION

The main purpose of this book is to suggest not only the possibility but the necessity of bridging the historic division between love and knowledge in the human approach to God. To affirm that spirituality and theology are related implies two things. First, and most importantly, our attempts to talk about the Christian doctrine of God cannot be separated from personal faith and spiritual experience. Second, there are signs of a contemporary convergence between theology and the new scholarly field of 'spirituality' which has replaced the older disciplines of ascetical and mystical theology. The present convergence is encouraging both for spirituality and for theology. It is important to set this movement within a wider historical context. This book will therefore offer a historical as well as theoretical and evaluative approach to the relationship between spirituality and theology.

The discussion of spirituality and theology is a broad topic. To make it more precise, the book offers reflections on the doctrine of God, the Trinity, as a theme throughout. I hope that this will demonstrate that the doctrine of the Trinity – and different approaches to this question – is absolutely central to the coherence and cogency of any properly Christian spirituality. This is important as much contemporary spiritual writing is open to the accusation that it amounts to little more than uncritical devotion quite detached from the major themes of Christian faith. My necessary disclaimer is that the book does not pretend to offer a comprehensive survey or evaluation either of the history of Trinitarian theology or of contemporary approaches to the subject. This will be addressed elsewhere in the series of which this book is a part. My approach is highly selective in that the Trinitarian theme is subordinated to the broader question of the nature of spirituality and its relationship to theology.

Some people may question the appropriateness of taking the Trinity as the main theological theme. It is often assumed that theologies of the human person (Christian anthropology) or sacramental theology provide the best starting points for examining the connection between spirituality and theology. These aspects of theology at least have the merit of beginning with 'the human condition'. This seems to accord most closely with the experiential basis of spirituality. It also fits the contemporary emphasis in theology on inductive method and on experience as the starting point for reflection. However, I would suggest that to take the doctrine of God as the main area of reflection need not involve a retreat into abstraction away from such methods or emphases.

The justification for this assertion is not difficult to describe. For the Christian it is impossible in practice to separate experiences of self from experiences of God or vice versa. While it may be said that *the* fundamental human experience is of the self or of one's own being, it may also be said that at the heart of this experience lies the Absolute. Put in more explicitly Christian terms, human beings experience themselves most completely as recipients of God's self-gift. There may then be a movement from the human self as gifted to the nature of God as the giver of gifts and as one who communicates to the world in love. The way Christians name this God, whose very life is to give and to reveal, is Trinity. It is to be hoped that what follows will show that the doctrine of the Trinity (especially as developed in modern theology) is not an *a priori* abstraction with no implications for Christian living – the 'life in the Spirit' that lies at the heart of what we define as spirituality. On the contrary, the naming of God as Trinity, more than any other belief, enshrines the specific riches of the Christian spiritual tradition. The problem is that a superficial examination of our contemporary Western cultural contexts reveals a suspicion of religious dogma. The openings for the development of a doctrinally rich spirituality do not seem promising. Yet as the opening part of this book attempts to demonstrate, such an analysis of contemporary attitudes may be unnecessarily pessimistic.

STRUCTURE OF THE BOOK

The book is divided into two main sections. Section One considers methodological questions. Chapter 1 initially examines some relevant aspects of Western culture particularly the experience labelled 'postmodernity' and the theories that claim to describe it. The chapter then sets out some general questions regarding the relationship between spirituality and theology within these contemporary intellectual horizons. The relationship of spirituality and theology has a long and chequered history. Thus Chapter 2 offers a selective historical overview of the relationship with some specific reference to the doctrine of God. The period since the 1950s has seen not merely the emergence of approaches to theology that are more sympathetic to spirituality but also the development of spirituality as a renewed discipline. Chapter 3 examines the attempts to reintegrate theology and spirituality. It begins by evaluating some modern theologians and schools of theology that have been most influential in this regard.

These will include such people as Bernard Lonergan, Karl Rahner, Jürgen Moltmann, Hans Urs von Balthasar, Wolfhart Pannenberg and David Tracy as well as the growing body of writings in feminist and liberation theologies. The chapter continues with some remarks on how the modern re-evaluation of the doctrine of the Trinity is having a particular impact on the reintegration of theology with spirituality. It is important to consider some of the differences of opinion about this and the main lines of the current, and as yet inconclusive, methodological debate will be analyzed. Finally, the chapter considers how spirituality and theology offer guidelines for the mutual evaluation of each other. Particular attention will be paid to theological criteria (not least theologies of God) for evaluating the adequacy and appropriateness of the wisdom of spiritual traditions.

Section Two of the book moves on from methodological questions to ground some of these in concrete examples or case studies. It is worth spending a moment to reflect on the ideas and principles that lie behind the choice of examples. Contemporary Western culture is often thought of as religiously apathetic. Yet there is also a phenomenon that the American theologian David Tracy has described as 'the strange return of God'.[1] This return is best expressed in a theology and spirituality that base themselves strongly on some challenging themes. The vision of God is of both an eschatological God and (following Bonhoeffer and theologians of liberation) a suffering God on the cross who disrupts any temptation to believe that humanity can somehow capture the Absolute Other. This God, who is strange and elusive rather than familiar or 'domestic', may be approached through longing and yet cannot be possessed and seems to overflow in particular into human frailty, woundedness, imperfection – the margins in fact. In Christian terms, the postmodern search for mystical union with a God who is and does more than we can conceive, for association with the Christ who suffers abandonment yet is the invincible ground of hope and for a prophetic message of liberation rooted in the experience of margins is reflected in important elements of the spiritual tradition.

The case studies begin with two chapters that examine the writings of three important spiritual teachers from different times and places. Apart from the fact that the doctrine of God plays a central role in each of the traditions chosen, their themes and approach fit rather well with the preoccupations I have just mentioned and will discuss in the first chapter. The three texts are the *Showings* of fourteenth-century English mystic Julian of Norwich, *The Spiritual Exercises* of Ignatius Loyola, one of the most significant figures of the sixteenth-century Catholic Reformation and finally the poetry of the seventeenth-century Anglican priest and poet George Herbert. It would have been quite traditional to associate Julian of Norwich with George Herbert as representatives of a distinctively English spiritual tradition. However it is perhaps more interesting to link Herbert with Ignatius Loyola and to compare them as two major figures of the Reformation era on different sides of the denominational divide.

The third case study concerns an important but neglected spiritual and theological theme, our understanding of place, rather than a specific spiritual tradition. The nature of place is not only a central aspect of human experience but is also an important preoccupation in much contemporary discussion about human identity and our quality of life. The chapter offers a reflection on how the theme of place, not least the contemporary crisis of place, may be illuminated by the Christian spiritual tradition and the doctrine of God.

Finally, this book has a dual purpose. The main readership is intended to be people who are studying spirituality and theology as well as other readers who have a love of the subjects. An important development over the last decade or so has been the growth of courses in Christian spirituality in a variety of contexts. These need to have a substantial theological element. The notes and a full bibliography are intended to help readers to pursue the subject matter further. When it came to classical sources it seemed appropriate to confine my references mostly to modern translations that were readily available. However, there is a second purpose. While the book does not pretend to be highly academic in a specialized sense, I hope that it may nevertheless make a modest contribution to the continuing discussion among English-speaking scholars about the relationship between spirituality and theology.

PART ONE

THEORETICAL QUESTIONS

1

ooooooooo

Living Our Theology

The great American Jewish theologian, Abraham Heschel, once wrote that 'The issue of prayer is not prayer; the issue of prayer is God'.[1] In other words, the question that lies behind every religious theory or practice is a God question. Who God is and how God is disclosed are questions that lie at the heart of Christian faith. They are, therefore, connected to our religious experience. Attempts to speak about our understanding of God (theology) and our efforts to live in the light of that understanding (spirituality) cannot be separated. This belief is the thread that runs through this chapter. We cannot do theology without risking faith commitment and we cannot be committed to Christian practices without attending to the fundamental beliefs that underpin the Christian story. Hence the title of this chapter, 'Living Our Theology'.

A theology that is alive is always grounded in spiritual experience. If it is to be complete, theology needs to be *lived* just as much as it needs to be studied and explained. To some people this will appear to be a statement of the blindingly obvious. However, intellectual assumptions born of the Enlightenment are still pervasive in theological circles and are not always at ease with the notion of 'experience', 'practice' or 'application'. Such words seem to imply uncritical subjectivity or a dangerous sectarianism. People who are not trained as theologians and who seek spirituality may in turn be equally suspicious of theological theory. They feel that it encourages a kind of dogmatism that can enslave us or a dry rationalism that inhibits our attention to experience.

SPIRITUALITY AND BELIEF

Western Christianity has to survive nowadays in a fluid and intellectually uncertain culture. Yet Christian faith has traditionally been quite detailed in its attempts to articulate what it understands to be the nature of God as revealed in Jesus Christ. Is this now a problem? Has there been too much dogma in Christianity for its own and everyone's good? The word 'theology' is now quite regularly used, outside as well as inside religious circles, to indicate a fiddling concern with any kind of irrelevant or unverifiable detail. For example, even within the Christian community some people see the doctrine of the Trinity as a redundant relic from a time when theology was disengaged from the real world. It was so disengaged that theology had all the time in the world (and, perhaps, eternity) to spend in trying to solve God's own crossword puzzle. Trinitarian doctrine is worth a great deal more than this but I confess to having a sneaking sympathy with the problem.

As a result of such negative perceptions, there is a great deal of 'practical Unitarianism' around these days. By that I mean that modern religious sensibilities are often content with a fairly undefined 'God' and with Jesus as a great spiritual and moral teacher. If there is a sense of God's Spirit operating within time and space it is likely to be confined to a kind of pantheistic understanding of the spiritual qualities of the Earth or of matter generally.

For contemporary Christians, spirituality is no longer simply a logical consequence of doctrines within a theology that is logically deduced from first principles. Yet, while such abstract ways of thinking about theology are

4

unhelpful, we cannot escape from questions of belief. Our whole sense of the world in which we live is the product of the frameworks of belief that we carry with us. These affect our experiences, not least our spiritual ones, and how we interpret them. To some extent, the separation of theology from human experience came about because believers internalized a post-Reformation, post-Enlightenment opposition between the 'secular' and 'sacred' spheres of human life. For example, the radical separation of Church and State in the United States' Constitution is as much an expression of this intellectual position as it is of a desire to protect society from sectarian divisions. Strangely both the approach of liberal believers (public secularity combined with private religion) and fundamentalist rejections of the world as sinful and Godless are logical consequences of this separation.

Paradoxically, a widespread decline in traditional religious practice in the West runs parallel with an ever-increasing hunger for spirituality. The question at the forefront of most of the great spiritual classics used to be 'What or who is God?' Nowadays the characteristic question of the contemporary spiritual seeker is more likely to be 'Who am I?' Great Christian teachers of the past such as Julian of Norwich understood quite clearly that these two questions are inextricably linked.

> And I saw very certainly that we must necessarily be in longing and in penance until the time when we are led so deeply into God that we verily and truly know our own soul.[2]

To be led into God and to 'know our own soul' are two sides of the same coin.

At present there is a kind of doctrinal vacuum both inside and outside Christian communities. In the past there may, in practice, have been more variety in belief within the Christian Churches than appeared on the surface. However, there was a clear bedrock of beliefs that was taken for granted by Christians even if infrequently or never explicitly examined. This former consensus about the language of faith can no longer be taken for granted. Within the Christian community some people question the continued validity of objective ways of thinking or speaking about God. 'God' is merely the word we use to describe the deepest level of value within ourselves.[3]

Beyond the boundaries of the Christian Church, the situation is even more uncertain. Many people are suspicious of religious dogma. A coherent system of belief, and complex language about the nature of God are no longer presumed to be necessary for a fruitful spiritual journey.[4] Alongside the breakdown of former religious certainties there is a more broadly-based cultural fragmentation. This makes public consensus about moral beliefs and behaviour extremely difficult. It also tends to inhibit any sense of common experience. As a result, some theorists argue that it is no longer possible to describe or defend any overarching framework of explanation or of values. Religious doctrines appear as eccentric options with no natural spiritual consequences. This results in a privatization of spirituality and a concentration on interiority. Spiritual experience becomes separated from a social or public vision of ethics. The phrase often used to describe this contemporary experience of fragmentation is postmodernity.

THE EXPERIENCE AND THEORIES OF POSTMODERNITY

There are a variety of theories of postmodernism but all of them reflect upon a common experience known as 'postmodernity'. Its roots appear to lie in the human experience of loss. A sense of loss, it is suggested, has

become more prevalent in the West as we approach the
end of the second millennium. What has been lost and
what is being grieved? Essentially it is the spirit of optimism
and certainty born of what, at the beginning of the twentieth century, appeared to be a stable social, religious,
intellectual and moral order. Continuous social and economic progress seemed to be guaranteed. The human
mind and will were deemed capable, in principle at least,
of addressing any question or of solving any problem that
would present itself. Nowadays it is precisely the nature of
'progress' that appears to be the problem. In the popular
mind, science once offered clear solutions but now raises
the sharpest and most baffling questions. Many of the
factors that eventually undermined our collective sense of
certainty and human self-sufficiency have their origins in
the nineteenth century. However the decisive breakpoint
was marked by the two world wars of the twentieth century.
This period reached an appalling climax in the Nazi extermination camps and the bombing of Hiroshima.[5] We have
lost our innocence. We can no longer afford to be naive
for we have learned too much about the ambiguities of
human behaviour.

The terms 'postmodernity' and 'postmodernism' are
notoriously slippery because they inevitably involve theory
as well as the observation of events. Theorists seem broadly
to support two versions of postmodernism. The first concentrates on demolishing previous assumptions about the
nature of the world and is especially prevalent among
French intellectuals such as Jacques Derrida and Michel
Foucault. These writers are radically suspicious of any normative interpretations of culture. The second form of
postmodernism (represented for example by the German
Hans-Georg Gadamer) recognizes our present social and
cultural fragmentation but seeks to find a strategy to
enable us to reconstruct some kind of authoritative inter-

pretation of events. However this is no longer a question of establishing universal norms. Any new interpretation must encompass the fact that human experience is plural and diverse. It will, therefore, necessarily be complex and untidy.

Both versions of postmodernism have something in common. They reject the intellectual optimism of what is known as 'modernity'. This word refers to Western culture since the Enlightenment and Industrial Revolution. In other words, postmodernism criticizes our confidence in the powers of human reason, in principle, to solve all problems, to discover essential truths or to establish definitive meanings. Postmodernism recognizes that all interpretations of 'truth' are culturally-conditioned, contingent and morally flawed as well as intellectually partial. Some theorists refer to an 'incredulity towards metanarratives'.[6] Such an approach is suspicious of any system of thought, whether philosophical or theological, that seeks to escape totally from the limitations of context. For some people, it is a short step from this suspicion to a rejection of the God of conventional religious institutions. Viewed more broadly, it appears that Western culture is not merely unclear about what it knows but uncertain of what it is to 'know' at all. To people brought up on a diet of what can be proved this is a confusing experience.

DIFFICULTIES IN POSTMODERNISM

As a way of interpreting the world, postmodernism has its dangers and limitations. Of course, even if we accept many of these criticisms of 'modernity' few of us would wish to turn our backs on the freedom that lies at the heart of the vision it created. Positively speaking, modernity has resulted in many social, political and technological achievements. Nor, indeed, can we ignore the ways in which modernity has enriched religious faith by challenging believers to question inappropriate understandings of religious traditions or doctrines.

The health of theology and spirituality is not well-served by a wholesale dependence on postmodern theory.[7] One obvious difficulty is that there are several theories of postmodernism. This fact in itself immediately demands that we exercise critical discernment when examining them. Postmodernism can also fall into the very traps it criticizes. It continually reminds us that for everything we say or do there is a context. It is rightly suspicious of dogmas or ideologies that proclaim a single way of expressing truth for every possible time and place. Such 'metanarratives' (to use a postmodernist term) tend not to acknowledge their own historicity and partiality. However, the theologian Nicholas Lash refers to a postmodern 'veneration of implacability'.[8] What he means is that postmodernism sometimes suggests that there are social and economic forces or structures that affect us in ways quite distinct from our ability to understand or control them. There is no theory to account for these autonomous forces. This can sound remarkably like another kind of ideology.

There is another danger in postmodernism. A suspicion of overall frameworks of explanation can easily lead to a detachment from ethical or political responses to suffering in the real world. The paradoxical flaw at the heart of some postmodernism is its almost dogmatic determination to defend the impossibility of any clear explanation for the way the world is. This inhibits attempts to redevelop a 'responsible (that is, ethical) self'.[9]

We also need to be cautious about the way the terms 'postmodernity' and 'postmodernism' are used. It is inappropriate to use 'postmodernism' to refer to any and every backlash against the rationalism or uncritical liberalism of modernity. Some conservative Christians adopt the terminology of postmodernism in support of vigorous proselytising. They are far removed from many of the values postmodernism stands for. It is true that postmodernism seems to enable religious traditions to be themselves. It frees the notion of 'God' from the constraints of rational philosophy and the need to justify belief in rational terms. On the other hand, properly understood, postmodernism implies a rejection of any kind of literalism. It also rejects authoritarianism and prefers dialogue with strangers and what is 'other' rather than to colonize alien experiences or to convert those who understand the world differently.

SPIRITUALITY AND POSTMODERNITY

From a Christian point of view, does postmodern culture offer an opportunity for spirituality? Some theologians disparage postmodern theory as a basis for deepening faith. For them postmodernism offers no spiritual depth. From this point of view, the postmodern approach to the possibility of 'truth' is inadequate given that Christianity makes universal claims. There is a battle here between two conflicting viewpoints about knowledge.[10] On the one hand, postmodernists (even moderate, theologically-minded ones) affirm that human contexts of history, culture and language are intrinsic to all knowledge. On the other hand, their critics want to continue to affirm a perspective that can speak of truth in a definitive rather than contingent way. It may be that, from the point of view of Christian faith and spirituality, postmodernism offers an important corrective to the tendency to believe that particular words are capable of saying *what is the case* about God in definitive ways. In reality all that we can ever do is to seek to express, haltingly, the inexpressible. The fact will always be that the depths of 'God' ultimately elude our grasp.[11]

When we turn to postmodern writers who are interested in spirituality some are deeply suspicious of traditional religious language. They reject the usefulness or necessity of transcendent realities such as 'God'.[12] However, postmodern culture is not necessarily opposed to religion, to concepts of 'truth', or to ethics and Christian spirituality. Indeed there is often a strange affinity between aspects of postmodern theory and Christian language. Far from being committed exclusively to a kind of nihilism, contemporary Western intellectual enquiry is often fascinated with 'the sacred'. Some Christian observers see in postmodernism the potential to free religion from notions of respectability determined on purely rational grounds. Because postmodernism at best is thoroughly contextual, it can cope more easily than modernity with the distinctive wisdom of particular traditions. Thus postmodernity allows Christianity to be itself in a way that modernity never could.

The roots of contemporary spirituality are to be found in an emphasis on human experience. In all its variety and pain, our ordinary human experience becomes the immediate context for God's self-disclosure. Interestingly, some recent writing on spirituality has adopted from postmodern theorists the suggestion that Auschwitz is *the* symbol of the death of modernism.[13] Auschwitz stands for the 'unrepresentable' and 'unnameable'. Modernism's attempt to reduce reality to the 'rational' is destroyed in the utter irrationality of the Nazi death camps. Paradoxically, at Auschwitz the God of religious systems dies, yet God somehow becomes present in absence. If it is valid to think of Auschwitz in this way, the 'saints' of the wartime era are looked to as prophets of a new spirituality. Some of them, such as the German Lutheran pastor Dietrich Bonhoeffer, adopted a radical stance against politically compromised versions of the Church. Others such as the Jewish writers Simone Weil or Etty Hillesum, because of

11

the complexity of their spiritual vision, existed ambiguously on the margins of institutional religion.

The fact that a political resister such as Dietrich Bonhoeffer can be cited as a prophet of postmodern spirituality is reassuring. Postmodern culture has sometimes been criticized for being incapable of taking an ethical stance, especially what some have called an 'ethics of resistance'.[14] In Bonhoeffer's case this involved a rejection of the social and political conformity of the Church under the Nazis. In other contexts, postmodernism may encourage us to uncover the often unacknowledged agendas that underpin our world views. By resisting attempts to reduce events or people to mere instances of some overarching theory, postmodernism defends the otherness, particularity and difference of all people.

> The others and the different – both those from other cultures and those others not accounted for by the grand narrative of the dominant culture – return with full force to unmask the social evolutionary narrative of modernity as ultimately an alibi story, not a plausible reading of our human history together.[15]

Social and cultural agendas are just as present in particular approaches to spirituality and its history as anywhere else.

The most important lesson that postmodernity can teach spirituality is the need to reject an unhealthy division between the sacred and the secular. There are two extremes. We can simply assimilate Christianity to surrounding culture or, like some radical fundamentalists, reject human culture entirely. Both of these are inadequate models.[16] A balanced spirituality must take the 'secular' order seriously as an essential ingredient of Christian faith and practice.

Notions of society or community are important because, for Christians, religious experience is never simply the

product or possession of an individual person who is isolated from a community of faith or from an inherited
religious tradition. Overall, the 'modern' Enlightenment
idea of the human self tended to emphasize our essentially
rational and autonomous qualities. If the word 'society' is
used, it may be adequately explained by the accumulation
of the individual purposes of essentially free-standing,
rational agents. In that sense, Margaret Thatcher seems to
be a thorough-going modernist when, while British Prime
Minister, she asserted in a now famous interview that there
was no such thing as society, merely individuals and
families.

Postmodern thought at its best exposes the illusory
quality of this understanding of human identity. 'That self-
grounding, self-present modern subject is dead: killed by
its own pretensions to grounding all reality in itself. Thanks
to the postmoderns, that subject should be unmourned by
all.'[17] In contrast, the postmodern image of the self is not
isolated or disengaged from the social world but is in some
sense brought into existence by it. Because the self exists
in a complex and mobile network of relationships, there
cannot be said to be such a thing as a complete or completed self. On the face of it, this view may appear merely
as another reaffirmation of overwhelming fragmentation.
However, the Christian dynamic implied by the doctrine
of redemption also requires that we see 'the self' as 'the
concern and the theatre of God's work'. We must also
grasp that

> the self at any given moment is a *made* self: it is not a solid,
> independent machine for deciding and acting efficiently or
> rationally in response to stimuli, but is itself a process, fluid
> and elusive, whose present range of possible responses is
> part of a developing story.[18]

Postmodernism may encourage spirituality to reject

explicitly the individualism that has frequently characterized previous perspectives. Our identities are constituted by being in relationship. All things are interconnected and interconnection is the inner reality of things, and persons, in themselves. In Christian terms this understanding offers significant connections between our understanding of human identity and the doctrine of the Trinity. 'Relatedness is not something simply external to the divine reality but is something internal to the divine life as well'.[19]

SPIRITUALITY AND THE DOCTRINE OF GOD

We are faced with the question whether there is a view of theology and Christian spirituality that can help us to respond to the contemporary intellectual and spiritual climate. There is one unavoidable starting point. Christians always confront a fundamental horizon within which the meaning of human life and all reality is judged. This horizon is a person – the Jewish teacher, Jesus of Nazareth, who lived in Roman-occupied Palestine during the early part of the first century CE. However, the story of Jesus of Nazareth is paradoxical. On the one hand it concerns contingent events in that it portrays someone who existed in a quite specific time and place. However, in a 'scandal of particularity', these contingent realities were experienced by Jesus' early followers as universal in their implications. Jesus is 'of Nazareth', the rabbi who is a carpenter's son. Yet, in the light of the Easter events, he is also known as 'the Christ', the anointed one of God, the saviour. The Christian community affirms not simply that *through* the human Jesus God speaks but rather that *in the very person* of Jesus is God-become-flesh. Christians cannot avoid the fact that this story does offer an overarching explanation for the 'meaning' of history. However, the language we use to talk about this is limited by our contexts. Equally, such an explanation does not need to be understood in an authoritarian or absolutist way.

Christian spirituality will always treat this perception about Jesus as *the* basic reference point. However, what is significant is that this belief embodies a specific understanding of God and God's self-disclosure. This understanding is sustained in a community of faith, the Church. Thus, our personal stories and experiences are continually brought into conversation with *this* story, with this original experience of the believing community and the many attempts across time to reflect upon it.

It is important to know what Christian doctrines are really attempting to express about God. The point of seeking doctrinal clarity (for example in the early Christian era) is always to express, promote and protect a quite distinctive experience of God along with its practical implications for life and prayer. Experience, in terms of a Christian understanding of revelation and incarnation, is initiated by God and not simply by our subjective needs. It is, therefore, challenging and profoundly disturbing.

Christian spirituality attempts to respond to the question, 'What kind of God do we have and what difference does it make to us?' The key doctrines formulated by the early Christian Church were those of God as Trinity and of Jesus Christ as truly God and truly human. All human statements about God have practical implications; we live what we affirm. Ineffective or even destructive spiritualities inevitably reflect inadequate theologies of God. In that sense, the quality of spirituality is one test of the adequacy of the theology of God that lies behind it. The Christian doctrine of God seeks to maintain a delicate balance of transcendence and immanence. This governs the way we understand and respond to the material universe. The classical heresies of the early Christian era were not considered unorthodox purely in terms of their technical language. Rather, they were felt to upset that delicate balance with ultimately destructive results. In different ways such heresies appeared to undermine the reality of the incarnation, that God truly became flesh in Jesus.

The language surrounding the traditional Christian belief in God's distance and detachment (known as God's 'impassability') derived largely from Greek philosophy. Plato's definition of perfection and Aristotle's idea of the creator as Unmoved Mover were especially influential. The language of 'impassability' does protect God's essential freedom. Yet, it needs to be held in tension with biblical images of God's engagement with creation and with humanity. Otherwise, human beings would be left with a disconnected God who could not truly enter human history and who offered no final redemption for the human condition. A spirituality that reflects such a lack of balance becomes divorced from human experience. Equally, such a disconnection of God from creation is a short step from a despotic God with whom there is no real communication and whose actions and demands are arbitrary.

Any version of Christian spirituality that is individualistic in tone fails to reflect the communion of equal relationships that is God-in-Trinity. It is not surprising that the nature of the Christian life was always an issue at the heart of early debates about the doctrine of God. To think of God as Trinity is fundamentally to assert, among other things, that within God there is society or relationship. To affirm that human beings are created in the image of that God implies that they are called to share more and more in the deep communion that is divine life itself. The crucial issue is the intimate link between the fundamental nature of God and God as revealed through creation and salvation.[20]

Spiritualities that are disengaged from the world rather

than committed to it, and to its transformation, fail to
reflect the irrevocable commitment of God to the world
in Jesus Christ. This is what the doctrine of the incarnation
seeks to express. Belief in the incarnation also invites
people to adopt a balanced approach to human nature
and especially to its material dimension, the body. This
should be neither radically pessimistic nor naively optimistic. The incarnation is more than a defence of the
reality and importance of the human nature of Jesus
Christ. It is a governing principle of Christian living; of
God's way of relating to creation and our way of response.
This means that the Christian vision of God, and God's
self-disclosure, forces spirituality to accord a fundamental
importance to human history and material existence.

Furthermore, in terms of God's self-disclosure, it is
impossible to avoid the intimate connection between the
life and ministry of Jesus of Nazareth and the cross of
Jesus. The vulnerability and powerlessness of the cross is a
radical challenge to an unbalanced emphasis on God's
glory. Equally it challenges the ultimate meaninglessness
and hopelessness of human suffering. The self-giving,
mutuality and interdependence at the very heart of the
Trinity is revealed in the cross. Here we are invited to
realize that God's self-giving love and vulnerability, rather
than human definitions of power, are what transform us
and transform the world.

Without denying the reality of suffering, God revealed
in the cross offers us the hope of reaching the fullness of
humanity. We come to share in the glory of God through,
and not merely despite, the apparently death-dealing
experiences of our lives. A theology and spirituality that
bypasses the cross will have nothing much to say about
the real presence of God in human suffering, failure and
sinfulness. These realities become intolerable. Consequently they are ignored by some excessively optimistic

spiritualities. Their main role seems to be to protect people from the possibility of final despair.

As we shall see in more detail later, the doctrine of the Trinity is of vital significance for Christian spirituality. 'Trinitarian' is not an adjective that qualifies only *some* Christian spiritualities. Rather, 'All authentic Christian spirituality is *ipso facto* Trinitarian' ... and 'the doctrine of the Trinity, with its far-reaching practical implications, constitutes the heart and soul of Christian spirituality'.[21] The doctrine of the Trinity is the cornerstone of Christian belief because it synthesizes the whole 'economy' of God's relationship with creation, including humankind. Christian spiritualities reflect the nature of that divine-human relationship and so the doctrine of the Trinity is the key element. It relates to humanity's openness to transcendence, to our capacity for a personal relationship with God and to our existence in God at all times and in all places. Creation is the outpouring of the life of *this* God. The doctrine of the Trinity is a paradigm for the fundamental unity of all reality. The Christian understanding of the basic vocation of humanity (the end product of spirituality) is 'deification', to become like God. In Trinitarian terms, this implies being drawn collectively into the very community of Father, Son and Spirit.

SPIRITUALITY AND CHANGING THEOLOGY

Beyond this starting point, there are a number of particular things to be said about the contemporary horizons of theology and spirituality. Over the last thirty years spirituality has freed itself from the constraints of abstract theory. There has been a serious attempt to re-engage Christian experience of God and Christian practice with doctrine. Matters have progressed a great deal since Thomas Merton suggested in the 1950s that the technical language of theology, as opposed to literature for example, conspicuously failed to provide him with what he needed to articulate his understanding of contemplation. In citing Merton's disquiet about theological categories, the theologian Sandra Schneiders admits that our understanding of theology in the 1990s is unlikely to be that of Thomas Merton. Yet she would still say that

> his insight into the fact that systematic theology, however precise and clear it might be, was not adequate to the concrete experience of the spiritual life which, as experience, is far more inclusive, was quite accurate. In other words, the task of spirituality as a discipline is to study Christian spiritual experience which, in our day, cannot be reduced to the exclusively Christian or the exclusively religious even when it is the experience of the committed Christian.[22]

At this point I do not want to discuss in detail whether spirituality is distinct from or part of our attempts to speak theologically. However, I do wish to raise two issues provoked by Schneiders' statement. First, it seems possible to understand 'theology' in ways that are broader and more inclusive than the one Schneiders criticizes. Second, while it is true that the spiritual experience of Christians is broadly-based, such experience raises specifically theological questions precisely because it is the experience of *committed Christians.* Sandra Schneiders is certainly correct in opposing abstract and rationalist approaches to theology. This view of theology subordinates other areas of knowledge and experience to its own method and denies them their integrity. One recent, brilliant attempt to restate the independence of theology is *Theology and Social Theory: Beyond Secular Reason* by the Cambridge theologian John Milbank. What is of interest here is that Milbank appears to support the reconciliation of theology

and spirituality.[23] Thus he defends the primacy of practice and a theology of grace that affects the whole of
human existence. He seeks 'to overcome the pathos of
modern theology, and to restore in postmodern terms, the
possibility of theology as a meta discourse'.[24] What Milbank
means by 'pathos' is theology's false humility and its surrender to 'secular reason', notably social and political
theory.

It is quite correct to suggest that one of the great challenges facing the contemporary Church is the restoration
of theology and spirituality as forms of public discourse.
However, if Christian theology alone can explain everything, the effect is to collapse all significant wisdom into
theology. There is obviously nothing positive to be said for
a *reduction* of theology and spirituality to 'secular reason'.
However, Milbank's adversarial approach to the question
undermines the possibility of *real* conversation between
Christianity and contemporary culture or between the
insights of theology and other wisdom. Milbank's theory
tends to separate the sacred from the secular; a truth-
bearing inner world from a sterile outer one; Christian
truth and moral virtue from historical and cultural contexts. In this case the reintegration of theology with
spirituality would be inhibited rather than enhanced.[25]

Contemporary theology and spirituality also seek to overcome the exclusive categories of the older sectarian
approaches. It may be argued that different approaches to
the nature of theology reflect the classical divisions
between the Roman Catholic and Protestant communities.
It seems clear that the theologies of the great sixteenth-
century Reformers were profoundly and inherently concerned with what we nowadays call 'spirituality'. The
central focus of the Reformation, while expressed differently by Luther and Calvin, was to address God's ways of
relating to the human condition, our experience of this

and our response to it. Early Anglicanism shared this concern in its own way. However it also developed a particular mixture of doctrine, ethics, pastoral reflection and spiritual teaching in its characteristic way of 'doing theology'. This tended to be expressed more in sermons, meditations and poetry than in systematic treatises.

If we study 'spirituality' these days, its focus tends to be the (Christian) spiritual life as experience.[26] Contemporary styles of theology also consider 'spiritual experience' as the legitimate starting point. Indeed, the fundamental method of such approaches as liberation theology explicitly takes a spiritual and experiential starting point – albeit in a collective rather than individualistic way.

Yet, we need to be careful when we talk about the priority of experience or of a return to 'experience' in theology. Theology cannot be reduced to a second-order reflection on prior (naked) experience. Religious experience presupposes a context of beliefs and symbols within which it can be known precisely as *religious* experience. To put it more simply, *some* understanding of Christian belief and of Christian symbols precedes any sense that experience has a Christian explanation. Equally, there can be no direct access to 'pure experience' for students of either theology or spirituality.[27] Our contact is only with what is remembered or deemed worthy of recording. This underlines the fact that what we study is not only historically conditioned but already theologically interpreted. Spirituality may be concerned with 'Christian spiritual life as experience' but our understanding of 'Christian', 'spiritual', 'life' and 'experience' are dependent on our theological assumptions. Theological criteria of interpretation and evaluation have already implicitly come into play.

At this point, it is useful to make a distinction. On the one hand we are free to opt into or opt out of certain ways of interpreting reality. For example, many of us choose to remain ignorant of literary theory. On the other hand we live, reflect and operate within certain *irreducible* horizons. These function as the fundamental boundaries within which we evaluate our experiences of the world around us. Thus, all human beings exist within historical horizons and have some implicit historical sense even if they are ignorant of historical method. For a Christian, the same applies broadly to a theological sense. We may need to be wary of uncritical approaches to Christian tradition but for Christians there is, as we have seen, a basic narrative that we cannot bypass.

THEOLOGY IN PRACTICE

Theology as a whole, not merely spirituality, is practical and needs to be practised. In the context of academic study, this view implies that what is sometimes called 'applied' or 'practical' theology should not be an optional extra within the theological core curriculum. However, the place of practice in theology means something more. Theology is not merely concerned with particular content or specific resources. For the Christian interpreter, personal faith is an irreducible horizon present at every moment of experiencing and interpreting.[28] This implies that to do theology means being a *theological person* not merely using theological tools.

Being a theological person implies more than an intellectual exercise. *Theologia* is a much broader concept than theology as an academic discipline. It inevitably involves what Eastern Orthodox Christianity has called *theoria*. At first sight, this word is misleading to Western eyes. It is more accurately translated as 'contemplation' rather than 'theory'.[29] The committed believer is one who *lives* theology rather than 'does' it as an activity detached from who he or she is. Sadly there is still a tendency in Western thought to think and act as if knowledge means something purely objective and rational. But theology is in its richest sense essentially performative as well as informative; is concerned with action as well as ideas. Consequently, the title 'theologian' does not imply someone who provides specialized analysis and information while standing at a personal distance from the object of reflection. 'Being a theologian' involves a quality of presence to the reality we reflect upon as much as a concern for the techniques of a specific discipline. This raises challenging questions concerning an essential relationship between the academic activities of research and teaching and such practical 'applications' as prayer, preaching, pastoral care and evangelization.

The ancient meaning of a theologian as a person who sees and experiences the content of theological reflection connects well with contemporary understandings of the self-implicating nature of study. Theology and spirituality in their fullest sense are self-implicating. This does not imply anti-intellectualism. There needs to be a critical approach to both theology and spirituality. However, this is not the heart of the theological enterprise. Critical analysis is the servant of good theology but is not, surely, what theologians do or live theology for. The same question needs to be asked of both theology and spirituality as areas of knowledge. Why does anyone bother to understand them at all? In both disciplines the answer would seem to be that a kind of transformation is implied by the search for knowledge. ' "Saying the truth" is distinct from, although never separate from, "doing the truth" . . . More concretely, there is never an authentic disclosure of truth which is not also transformative'.[30]

An implied question, of course, is whether a faith-based understanding of theology excludes it from the academic world. If we do not approach Christianity or any great religion as *faiths* we do not understand them at all. This

does not imply that we must exist within a faith community
or seek to serve it before we can legitimately study theology.
However it does imply that to study any religious faith
seriously is to allow oneself to be confronted by the truth
claims it embodies. The 'non-judgemental neutrality' that
sometimes characterizes university teaching of many disciplines, not merely theology, is ultimately corrupting of
academic ideals. In that sense, it is vital for the academy
to re-engage with matters of truth.[31]

SPIRITUALITY, MYSTICISM AND A THEOLOGY OF UNKNOWING

One of the most fundamental aspects of the Christian
doctrine of God is that human relationships with God
embrace a paradox of knowing and not knowing. This has
particular force in the context of mysticism and with a
conversation not only between spirituality and theology
but also between the Christian tradition as a whole and
contemporary culture.

The history of Christianity is often presented purely in
terms of ever greater doctrinal refinement and definition.
However, Christianity has always affirmed that God is
beyond the capacity of anyone to define or finally to *know*.
One striking New Testament image is the story of Peter's
vision before his visit to Cornelius and his family as
described in Acts, chapter 10. As an observant Jew, Peter
'knew' what God wanted in terms of dietary laws. However,
in the vision at Caesarea, he was challenged to eat what is
profane and unclean. When Peter queried this, he heard
a voice say, 'What God has made clean, you must not call
profane'. In visiting the 'unclean' Gentile, Cornelius, Peter
made an important connection. He came to realize that
with God there are no favourites and that God is as much
the God of the Gentiles as of the Jewish people. According
to the story, God profoundly challenged Peter's assump-

tions about where God was to be found and how God acts. This point is most strikingly underlined by the detail that Cornelius and his family received the Holy Spirit even though not baptized (Acts 10:44–8). The story also affirms the power of the Spirit to blow where it wills and so to lead us into all truth. Throughout its history, Christianity has struggled with its discomfort at the wild and disruptive side of God and with the unpredictability of God's way of leading.

Human attempts to think about God seek a balance between imaging God and a recognition that the reality of God is ultimately beyond images. The words 'cataphatic' and 'apophatic' have often been used to describe the two sides of human relations with God. The cataphatic element emphasizes the way of imaging. It is a positive theology or a theology of affirmation based on a high doctrine of creation and of human life as contexts for God's self-revelation. The apophatic element, in contrast, emphasizes 'not knowing', silence, darkness, passivity (to a degree) and the absence of imagery. It is a negative theology, or a theology of denial. A sixth-century Eastern Christian writer known as Dionysius (or Denis) the Areopagite was one of the most influential exponents of the concepts of apophatic and cataphatic theologies.[32] He had a major impact on Western theology and mysticism.

In Dionysius' approach to God, knowing and unknowing are mutually related rather than mutually exclusive. The whole of creation is brought into being by God to show forth divine glory. The cosmos is to be viewed positively as the self-revelation of God's goodness. 'Good' is, therefore, the first affirmation (or image) of God discussed by Dionysius. Again, in Dionysius' theology the Trinity is first realized in terms of distinctions between the 'persons' whereby we can know something of God. However, underlying these distinctions, or contained within them, is a

25

unity or synthesis that we cannot ultimately comprehend. Therefore, the theology of the Trinity is a way of knowing because it seeks to affirm something about God. Yet, at the same time, it is a way of unknowing because the affirmations we make immediately push us beyond what we can grasp. Paradoxically, the doctrine of the Trinity both reveals God and yet reveals God as beyond human knowing. Through our relationship with God as revealed in creation, and in the midst of our affirmations, we come to realize that God never becomes our possession or an object of rational knowledge.

To seek God through images prevents us from losing touch with God's movement towards us in and through creation, through our own lives and in the incarnation. Created reality is not a distraction from which God is utterly removed. Yet we cannot reduce God to human categories. God has always received many names and yet always remains beyond every name. Indeed the apparently endless 'naming' of God finally draws us back into the mysterious divine depths beyond the limitations of naming, reason and subjective experience. Difficult though it may be, the Christian tradition suggests that we must hold in creative tension the process of imaging God and the process of denial that any image *is* God. For some people, apophatic or negative theology is ultimately normative. This is because the apophatic way should not be seen simply as a way of correcting an unbalanced 'positive' theology. 'Apophasis is "not a branch of theology", but an attitude which should undergird *all* theological discourse, and lead it towards the silence of contemplation and communion.'[33]

It is interesting that a number of contemporary analyses of the implications for spirituality of postmodern experience reflect these central paradoxes in the doctrine of God. It is true that one aspect of postmodernism highlights fragmentation. However, the recipe for recovery points towards, rather than undermines, a fuller appreciation of the riches of the Christian doctrine of God. We may now realize once again that the world is 'ultimately incalculable and beyond the laws of the human mind'. This is not necessarily a recipe for despair. It opens the possibility of a return to wonder and worship at the heart of theology and spirituality.

One recent analysis of spirituality in postmodern context speaks of a number of crucial needs that relate directly to the doctrine of God. Spirituality must be strongly incarnational and engaged with the ordinariness of materiality; emphasize the existential quality of God's relationship to us; encourage a radical belief in the unconditional love of God behind all reality, including 'the monstrosities of history'; and speak of the cross as the suffering of God within human suffering. Some postmodernist writing (for example, by Jacques Derrida) has been described as a form of apophatic or 'negative theology'.[34] Whether or not this is appropriate, contemporary theology and spirituality certainly need to reflect upon the tradition of the hiddenness of God in the context of a contemporary 'absence of God' in the lives of many people. This sense of the hiddenness of God may help to purify our false images of God.

Modern religious poets such as the Welsh priest R.S. Thomas eloquently capture a kind of postmodern 'dark night of the soul'. Faith is stripped to bare essentials and God's presence is paradoxically experienced only in absence.

> Why no! I never thought other than
> That God is that great absence
> In our lives, the empty silence
> Within, the place where we go
> Seeking, not in hope to
> Arrive or find . . .[35]

The hidden face of God plays a particularly strong role in the Christian tradition of mysticism. The believer is brought to the frontiers of language or conceptual thinking and to the edge of mystery – a Mystery which is, none the less, intensely present. It is not surprising that the great French intellectual, the late Michel de Certeau, drew parallels between postmodern culture and the mystical tradition. Both the mystic and the postmodern person live in a kind of movement of perpetual departure. They are wanderers and pilgrims lost in 'the totality of the immense'. Each of them 'with the certainty of what is lacking, knows of every place and object that it is *not that*, one cannot stay *there* nor be content with *that*'.[36]

'Modernity' places a powerful emphasis on intelligibility, not least that of God language. Because of this, those people whose lives affirm the essential otherness of a mysterious God are seen by de Certeau as outsiders to the 'modern' project.[37] Echoing de Certeau, the American theologian David Tracy suggests that hope lies particularly in the challenge to traditional power and privilege offered by an 'otherness' that is present in marginal groups. He points particularly to the mystics and the mad.[38] Perhaps this is why de Certeau was fascinated throughout his writings by the seventeenth-century Jesuit mystic Jean-Joseph Surin (whom he called 'my guardian'). Surin was for many years also profoundly disturbed psychologically and consequently isolated and oppressed.[39]

At present there is a great curiosity about mysticism in Western culture. This is a recognizable part of postmodern religiosity. It seems to express a desire for immediate contact with the spiritual and transcendent. This is presumed to be beyond what is thought of as the cold objectivity of the life and teachings of the institutional Church.[40] Mystics of every age have understood that the

way to true understanding and fulfilment is the way of
unknowing and dispossession.

> To reach satisfaction in all
> desire its possession in nothing.
> To come to possess all
> desire the possession of nothing.
> To arrive at being all
> desire to be nothing.
> To come to the knowledge of all
> desire the knowledge of nothing.[41]

The postmodern affirmation that all religious language
is relative reminds us that religious definitions are to be
treated as provisional. The reality we name as 'God' exists
beyond all categories – even beyond the familiar category
of Being.[42] It is a central belief of Christianity that God is
not 'intelligible' and cannot be 'known' in terms of
rational thinking. Yet, as mystics of every age have intuit-
ively grasped, the God-who-is-Love may be touched
existentially in our desiring and in longing love.

> Now all rational creatures, angels and men alike, have in
> them, each one individually, one chief working power which
> is called a knowing power, and another chief working power
> called a loving power; and of these two powers, God, who
> is the maker of them, is always incomprehensible to the
> first, the knowing power. But to the second, which is
> the loving power, he is entirely comprehensible . . .
>   No man can think of God himself. Therefore, it is my
> wish to leave everything that I can think of and choose for
> my love the thing I cannot think. Because [God] can cer-
> tainly be loved but not thought. (*The Cloud of Unknowing*)[43]

This dynamic love that exists at the centre of our being
and which is in perpetual search of fulfilment is, as many

mystics teach, also the very heart of the mystery of the Trinity.

> This is very strange that God should want. For in Him is the fullness of all Blessedness: He overflowed eternally. His wants are as glorious as infinite: perfective needs that are in His nature and ever Blessed because always satisfied. He is from eternity full of want, or else He would not be full of Treasure. Infinite want is the very ground and cause of infinite Treasure. It is incredible, yet very plain. Want is the fountain of all His fullness. (Thomas Traherne)[44]

It is worth noting that a number of modern theologians have been fascinated by the theological possibilities of mystical writings. The American David Tracy, for example, suggests that in our postmodern era 'we may now learn to drop earlier dismissals of "mysticism" and allow its uncanny negations to release us'.[45] This reflects Tracy's own journey towards a belief that the apophatic language of the mystics is where theologians must turn in our present times.

> As critical and speculative philosophical theologians and artists learn to let go into the sensed reality of some event of manifestation, some experience of releasement and primal thinking, a sense of the reality of mystical experience can begin to show itself in itself. Even those with no explicit mystical experience, like myself, sense that thinking can become thanking, that silence does become, even for an Aquinas when he would 'write no more', the final form of speech possible to any authentic speaker.[46]

Karl Rahner and Rowan Williams remind us that spirituality is integral to the theological enterprise.[47] Because it cannot be reduced to subjective affectivity, spirituality points towards another way of knowing and learning. In fact, the key to good theology is prayer, understood in its fullest sense as a relationship with, or contemplation of, the divine rather than simply devotions and techniques of meditation. Perhaps we may go further still and say that all true prayer is true theology and vice versa. For true prayer and true theology are both matters of the heart and the head. They each point to a unity of love and knowledge beyond the traditional post-Enlightenment division.

In the West we have inherited a tendency to believe that 'knowledge' means only abstract intelligence and objective analysis. The problem with theological 'knowledge' is that while we may be impelled to speak of God, we cannot in the end speak definitively *about* God in the sense of capturing the divine. The problem with a purely intellectual search for God is that it necessarily regards what is sought as an object or a conclusion and an objective that can be reached. Equally, the determining factor of such a search is *me* and *my* understanding rather than the action of God. In so far as we can, in Christian terms, speak of the human search for God, it will be a search that involves a continuous failure to 'find' God in a definitive sense. Thus Gregory of Nyssa could suggest that a 'true' vision of God always involves a movement onwards.

> This truly is the vision of God: never to be satisfied in the desire to see him. But one must always, by looking at what he can see, rekindle his desire to see more. Thus, no limit would interrupt growth in the ascent to God, since no limit to the Good can be found nor is the increasing of desire for the Good brought to an end because it is satisfied.[48]

CONCLUSION

In conclusion, from a Christian perspective we cannot separate our attempts to speak of God and our desire to live spiritually. At first sight this does not appear to sit easily with a tendency in modern Western culture to separate spirituality from coherent systems of belief or from commitment to traditional religious groups such as the Church. As we have seen there is also a suspicion of what are sometimes called 'metanarratives' or complete and exclusive systems of thought that claim to explain the meaning of life. Yet Christianity cannot escape from its fundamental frameworks of belief. These frameworks, expressed particularly in the doctrines of Trinity and incarnation, act as the boundaries within which we understand ourselves, other people and the world around us. In that sense, the Christian story of God revealed in Jesus Christ is a kind of 'metanarrative' in that it offers an explanation for the meaning of existence.

Having said that, the Christian tradition rather importantly suggests that the language it uses is always provisional. The Christian way of seeing reality has sought a balance between the desire to speak of God and the need to recognize that God is ultimately beyond all we can say. This elusive aspect of God has been best expressed in the traditions of mysticism and spirituality. Spirituality without theology runs the danger of becoming private or interior. Theology, however, needs the corrective of spirituality to remind us that true knowledge of God concerns the heart as much as the intellect.

2

The Divorce of Spirituality and Theology

'Spirituality' is a word that is commonly used yet difficult to define. For a number of reasons, theologians have particular suspicions concerning the precise subject matter. Some of the suspicions, as we shall see, are rooted in a long history of separation between theology and spirituality. This has led to the two words being interpreted as concerned, respectively, with the intellectual and devotional dimensions of Christianity. Nowadays, however, spirituality demands to be taken seriously as an area of study and knowledge in its own right. This raises difficulties for theologians especially when spirituality refuses to see itself simply as subordinate to theology. Spirituality also invites theologians to take seriously the role of their own faith in their reflections and to realize that in general terms spiritual experience lies at the heart of the theological enterprise.

Spirituality appears to want to cross all kinds of disciplinary boundaries that were previously considered as 'hard'. It also seems to lay claim to almost unlimited resources (for example, historical, theological, philosophical, psychological and anthropological). Spirituality has been accused of not defining its own methods very precisely. As a matter of fact, significant attempts have been made by scholars in recent years to provide a coherent definition and methodology from both a theological and historical standpoint.[1] As an area of study and reflection,

33

spirituality is emerging more clearly as interdisciplinary but with a special relationship to theology. It is concerned with the specifically 'spiritual' dimension of human existence.

First of all we need to explore briefly the history of the relationship between theology and spirituality and particularly the reasons for the great divorce between them. At that point it is helpful to look particularly at the specific relationship between spirituality and Trinitarian theology. We can then turn to the contemporary attempts to rebuild an intimate connection between spirituality and theology. In the process, we shall come to see some of the most significant dimensions of the contemporary approach to spirituality. Finally, we can look briefly at how the boundaries between disciplines are becoming blurred and a more interdisciplinary approach is emerging. This has special relevance to the relationship between spirituality and theology.

THE CONCEPT OF SPIRITUALITY

The concept of 'spirituality' is not limited to the Christian religion and is in fact increasingly used even beyond explicitly religious circles. As a result, there have been attempts to define 'spirituality' generically. Such definitions seek to transcend the assumptions of specific religious traditions. It is clearly useful to reach some rather general definition for the purpose of conversations between faiths and between disciplines. However, overall, generic definitions have severe limitations. The way we understand the concept of 'spirituality' is ultimately dependent on quite specific religious perspectives. In Christian terms, 'spirituality' concerns how people subjectively appropriate traditional beliefs about God, the human person, creation, and their interrelationship, and then

34

express these in worship, basic values and lifestyle. Thus, spirituality is the whole of human life viewed in terms of a conscious relationship with God, in Jesus Christ, through the indwelling of the Spirit and within the community of believers. As a field of study, 'spirituality' examines this dimension of human existence from a variety of standpoints of which the theological, historical and phenomenological are the most common.

The word 'spirituality' has a relatively short pedigree and was confined, until recently, to Roman Catholic and Anglican circles. What it seeks to describe has changed shape over the centuries, whether subtly or substantially, as understandings of God, Church and human person have evolved in different contexts. Most significantly, in recent decades there has been a paradigm shift in theological method which has had a major effect on how spirituality is understood. Previously, theology was predominantly analytical, logical, deductive in approach, with a stable body of knowledge, rich in tradition and equipped to answer all questions from an *a priori* standpoint. Approaches to the 'spiritual life' were similarly structured and separated from concrete human experience.

As we shall see, greater reflection on human experience as an authentic theological starting point has encouraged a movement away from static understandings of the Christian life. At the same time that theological thinking has moved towards a more inductive, experiential method, 'spirituality' has become more of a dialectical tension. On the one hand, there is the concreteness of revelation in Jesus Christ and subsequent tradition and, on the other, the appropriation of the gospel by each person within specific historical and cultural contexts. Spirituality operates on the frontier between religious experience and inherited tradition. It should not attempt to subordinate the former unquestioningly to the latter.

Consequently, it has become increasingly clear that spiritual traditions are embodied first of all in people rather than in doctrine and begin with experiences rather than abstract ideas. The problem of defining 'spirituality' in recent years is in part because it is no longer a single, transcultural phenomenon. Rather it is rooted in experiences of God that are framed by the always *specific*, and therefore contingent, histories of individuals and communities.

HISTORICAL DEVELOPMENTS

In the West, what we nowadays call 'spirituality', and used to be called ascetical and mystical theology, began as part of an undifferentiated reflection on Christian sources and their application. From the patristic period until the development of the 'new theology' of scholasticism around the twelfth century theology was a single enterprise.[2] To say that theology was a unified enterprise does not simply mean that the later distinctions between *intellectual* disciplines were not present. The unity of theology implied that intellectual reflection, prayer and living were, ideally speaking, a seamless whole. Patristic theology involved the constant reading of Scripture which was then shaped in the liturgy and in critical dialogue with Greek philosophical culture. This issued in reflection on such central themes as prayer, martyrdom, the state and stages of the Christian life and so on. A variety of genres provided the medium for such theology: sermons, letters, lives of saints and monastic rules.

To be a theologian meant that a person had contemplated the mystery of the incarnation and possessed an experience of faith on which to reflect. Theology was always more than an intellectual exercise. Knowledge of divine things was inseparable from the love of God deepened in prayer. For Augustine (*De Trinitate*, Books XII-

XIV), God is known not by *scientia* but by *sapientia* – that is to say, not by objectification and analysis but a contemplative knowledge of love and desire. Patristic theology was not an abstract discipline separated from pastoral theory and practice. The unifying feature was the Bible and the patristic approach to Scripture ultimately developed, in the West, into a medieval theory of exegesis.[3] Thus, theology was a process, on different levels, of interpreting Scripture with the aim of deepening the Christian life in all its aspects.

This approach encompassed a synthesis of exegesis, speculative reasoning and mystical contemplation. Doctrinal theology arose from this biblical base and attempted to provide a language to express an essentially mystical apprehension of God revealed in Christ and as the Spirit within every Christian. Early theologians did not write about 'spirituality' or 'mystical theology' as distinct areas of knowledge. The very heart of patristic theology was mystical.

Patristic 'mysticism' is not to be confused with later Western interest in subjective religious experiences or in detailed itineraries for the spiritual journey. 'Mysticism' was fundamentally the life of every baptized Christian who came to know God revealed in Jesus Christ through belonging to the 'fellowship of the mystery', that is, the Church. This life was supported by exposure to Scripture and participation in the liturgy. In the sixth century this insight fused with neo-Platonic elements in the writings of an anonymous theologian known as Pseudo-Dionysius or Dionysius, to produce a more explicit 'mystical theology'. Although, to some degree, he pointed towards the later medieval development of mystical theory, he essentially summarized patristic approaches.[4]

The Eastern Orthodox tradition, unlike the Western tradition, continued to follow the patristic model of 'mystical theology'. This synthesized ethics, spirituality and doctrine. Orthodox theology may be defined as a spirituality that expresses a doctrinal attitude. In a sense, doctrine has priority and leads to practice as a natural outcome. Yet, theology itself is inseparable from contemplation and is mystical in that its overall aim is to show forth the divine mystery. True theologians are those who *experience* the content of their theology. On the other hand, mystical experiences, while personal, are nevertheless the working out in an individual of a faith that is common to all.[5]

The unity between knowledge and contemplation found its supreme expression in the West in the Golden Age of monastic theology. This stretched from Gregory the Great in the sixth century through Anselm of Canterbury in the eleventh century to Bernard of Clairvaux in the twelfth century.[6] This patristic-monastic style of theology drew its inspiration and method from the traditional meditative reading of Scripture known as *lectio divina*. Medieval readers of Scripture based themselves on a theory of interpretation that can be traced back to Origen. In broad terms, this proposed four 'senses' of Scripture or dimensions of meaning. There was, of course, a literal sense which considered the biblical events and realities in 'history'. Then there were three 'spiritual' senses which interested medieval readers far more. The allegorical sense revealed the explicitly Christian, that is theological, meaning of the biblical text. The tropological, or moral, sense considered how the text of Scripture should be applied to the Christian life. Finally, the anagogical sense offered a mystical or eschatological meaning. This focused on what might be thought of as the deepest, ultimate or 'finally realized' meaning of the text.

Within these overall boundaries, considerations of what might be called spiritual theology appeared simply as collections of homilies or scriptural commentaries. Apart from this, there were some writings specifically associated with the way to God appropriate to monastic life. Studies of prayer and asceticism, therefore, took for granted a context of separation from everyday life.

It is difficult to be precise about the date when a rational or 'scientific' approach to theology in the West was born. This is because change is always an extended process rather than an event. However, from approximately 1100 onwards, scholars such as Peter Abelard (1079–1142) began to understand theology to be essentially a process of intellectual speculation. In the construction of systematic theology, philosophical categories (especially those of Aristotle) began to rival biblical ones. The 'new' theologians treated Scripture and patristic writings in a more propositional way, began to compare the propositions with each other and then to apply the rules of Aristotelian logic. Contradictions were to be eliminated by means of carefully constructed distinctions. The theologians who advocated this approach were known as dialecticians.

Not surprisingly there were serious conflicts between those who espoused a dialectical approach to theology and those who continued to oppose it.[7] The latter feared excessive rationalization. The centres of theological enquiry increasingly moved during the twelfth century from the monasteries to new cathedral 'schools' that eventually gave birth to the great European universities. This involved a geographical shift from the countryside to the new towns but the move involved more than geography. The theological enterprise was no longer to be focused in centres that were explicitly dedicated to a religious way of life. The new scholarship in the narrow sense created centres that existed primarily to foster teaching and learning. The new theology gradually gave birth not only to distinctions between disciplines such as biblical theology, doctrinal theology and moral theology. It also produced a belief that the discipline of the mind could be separated from the discipline of an ordered lifestyle or *ascesis*.

The fears of the traditional monastic theologians such as Bernard of Clairvaux and William of St Thierry were not without foundation. It is true that the greatest figures of the theology of the new schools (scholasticism) such as Aquinas and Bonaventure still sought to unite theological reflection with contemplation. Yet Thomas Aquinas divided his *Summa Theologiae* into various component parts. In some senses this heralded a slow process of division which would climax in the development of different theological 'disciplines' centuries later. The new theological method, with its more 'scientific' approach, led to a slow but inexorable separation of spiritual theory from the hard core of theology. Aquinas placed what we might call spirituality in the second part of his *Summa Theologiae* as a subcategory of moral theology and distinct from dogma.

Whatever the intentions of the early theologians of the schools, dogmatic theology finally grew apart from what we would call spirituality. This was a tragedy for both. Secular reason has traditionally been considered the child of the Reformation and the late seventeenth-century and eighteenth-century Enlightenment. However, its intellectual origins lie in the theological developments in the High Middle Ages where 'thinking' began to be understood as a mastery of facts and details rather than attention to the truth expressed in symbols. To put it more simply, reason began to triumph over imagination and the ability to define truth over experiences of the sacred. It has been noted by a number of writers that in the patristic and monastic theological traditions, theologians were frequently saints. According to the theologian von Balthasar it was only after the epoch of Albert the Great, Thomas Aquinas and Bonaventure towards the end of the thirteenth century that we can see 'the disappearance of the 'complete' theologian ... the theologian who is also a saint'.[8]

The recovery of interest in the mystical theology of Dionysius during the High Middle Ages became associated with a new attention to affective experience and the birth of mystical literature. This had several sources, including an aesthetic and romantic sensibility born of the twelfth-century 'Renaissance'. The theme of love, secular and religious, was cultivated to a heightened degree. There was also an increased awareness of the inner human landscape even if not precisely of the modern concept of the individual 'self'. These shifts of consciousness encouraged an interest in spiritual guidance which in turn generated treatises by spiritual directors for those under their care. The interest in subjective experience combined with the 'scientific' theology of the schools in the writings of the Victorine monastery in Paris. The two great writers Hugh and Richard of St Victor exercised a major influence on the development of a distinct spiritual theology. This gave birth to a new genre of spiritual treatises. *The Cloud of Unknowing*, the fourteenth-century English mystical text, is a well-known example of a treatise of spiritual guidance strongly influenced by the spiritual theology of the Victorines.[9]

Even if there was an increase in interest in the spiritual journey of the individual person, medieval mystical theologians did not expound subjective mysticism in our contemporary sense. The term 'mysticism', referring to a certain kind of subjective *experience*, is the creation of nineteenth- and twentieth-century theorists. In practice, the medieval mystical theologian denied the ultimate importance of the experiential. The 'mystical' was a divine, hidden, wisdom beyond meditative method rather than essentially bound up with it.

Initially, a distinct field of mystical theology found a place within scholasticism. This was a systematic, doctrinal study of the contemplative journey of the soul towards union with God through the different stages of the spiritual life. A classic expression is the *De triplici via* (The Triple Way), composed in the mid-thirteenth century by the great Franciscan theologian St Bonaventure. However, as we have noted, the late thirteenth century saw an increasingly dialectical approach to theology that hastened the alienation of experience and reflection. One fifteenth-century Carthusian commented that mystical theology and scholasticism were no more related than painting and shoe-making!

Finally, the growth of a body of knowledge associated with asceticism, contemplation and mysticism led to the gradual emergence of systematic meditative techniques. The meditations of St Anselm in the eleventh century were still fundamentally unsystematic, based on prayerful reading of Scripture. In contrast, the treatises of the four-teenth- and fifteenth-century movement known as the *devotio moderna* discussed methods of prayer and structured them into regular exercises. This growth of methodical prayer gave rise to a considerable literature over the next few centuries. The monastic practice of *lectio divina* sought, in a fluid way, to guide the whole of life by means of meditative reading of Scripture. However, by the end of the twelfth century the Carthusian writer Guigo II in *The Ladder of Monks* had begun to turn it into a structured, four-stage analysis of the spiritual life. In Guigo there are four clear stages: reading (*lectio*), reflection (*meditatio*), prayer (*oratio*) and contemplation (*contemplatio*). These stages are not only consecutive and distinct. They are also associated with different levels of spiritual proficiency progressing from 'beginners' to 'the elect'.[10]

By the end of the Middle Ages, there were few significant thinkers who stood out against the separation of theology and spirituality. Two exceptions were Jean Gerson and

Nicholas of Cusa. Gerson was a diocesan priest and Chancellor of the University of Paris from 1395–1418. He continued to draw upon the patristic tradition (especially Dionysius) and the monastic theology of the Victorines, Bernard and Bonaventure. In this context, Gerson's three most significant works were *De mystica theologia speculativa*, *De mystica theologia practica* and *De vita spirituali*. During the Council of Constance in 1415 Gerson also wrote *De probatione spirituum*. The book provided a theological framework for analysis and judgement concerning the validity of mystical visions. Nicholas of Cusa (1401–64) was one of the most original thinkers of the fifteenth century. Like Gerson he became a priest who was both a major figure in the Conciliar movement and later an ecclesiastical reformer, papal legate and bishop. Again like Gerson, Nicholas of Cusa was strongly influenced by the thought of Dionysius as well as medieval mystical theologians such as Bonaventure and Eckhart. Intellectually he crossed the boundaries between theology, philosophy, mathematics and political theory. His major writings on the theology of spirituality have only recently become available in English.[11]

In summary, the High Middle Ages in the West were characterized by growing divisions within theology and the gradual separation of spirituality from theology. This division went deeper than method or content. It was, at heart, a division between the affective side of faith (or participation) and conceptual knowledge. Further, within what we think of as spirituality there was a concentration on interiority that separated it from public liturgy and from ethics. By the end of the Middle Ages, the 'spiritual life' had increasingly moved to the margins of theology and culture as a whole. Although late medieval religion was not completely individualistic (the growth of lay confraternities is evidence of the importance of collective experience), there is no doubt that religious practice became more personal and internalized. It also began to demand a new specialized language, distinct from theological discourse as a whole, capable of expressing its separate existence.

By the sixteenth century the relationship between mystical theology and theology in general was at best ambiguous and at worst antagonistic. The divisions in Western Christianity in the aftermath of the Reformation encouraged theology to concentrate on dogmatics in order to become the guardian of the prevailing Catholic or Protestant orthodoxies. Roman Catholic dogmatic theology opposed not only the supposed unbalanced subjectivity of Protestants but also spiritual reformers and mystics in its own ranks.

The *Spiritual Exercises* of Ignatius Loyola, the founder of the Jesuits, were suspected of unorthodoxy because of the emphasis on inner freedom and personal inspiration. The addition of the 'Rules for Thinking with The Church' (including a defence of scholastic theology!) as an appendix to the *Spiritual Exercises*, the translation of the text from Spanish into an official Latin version, as well as the over-all direction taken by Ignatian spirituality after the death of Ignatius, may well have something to do with the prevailing theological climate.[12]

Roman Catholic writers in the immediate post-Reformation period, such as Ignatius Loyola, Teresa of Avila or Francis de Sales, did not yet possess the terminology of later 'ascetical' or 'mystical' theology. A specialist vocabulary developed in the eighteenth century and had become common currency in the late nineteenth century. Even so, their writings showed the beginnings of a distinctive language concerning knowledge of the spiritual life. Parallel to this, the late scholasticism of the Baroque period tended to divide theology into evermore discrete disciplines.

The period of the Enlightenment in the late-seventeenth
and eighteenth centuries saw the growth of scientific
enquiry as a way to truth and certainty. This further aggra-
vated the split between spirituality and theology. Roman
Catholicism in particular espoused a defensive positivism.
That is to say, faith was increasingly expressed in terms of
propositional 'truths'. To theologians, spirituality became
an object of suspicion. It was unrealistic because associated
with theologically dubious devotion and was of optional
interest because it seemed to relate only to a certain cast of
mind. The value of abstract intelligence was overestimated.
Consequently the experiential dimension of human life
was to be questioned continuously throughout an analytical journey towards what could be proved. The notion
that theology was a science became linked to the belief that
science could generate value-free knowledge. This pointed
theology towards a position of isolation from context or
personal feeling.[13]

During the next hundred and fifty years a vocabulary of
Christian life and prayer stabilized and a field of study
defined as 'spiritual theology' was established, particularly
in Roman Catholic circles. There were, of course, Anglican
and Protestant mystical writers who, particularly in seventeenth-century Anglicanism, produced works of spiritual
guidance or meditation. Among Anglo-Saxon Protestants
(not least the Puritans) and Lutheran Pietists there was a
vocabulary of 'piety', 'Godliness', 'holiness of life' and
'devout life'. A genre of devotional literature developed to
correspond to this.[14]

Until the modern era, within Protestantism, there was
no systematic approach to the spiritual life such as there
was in Roman Catholicism. On the contrary, there was
some antagonism to it. Protestant suspicions can be traced
to a number of factors. First, such approaches appeared
to justify a method of self-sanctification. Terms such as

'ascetical and mystical theology', 'spiritual theology' and 'spirituality' were thought to be tainted with the erroneous doctrine of salvation through works. In contrast, *the* fundamental mark of Reformation piety was the principle of divine monergism – that God alone initiates and accomplishes everything in the work of salvation. To put matters rather simply, the classic Protestant emphasis was on God as the sole source of holiness. The classic Catholic emphasis (leaving room for human actions made worthy by grace) was on the practical consequences in the life of the individual Christian of justification and redemption. Thus Protestantism reversed the conventional medieval pattern where the human soul sought God, the sinner strove to turn to God and the contemplative ascended a spiritual ladder towards divine light. Instead, God alone seeks us, strives after us and descends to us.[15]

A second reason why classical Protestantism did not develop an explicit spiritual theology concerns the Reformed understanding of the fundamental relationship between spirituality and theology. The major sixteenth-century reformers, most notably Martin Luther, were inherently opposed to the kind of divisions that late medieval scholasticism brought about between spirituality and theology, especially doctrine and ethics. From the very beginning, Lutheran and Calvinist theologies had at their heart a concern for what we now think of as spirituality. That is, the primary task was to describe the nature of the divine-human relationship and ways in which this should be expressed in the life of the individual Christian and in the Church. Understood in these terms, Luther's *The Freedom of a Christian* (1520) and Calvin's *Institutes of the Christian Religion* are fundamentally essays in 'spiritual theology'.

The English Reformation, specifically the Elizabethan Settlement, produced a rather different approach from that of Continental Protestantism. The 'godly, righteous and sober' life which *The Book of Common Prayer* enjoined of Anglicans expressed a particular approach to spirituality. During the seventeenth century, which saw the gradual emergence of a distinctive Anglican identity, what we nowadays call spirituality was linked closely to ethics. This was apparent in such works of Jeremy Taylor as *The Rule and Exercises of Holy Living* and even more sharply in the anonymous 1657 *The Whole Duty of Man*. The nearest that early Anglicanism came to a kind of theology of spirituality was present in parts of Richard Hooker's (unpromisingly titled) *Of The Laws of Ecclesiastical Polity* (especially Book V). Overall, Anglican spirituality was not described technically or systematically until the twentieth century. It was expressed in a rather diffuse way through books of devotion, homilies and works of pastoral care.[16]

SPIRITUALITY AND TRINITARIAN THEOLOGY

As we look back at the history of the relationship between theology and spirituality from the patristic period to the eve of the modern era, one specific question stands out which demands brief attention. How far did the doctrine of God play an explicit role in approaches to the Christian spiritual life? One would assume that a Trinitarian vision always lay at the heart of Christian faith and therefore of spirituality as well.

> The life of God – precisely because God is triune – does not belong to God alone. God who dwells in inaccessible light and eternal glory comes to us in the face of Christ and the activity of the Holy Spirit. Because of God's outreach to the creature, God is said to be essentially relational, ecstatic, fecund, alive as passionate love. Divine life is therefore also our life. The heart of the Christian life is to be

47

united with the God of Jesus Christ by means of communion with one another. The doctrine of the Trinity is ultimately therefore a teaching not about the abstract nature of God, nor about God in isolation from everything other than God, but a teaching about God's life with us and our life with each other.[17]

Yet it is sadly the case that the doctrine of the Trinity in the West, with some notable exceptions, became disconnected over time from the theology of salvation and consequently from any practical or spiritual outcome.

The blame for this disconnection has often been laid at the door of Augustine of Hippo. His prodigious influence in the West has led some commentators to consider subsequent Trinitarian theology as little more than 'a series of footnotes on Augustine's conception of the Trinity in *De Trinitate*'.[18] His Trinitarian theology has been described not only as different from Greek theology, particularly the Cappadocians, but also radically incompatible with it. The divergences are presumed to be twofold. First, the Cappadocians began their Trinitarian theology with a consideration of the persons in their distinctiveness while Augustine began his scheme with the unity of the one God. Second, and consequently, Augustine sacrificed a relational and economic theology of the Trinity. The impact on later Western theology was that the fundamental relationship between God's inner reality and God's self-communication broke down.

This simplistic judgement concerning Augustine has rightly been severely criticized.[19] Equally, it ignores Augustine's debt to the East, not least to the Trinitarian theology of Gregory of Nazianzen. It cannot be denied that Augustine, in his concern to combat Arianism, emphasized the single divine nature and then moved on to consider this divine essence as constituted equally by all three persons.[20]

48

However, it would be unfair to limit statements about Augustine's approach to the Trinity to this one point. The further question is whether this approach contradicts in some vital way the greater emphasis in the Greek tradition on persons and relations within God and God's self-communication and creative dynamism. The Greek Trinitarian model was founded not on a single divine 'essence' or 'nature', with its tendency to become a static concept, but on the person of God the Father. As the unoriginated origin, the Father was the active source of the dynamic inner life of the Trinity. In this way of thinking about God, the Trinity is infinitely fruitful and infinitely creative in its own inner life. This inner dynamism of God necessarily breaks forth into creation and revelation.

However, it is possible to argue that behind the Augustinian Trinity lies a potential for dynamism equal to that of the Cappadocians. Augustine concentrates *both* on the unity of the divine nature and on the distinctions between the persons of the Trinity. This suggests that there is, as it were, a creative tension within God that is inherently dynamic rather than static. The language we can then use concerning the mystery of God holds together unity and diversity, oneness and distinction, communion and individuality, fixed ground and fluid relations.

It is possible to argue that there is a complementarity rather than a conflict between Greek and Augustinian theologies. The dynamism of the Greek Trinity is expressed in terms of emanation, with all things flowing ultimately from the Father. Augustine focused on the traces of the Trinity (*vestigia Trinitatis*) found in everything and particularly in the soul of the individual human being. In a certain sense, this relocation of the 'economy' of God strongly emphasizes interiority. The question is whether this effectively undermines a connection between the Trinity and salvation. As we shall see later in reference to the Trinitarian theology of Julian of Norwich, it is not necessarily a serious problem.

Augustine's Trinitarian theology has an impact on spirituality in a number of significant ways. People are made in the image of God-as-Trinity and are called to be restored to that image which has been obscured by sin (*De Trinitate* 14.19.25). Further, being created in the image of the Trinity involves a vocation both to intimacy with God (living in the love of the Trinity) and to community (sharing the love of the Trinity). It is not that Augustine did not consider that the 'economy' of God was revealed in external activity such as the incarnation and the outpouring of the Spirit at Pentecost. However he was more concerned with how Christians are transformed interiorly by the invisible indwelling of the Trinity in human souls. This indwelling of the loving communion of the Trinity brings about charity. In a profound sense the purpose of contemplation (intimacy with God) and of human activity (charity) are intimately connected.[21]

Sadly, in much later medieval scholastic theology, the doctrine of the Trinity became a kind of sacred mathematics. This placed the life of God at a distance from the world of human events and needs. In the long term, theologians who drew on Augustine (rather than Augustine himself) tended to favour a static, remote Trinity with abstract rather than dynamic relations between the persons. Augustine's own model of love as the way of understanding Trinitarian relations was submerged. The exceptions were those significant mystical and spiritual writers such as Richard of St Victor who developed it creatively.

Richard of St Victor, the theologically outstanding twelfth-century canon at the Abbey of St Victor in Paris, had a profound influence on spiritual writings throughout the Middle Ages. At the heart of his mystical teaching

lay the Trinity. Inspired by Augustine, Richard emphasized
that love was the centre of relations within God. For him,
the perfection of love demanded not only the mutual love
of two persons but a third person with whom this joy of
mutual loving can be shared (*De Trinitate* 3.19). True love
expresses itself not in the closed introspection of two
persons but in sharing this love. In a reflection of God the
Trinity as love, human interpersonal love is essentially self-
transcending. This is brought about particularly by the
action of God's Spirit within the human spirit (*De Trinitate*
6.14). Love, therefore, is at the heart of Christian living and
is much more than a source of satisfaction or fulfilment. It
brings into being a community based on communication
and mutuality.

One of the other great mystical theologians of the
Middle Ages is the fourteenth-century Flemish Church
reformer, John Ruusbroec. In many respects, he was closer
to the Augustinian tradition, mediated through Richard of
St Victor, than to his near contemporaries of the Rhineland
school of mystics such as Meister Eckhart. Ruusbroec did
not mimic Eckhart's apparent tendency to distinguish
between the image of God and the deeper, inaccessible,
Godhead. His mysticism was consistently Trinitarian as he
did not differentiate between oneness in the depths of
God and the communion of divine persons. In the highest
part of the human soul lies the *imago Trinitatis*. Although
he understood the Christian life as having three stages,
Ruusbroec does not describe the highest stage
(contemplative union with God 'without distinction') with
the starkness of Eckhart. Although ultimately God transcends all concepts, the Godhead nevertheless includes the
Trinity of persons (*The Spiritual Espousals* Book 1, Part 4).

> [God] subsists blissfully in eternal rest in accordance with
> the essential Unity of his being and also subsists actively in

eternal activity in accordance with the Trinity. Each of these
is the perfection of the other, for rest abides in the Unity
and activity abides in the Trinity, and the two remain thus
for all eternity.[22]

Consequently, while the soul enters contemplatively into
darkness, this brings with it a union with the Trinity in
eternal love (*The Spiritual Espousals* Book 3, Part 4).

Meister Eckhart has been considered by many commentators to be scarcely Christian because of his lack of
Trinitarian and Christological language. What he says concerning the Trinity appears very obscure. Eckhart is
suspicious of conceptual language about God and the simplicity and oneness of God receive by far the greatest
attention. Yet, the Trinity does appear quite extensively in
his works. Interestingly in his Commentary on John's
Gospel Eckhart seems to come closer to the Greek theory
of emanation than to the traditional Western theology of
Augustine. Eckhart describes the Father as the 'Beginning'
or 'Principle' of the Godhead from which all else flows. It
is not clear whether this implies that the Trinity is merely
part of a divine emanation rather than a part of God
intrinsically ('God' rather than 'Godhead'). In the same
passage he clearly links the divine reality or essence
(immanence) with the activity of creation (economy). Elsewhere in the Commentary (123) Eckhart follows Augustine
(*De Trinitate* 14.19.25) in considering that humanity is
made in the image of the whole Trinity. In his 'Book of
the Parables of Genesis' it is clear that the persons of the
Trinity are within the One from all eternity and that we
cannot separate God's works from God's essence.[23]

After the Reformation, theological developments within
both reformed Roman Catholicism and the Churches of
the Reformation failed until recently to make any significant connection between the Trinity and the Christian life.

Chapter 3 will consider the modern theological rediscovery of the importance of the doctrine of the Trinity to the Christian life. However, as in the Middle Ages, the gap between theology and spirituality was bridged to a degree by some post-Reformation spiritual traditions or writers. In their works we may find modest connections between spiritual wisdom and the doctrine of God. As one of the case studies in Part Two, we will examine two examples from opposite sides of the Reformation divide: Ignatius Loyola and George Herbert.

TOWARDS THE CONTEMPORARY ERA

The present debate about the precise relationship between spirituality and theology will be considered in more detail in the next chapter. At this point, it is helpful to sketch the general trajectory of the contemporary reintegration. In the late nineteenth and early twentieth centuries there was a revival of a purified form of Thomist theology after centuries of second-rate scholasticism. This encouraged some re-engagement between the subject matter of spirituality and theology. Numerous manuals of ascetical and mystical theology appeared in Roman Catholic circles throughout the twentieth century until the Second Vatican Council in the 1960s. Texts such as those by A.A. Tanquerey and R. Garrigou-Lagrange became *the* handbooks of ascetical and mystical theology in Roman Catholic seminaries and theology faculties. Attempts were made in Anglican circles in the 1930s to produce something comparable. These were also based to some degree on Thomist principles.[24]

Unfortunately, this form of reintegration had severe limitations. The starting point for 'spiritual theology' was the principles governing dogmatic theology. The overall approach was one of precise categories and definitions.

Despite the experiential subject matter, the theology was static and the method was deductive. Divine revelation and rational knowledge were the major sources because a 'scientific' study of the spiritual life needed universal principles. 'Spiritual Theology' first appeared in the official theological curriculum in 1919 and by 1931 was included in an official Vatican document on ecclesiastical education, *Deus Scientiarum Dominus.*

One classic definition of how spiritual theology related to the wider theological field appeared in Pierre Pourrat's influential three-volume history of spirituality, *La Spiritualité Chrétienne*, which appeared in the 1920s.

> Spirituality is that part of theology which deals with Christian perfection and the ways that lead to it. *Dogmatic Theology* teaches what we should believe, *Moral Theology* what we should do or not do to avoid sin, mortal and venial, and above them both, though based on them both, comes *Spirituality* or *Spiritual Theology.* This, again, is divided into *Ascetic Theology* and *Mystical Theology.*[25]

For Pourrat, spirituality was subordinated to both dogmatic and moral theology.

Immediately prior to Vatican II, writers such as Louis Bouyer moved away from the style of the older manuals. His work espoused a more scriptural, liturgical and even ecumenical approach.[26] Bouyer was concerned to define spirituality as a theological discipline but one that was distinct from dogmatic or systematic theology. Spirituality was not concerned with abstract ideas (although that precise understanding of systematic theology is revealing in itself). Rather it examined the way in which the objects of faith arouse reactions in religious consciousness. Bouyer departed from Pourrat's classic statements in another significant way because he suggested that moral theology concerned more than obligations, the 'dos' and 'don'ts' of human acts. For Bouyer, moral theology was also concerned with ideals and with perfection. It therefore overlapped with spirituality although the latter focused more directly on the human search for God. Overall, in Bouyer the boundaries between the theological disciplines are much more blurred than was the case with earlier writers such as Tanquerey or Pourrat. He was more aware than his predecessors that all theology has the potential to be 'spiritual' if it does not limit itself to scholastic rationalism.

In addition, the spirituality taught in Roman Catholic and Anglican Catholic circles until recent times primarily referred to various forms of monastic or clerical life such as Benedictine, Carmelite or Jesuit. This approach emphasized the priority of those people who sought a 'life of perfection' away from the world. It contrasted this with the 'ordinary life of faith' of the vast majority of Christians who lived in 'the world'. The initial impetus of the Second Vatican Council in the 1960s with regard to spirituality was to endorse a *resourcement*, a return to original sources, directed once again at members of religious orders. This process was still marginal to the wider theological project and continued to focus on special groups leading eccentric lives.

CONTEMPORARY PERSPECTIVES

In recent decades a major shift has taken place in Western theology. The move has been from a more deductive, transcultural theology towards serious reflection on experience of God in its particular and plural cultures. In harmony with this shift, and partly provoked by it, understandings of the Christian life have also changed. 'Spiritual theology' has given way to a more dynamic and inclusive concept known as 'spirituality'.

As a consequence, the separations noted at the end of the medieval period and reinforced by the Enlightenment have begun to break down. First, spirituality is not limited to elites such as monastic celibates. Spirituality has broadened beyond attention to a limited range of phenomena, for example mysticism, to include reflection on the values and lifestyles of all Christians. The term 'spirituality' has gained considerable ecumenical acceptance and so studies of it tend to draw on the riches of a shared Christian heritage rather than limit themselves to sectarian understandings of life in the Spirit. The term has also found favour in inter-faith dialogue and is no longer limited to Christian experience. More contentiously, the term 'spirituality' has been used to describe the deepest values of people professing no coherent religious belief system.[27]

Second, spirituality has become more fruitfully associated with mainline theology and biblical exegesis than it has been over the last few hundred years. A number of major theologians and theological schools once again take experience seriously as a subject for reflection. This is associated with a renewed theology of grace and of the human person. In some cases, reflection on experience, and the question of the relationship between experience and tradition, has become the heart of theological method. Further attention will be given in the next chapter to some theologians who have particularly contributed to the conversation between theology and spirituality.

One specific area where there is a fruitful dialogue is the interrelationship between spirituality and ethics or moral theology. This is paradoxical given that in the old Roman Catholic theology manuals ascetical and mystical theology used to be considered merely as a subdivision of moral theology. Indeed, it could be argued that traditional approaches to moral theology helped to reinforce the split between theology and spirituality. Both moral theology and ascetical theology were preoccupied with sinfulness and the enfeebled nature of the human condition. This over-powered any serious theological consideration of holiness and gave the impression that ascetical theology had very little if anything to say theologically in its own right. It appeared to deal merely with some subsidiary (even optional) aspects of the moral life.

Nowadays, however, moral theology has moved away from a concern primarily with the quality of actions to a greater interest in people's dispositions of character. There has been a shift from action to human agent. Here, spirituality and moral theology find a common language in a renewed theological anthropology and understanding of grace. There is an increasing awareness of the basic unity between the moral and the spiritual life. A number of writers have suggested that the joint task of contemporary spirituality and moral theology is to explore renewed understandings of 'virtue' (that is, what enables a person to become truly human within a commitment to Christ and aided by the action of grace) and 'character' (or what we should *be*, rather than do, if we are to become fully human persons).

Moral theologians increasingly emphasize that our ulti-mate guide to goodness is not objective codes of behaviour or moral rule books but the presence within us of the Holy Spirit. The indwelling of God grounds the recovery of a fruitful relationship between ethics and spirituality. Yet 'spirituality' and 'ethics' are not totally synonymous. Spiri-tuality in its widest sense includes the whole of a person's or group's spiritual experience or orientation. This may involve beliefs, ways of thinking, feelings and relationships. Because it is all-embracing and encompasses all aspects of living, spirituality may *include* behaviour and the attitudes that underlie it. In that sense, spirituality overlaps with ethics but cannot be reduced to it.

Some of the most fruitful reflection on the contrast between a 'Spirit ethics' and 'code ethics' and on the relationship between spirituality and ethics in general has been in the writings of Christian (particularly Roman Catholic) feminist theologians. Spirituality is, if you like, the main source of ethics just as it should be of theology as a whole. The traffic, however, cannot be one way. Doctrinal theology and moral theory may act as vital critiques of spirituality in a way that may transform it.[28]

Third, Christian spirituality is not so much concerned with defining 'perfection' in the abstract as with surveying the complex mystery of human growth in the context of dynamic relationships with God. If we add that spirituality is not limited to interiority but seeks to integrate all aspects of human experience, this affects its actual definition. The broader the compass, the greater the danger of making spirituality no different from religion in general. The British theologian Rowan Williams rejects an understanding of spirituality as the science of spiritual and private experience: 'it must now touch every area of human experience, the public and social, the painful, negative, even pathological byways of the mind, the moral and relational world'.[29] Contemporary theorists accept that definition becomes more complex once we cease to separate the spiritual dimension of human existence from everything else. Whatever the problems, contemporary spirituality as an area of reflection attempts to integrate religious and human values rather than to concentrate exclusively on such narrowly-conceived matters as stages of prayer.

We have seen that attempts to define spirituality in generic terms are problematical. In practice, spirituality cannot be separated from particular doctrinal reference points. This is what makes it possible to sift the authentic from the unauthentic in spirituality. Every religious tradition has tests for the authenticity of spiritual experience based not only on broadly human considerations but also on the foundational beliefs of the tradition.[30]

Context is an essential element of the contemporary study of spirituality and, indeed, of theology. It is a concept that is imported from the disciplines of history and the social sciences. Context has become a primary framework of interpretation in the study of theological and spiritual traditions. All experience, including spiritual experience, is determined to some degree by culture. Spirituality is never abstract or pure in form. The contextual approach to spirituality, in addition, seeks to address not merely explicitly religious issues but the situation of a spiritual tradition within the social context as a whole. 'Context' is not really a 'something' that may be added to or subtracted from spiritual experience but is the very element within which such experiences take their forms and expressions. Even though religions claim a transcendent dimension, all faiths throughout their long histories have been embedded in specific cultures.[31]

These comments about culture and context in relation to spirituality would now be widely accepted. However, the way in which contextual studies have developed raises serious questions for people who are concerned with the religious themes of spirituality. For example the history of spirituality has come to mean the study of how religious attitudes and values are conditioned by surrounding culture and society. This brings historical spirituality close to the study of *mentalités*, or world views, beloved of modern French historians. This 'social' version of history is itself informed by anthropology and religious sociology. The limitation is that such an approach to spirituality, if it is exclusive, tends to abandon theological sources and the questions raised by theological theory. We need a middle way between the older (exclusively theological) approach and the newer stress on changing social contexts.

A case study is provided by recent treatments of early Christian asceticism and monasticism. The dangers of abandoning traditional perspectives altogether have been noted. The modern contextual approach resituates asceticism in a broader world than that of monasticism or even of Christianity and approaches its history with questions drawn from a wide range of disciplines. The problem is that this approach *in isolation* often leaves no room for the theological goals that were the active horizons of Christian asceticism.[32]

Finally, our basic understanding of 'context' has become much more fluid in recent decades. On the one hand, religion still tends to be strongly linked to specific cultures. On the other hand, there is an increasing convergence of world cultures into what we may call a 'global consciousness' and 'the global village'. This cultural convergence changes the context for religion through a new global encounter of world faiths. This does not merely affect how religions exist but also how their traditions are to be interpreted and appropriated. One of the most original writers in the theology of religions, Raimundo Pannikar, argues that whereas Christian theology traditionally operated within what he calls a 'dialectical dialogue' (that is, by argument *against* 'the other') it now needs to accept a 'dialogic dialogue' that is open to the values of 'the other'.[33] The disturbing impact of this new context for Christian theology and spirituality has hardly begun to be explored.

In addition to the issues of context, there is another question. This concerns whether the shift towards human experience in spirituality necessarily involves a move away from doctrine. The former approach to spiritual theology was based on sources that were defined in essentially doctrinal terms: revelation, grace, the gifts of the Spirit, participation in the life of the Trinity, the life of grace and so on. However, the move to experience as the primary starting point is *not* an invitation to pure introspection. Rather it is an invitation into the experience of *faith*, the human self in relationship to the Absolute.

The emphasis on experience in contemporary spirituality does not exclude reference to tradition. There may be some common ground between different faith traditions (for example, between Christianity and Hinduism) regarding the meaning of 'spirituality'. Nevertheless contemporary expressions of Christian spirituality, as well as the study of them, are increasingly related to theological themes. Spirituality, in Christian terms, concerns not some other life but simply human life at depth. Yet, our understanding of what this means arises from what Christian revelation and tradition suggest about God, human nature and the relationship between the two. Christian spirituality derives its specific characteristics from certain fundamental beliefs. For example, Christianity affirms that human beings are capable of entering into relationship with a God who is transcendent yet dwelling in all created reality. Further, this relationship is lived out within a community of believers that is brought into being by commitment to Christ and is sustained by the active presence of the Spirit of God. Put briefly, Christian spirituality exists in a framework that is Trinitarian, pneumatological and ecclesial.

Spiritual experience is not 'naked' in the sense of free from values and assumptions drawn from faith traditions. Nor is it entirely private. It exists within systems of religious discourse or behaviour – even if these, in some cases, are implicit rather than expressed in membership of some faith community. This seems to indicate that members of different faith traditions do not simply *write about* the nature of spiritual experience differently but actually *have* different experiences in crucial ways.

Christians and Buddhists may be able to describe similarities in the *phenomena* of spiritual experience (for example, the physiological and psychological changes that accompany meditative practice). The changes in consciousness that may occur in contemplative contexts appear to produce a spiritual unity beyond our ability to conceptualize or to think discursively. However, this does not affect the fact that at the level of *experience as experience* our frameworks of interpretation, Christian or Buddhist, are inherent rather than accidental.

DISCIPLINES, BOUNDARIES AND THE INTERDISCIPLINARY

The shift to experience within spirituality and theology has led to a dialogue with other disciplines. The possibility of a fruitful encounter between disciplines actually owes something to the contemporary theories of postmodernism that have already been discussed. Postmodernism blurs the boundaries between disciplines. Within the academic world, the modernist approach to knowledge tended to produce a series of inwardly consistent but mutually exclusive disciplines. Specialization, purity and the isolation of specific areas of study was the order of the day. This emphasis on the differences between disciplines strongly discouraged interdisciplinary conversation. These assumptions have recently been questioned and the mood has changed. This has had its effect on the study of religion as much as on any other field. The identity of an area of study is no longer to be found in maintaining 'hard' boundaries and sharp distinctions but in blurred edges and boundaries that are crossed. This shift has been characterized as 'a centrifugal, rather than a centripetal, sense of disciplinary identity'.[34] Perhaps the word that best characterizes the new situation is 'conversation' between different perspectives, presuppositions and methods in the search for meaning.

In the specific field of spirituality, the emphasis on context has necessitated a conversation with the social and human sciences. The study of spirituality also frequently includes historical, psychological, sociological and literary approaches. The absolute necessity of a sophisticated historical approach is now widely accepted and employed. A socio-political approach has been particularly noticeable in liberationist, feminist and justice-focused approaches to spirituality. It is gradually becoming common coinage as one aspect of more general studies in the field. Perhaps the most recent 'conversation' is between spirituality and literature. Particularly in the English-speaking world modern literature has increasingly addressed deep issues of meaning and belief. This unthematic, and even agnostic, spirituality is attracting increasing attention.[35]

Apart from the interest in a dialogue between spirituality and science,[36] one of the most striking and controversial interdisciplinary conversations is the one with psychology. References are too numerous to list. While psychology is a legitimate and necessary dimension of an experiential approach to spirituality, it has distinct limitations if it is given disproportionate attention. For example, psychological terminology has at times become almost a substitute for serious engagement with the Christian theological and spiritual tradition. At other times it has encouraged a thoroughly *un*contextual and anachronistic approach to the wisdom of the past.

Most worrying of all, the seriousness of spirituality as a coherent field of study is undermined by the explosion of books that blend a superficial approach to the great traditions with 'popular' psychology. At worst, some of this writing is dangerously naive. At best it tends to perpetuate a theologically dubious, individualistic, self-help approach to the spiritual quest.[37]

It may be true that bookshops are full of literature on astrology, yoga, mysticism, parapsychology and science fiction under the guise of 'spirituality'. This phenomenon makes the continued nervousness of some theologians about 'spirituality' understandable. However the fear is ultimately unjustified because students of spirituality have equal misgivings about contrasting 'spirituality' and 'theology' rather than treating them as dependent on each other.

3

ooooooooo

Partners in Conversation

The time has come to examine in more detail the ways in
which spirituality and theology have once again entered
into serious conversation. First of all we will look briefly at
the way some significant twentieth-century theologians
have contributed to this re-engagement. The contemporary recovery of Trinitarian theology is not only
important for the whole theological enterprise but has
powerful implications for the conversation between
theology and spirituality. This leads us naturally to reflect
on the current debate about precisely how theology and
spirituality relate to each other. Whatever the continuing
controversies about this, there can be no longer any doubt
that theology offers criteria for evaluating spirituality and
vice versa.

A number of theologians or theological traditions in
recent decades have had a particularly important impact
on the reintegration of spirituality with theology. Several
have already been mentioned in passing. For example, the
Lutheran Paul Tillich and the Roman Catholic David Tracy.
Tillich is particularly interesting. Adolf Harnack coined
the dictum that 'a mystic that does not become a Catholic
is a dilettante'. This expresses concisely the belief of many
Protestant theologians in the early part of the twentieth
century that mysticism (including what we now call
'spirituality') was incompatible with evangelical faith. Paul
Tillich is, therefore, unusual in his consistent interest in

religious or mystical experience. However, Tillich wrote only scattered remarks on the subject rather than any substantial essays.

Among the most significant contributors to the conversation between theology and spirituality have been the Roman Catholics Bernard Lonergan, Karl Rahner and Hans Urs von Balthasar and the Lutherans Jürgen Moltmann and Wolfhart Pannenberg. A number of Anglicans have also addressed the issue. Attention should also be paid to two schools of theology as a whole, liberation theology and feminist theology. Both of them take as a *sine qua non* of their approach the fundamental connection between spirituality and theology.

CONTEMPORARY THEOLOGIANS

Bernard Lonergan (1904–84), the Canadian philosophical theologian, has been described variously as the greatest English-speaking theologian since Newman and a giant of modern Roman Catholic theology capable of standing alongside Karl Rahner.[1] Lonergan directed a great deal of his attention to theological method. His 'transcendental method' suggested that religious experience, and particularly conversion, was the heart of theological enquiry. For Lonergan, there is an invariable movement within human consciousness which begins with experience. All of us move from attention to our experience to an understanding of what has been experienced and then to judgement in the light of that understanding. Finally we reach a point of choice or decision in terms of what has been understood. In other words, human intentionality moves from desire to knowledge and finally to action. All this takes place within a process that involves personal consciousness being drawn towards the Ultimate, Love, God. This process of growth or conversion is an integrated one that finally involves the affective, imaginative, intellectual, moral and religious dimensions of our lives. Lonergan's language frequently sounds empirical. This may be explained by Lonergan's mathematical and scientific background – unusual in a theologian. Its self-actualizing emphasis (albeit self-actualization for the sake of others) also brings us close to the world of psychology. While Lonergan was concerned for a new language to mediate faith to a world of cultural pluralism, he was in all respects doctrinally conventional. His emphasis on experience as the first moment of conversion is, in practice, influenced less by modern psychological insights than by the classic tradition of patristic and early medieval theology. This tradition emphasizes that love precedes and is the foundation of knowledge.[2]

Perhaps more than other Western theologians of any tradition, Karl Rahner (1904–84) has made acceptable the language of 'openness to mystery' and 'self-transcendence'. Both of these concepts had long been familiar to students of spirituality. The mystery, of course, is God in whom is our origin, within whom we live and towards whom we are drawn in a continual movement of self-transcendence. In other words, simply by being human we are fundamentally oriented towards the mystery of God. Rather than starting with the idea of God, Rahner begins his theological enquiry with our shared human experience. In this sense he represents a theological response to modernity's emphasis on the human subject. There is a kind of knowledge that is acquired simply by being in existence. This is 'experiential knowledge'. Because we are social beings, this knowledge is not isolated but reaches the level of reflection and communication in us. One aspect of this existence and our experience of it is a sense of responsibility and a realization of our freedom to choose. To this extent we exist 'beyond' the world and its causes and in

this sense we transcend it. The questions that arise, therefore, concern where we come from (if not solely from the
world) and where our transcendence is leading us (if
the world cannot define our limits). It is this ultimate
question, or transcendental experience, that confronts us
at every turn. It is this question that Rahner reflects upon
as a starting point for speaking of God.

Despite this way of proceeding, at a more fundamental
level Rahner understands that God is always the starting
point. It is God's free communication of self (grace) that
actually *is* this capacity for transcendence within us. God's
grace encompasses the whole of our human existence in
such a way that our consciousness, our intellect and our
will are illuminated and guided. Thus God is both beginning (initiator) and end (gift). Because Rahner's approach
to self-transcendence applies to every human without
exception, he offers a balanced incarnational theology and
spirituality. Rahner rejects any dichotomy between sacred
and secular, private and public, 'extraordinary' and
'ordinary' religious experience. By stressing both the
mystery of God and an incarnational vision, Rahner unites
'negative theology' with the 'positive theology' in his theological language.[3]

Hans Urs von Balthasar (1905-88) in his later years
became famous (perhaps notorious) for his opposition to
liberal theologians. In particular he espoused a theology
'from above' and a traditionalist ecclesiology. Whatever
our theological standpoint, however, it is impossible to
ignore the power of his synthesis of classical theology and
spirituality.[4] Von Balthasar understood all theology to be
potentially 'spiritual theology' in that it should transcend
purely rationalist thinking. Equally, all spirituality is theological in that its 'meaning' is necessarily associated with
revelation. This view found classic expression in an article
by von Balthasar in one of the early editions of *Concilium*,

'The Gospel as norm and test of all spirituality in the Church'. For von Balthasar, revelation is the key to defining spirituality. He argued that 'within the Church it is the Gospel that is the standard and touchstone of all spirituality'. All human forms of spirituality are rooted in the revelation of a loving triune God. For Christians, no spirituality can be authentic if it is disconnected from Christ's revelation and the 'ultimate meaning' that is communicated and realized through that revelation.[5]

Unlike Lonergan and Rahner, von Balthasar was profoundly suspicious of the turn to 'experience' and to the human subject as the basis for theology and spirituality. In his view, this tended to make faith too subjective and detached it from its fundamental roots in revelation. Constructively, von Balthasar placed greatest emphasis on the importance of the visible form of Jesus Christ as the expression of God's inner-Trinitarian reality. The centrality of this idea pushes both theology and spirituality in an incarnational and sacramental direction. It also opens up a rich emphasis on beauty and aesthetics that became von Balthasar's hallmark.

We have already noted that continental Protestantism was at one time extremely suspicious of the language of spirituality or mysticism. However, in recent decades a number of significant Protestant theologians have begun to give attention to religious experience or to a theology of the spiritual life. Some people would suggest that all the major writings of Jürgen Moltmann bring together questions of Christian living with the great themes of Christian doctrine. Moltmann has also written one or two essays explicitly in what would these days be called the field of spirituality. The most notable is his little book *Experiences of God* and especially the chapter 'The Theology of Mystical Experience'. There are some brief but interesting remarks concerning the distinction between mystical and doctrinal theology. Moltmann also comments on the ethical dimension of the 'experiential wisdom' (*sapientia experimentalis*) that is associated with spirituality or mysticism. This concept is similar, of course, to Luther's own emphasis and is also close to Tillich's idea of 'participative knowledge'.

However, the most interesting aspect of Moltmann's essay is his approach to the dynamics, or stages, of the spiritual journey. Moltmann's theology of the cross enables him to express the purpose of 'mystical union' in terms that avoid any sense of separation from the world or of a necessary transcendence of material existence. On the contrary, Moltmann perceives mystical union as a preparation for action, for radical political commitment and for a deepened discipleship *in the world*. This is the pattern for Christian life determined by the cross of Jesus. Moltmann also pursues the theme of the relationship of mysticism to the theology of the cross in another, little known, essay on Teresa of Avila.[6]

Another German Protestant theologian, Wolfhart Pannenberg, has addressed questions of spirituality in more detail. He is particularly critical of the kind of academic theology that appears to be uninvolved with questions of application and practice or that intentionally separates itself from the experiential roots that underlie doctrinal issues. Clearly there is a reciprocal relationship between spiritual experience and doctrinal reflection. Equally clearly it is perfectly valid for Pannenberg to say that, in a certain sense, the contours of any Christian spiritual tradition will be determined by prior theological assumptions. However, Pannenberg also accords a certain priority to spirituality in the otherwise endless hermeneutical circle. Thus he suggests that every major historical form of spirituality implies a complete interpretation of the world. This will relate to whatever aspect of doctrine is central to the religious consciousness of the time. Yet at the same time, 'in the more important forms of Christian spirituality we encounter the substructures of theology'.

Pannenberg astutely notes that the Reformation was a response to a *spiritual* crisis rather than a purely intellectual one. When he describes medieval spirituality, he may be open to the criticism that he indulges in some historical over-simplification. Doubtless there was a profound sense of distance from God and of sinfulness in much (but not all) medieval piety. However, this is unlikely to have been the product merely of the development of auricular confession and penitential literature as Pannenberg appears to suggest. The spiritual climate was in practice the product of a much more complex mixture of factors. This included changes in religious practice over time, socio-economic realities and a general sense of human vulnerability that arose from regular cycles of plague, war and famine. Whatever the causes, the consequence was an urgent concern for immediacy with God and the cultivation of every form of mediation that might serve to bridge the divine-human divide. Thus the classic doctrines of Reformation theology, such as justification by faith alone, responded to profound spiritual needs and then themselves gave birth to a new spirituality. However, Pannenberg is concerned that subsequent Protestant spirituality failed adequately to protect the Reformers' theological emphases. This is especially the case with the freedom of the Christian person brought about by grace. According to Pannenberg, Protestant piety tended to perpetuate the familiar medieval guilt-consciousness and penitential piety in new forms. More recently, as a response to this problem, Pannenberg has suggested the need to renew Protestant spirituality through a re-engagement with sacramental, especially eucharistic, theology.[7]

If we turn to the Anglican tradition, a number of recent

writers have given explicit attention to the relationship between theology and spirituality. Andrew Louth, who may be broadly considered a historical theologian with a particular expertise in patristic theology, has shown a consistent interest in the Christian mystical tradition. He has written substantial works on Pseudo-Dionysius and on the origins of the Christian mystical tradition as a whole. Louth has also, like John Macquarrie, written a short essay on the relationship between theology and spirituality.[8] The spiritual writer Kenneth Leech has offered an impressive modern version of 'spiritual theology' based on different ways of imaging God.[9] However, arguably the most consistently important contributions to the relationship between theology and spirituality come from the writings of Macquarrie's successor at Oxford, Rowan Williams. A concern for the re-engagement of theology with spirituality is implicit in everything he writes and in the totality of his approach to theology. It is therefore difficult to select particular works as 'spirituality' in contrast to other writings. However, the book, *The Wound of Knowledge*, has become something of a classic in the field of spirituality. While the book's framework is broadly chronological from the New Testament to the sixteenth century where it ends, it is not intended to be a full narrative history of spirituality. Rather, it is a rich essay concerning ways in which some central themes of Christian theology intersect with particular moments or traditions in the history of spirituality. In his recent study of Teresa of Avila, Williams also has many important things to say about the relationship of theology and spirituality, not least concerning how mysticism is a way of 'knowing' that is important and real yet distinct from the rational discourse of speculative theology.[10]

LIBERATION AND FEMINIST THEOLOGIES

Apart from individual theologians, two contemporary
schools of theology demand attention. Perhaps more than
any other recent school of theology, the liberation tradition is concerned to affirm the spiritual roots of all
theology. The theological method involved in the liberationist approach is fundamentally inductive rather than
deductive – that is to say, it consists of reflection on human
experience in a general sense. However, it is reflection on
the quite *specific* daily experiences of Christian communities in Latin America, Asia and elsewhere that exist in
conditions of overwhelming poverty, suffering and
oppression. Liberation theology is also a form of reflection
that focuses on the experience of *a people*, a collective
experience rather than that of isolated individuals. In this
tradition, theology and spirituality are inherently inter-
twined from the start and at all points. There is no question
of needing to bridge a gap or of bringing two discrete
disciplines together. As Gustavo Gutiérrez suggests,

> the kind of reflection that the theology of liberation repre-
> sents is conscious of the fact that it was, and continues to
> be, preceded by the spiritual experience of Christians who
> are committed to the process of liberation.[11]

Finally, it is important to note that liberation theology
reflects on explicitly *spiritual* experience rather than
merely on a socio-political one. Equally, it is the case that
valid theology is *lived* (orthopraxis) and so the actual following of Jesus Christ in concrete circumstances, not
merely reflection on 'discipleship', is an essential theological 'moment'.[12]

Another contemporary movement, feminist theology,
also suggests the need for a profound reintegration of
experience and reflection.

As the experience of God's salvation in Christ and the response of individuals and groups to that salvation, spirituality can be understood as the source of both theology and morality.[13]

Again, this relationship is dialectical because theology and morality also work upon spirituality. This means that they may critique and transform spirituality which is often an unconscious pattern of convictions and behaviour in relation to God. All generalizations are hazardous. However, it seems reasonable to suggest that a critical element in much feminist theology is the desire to shift theological anthropology away from a dual-nature theory to a single-nature one.[14] For feminist theology there may be observable differences between the sexes regarding styles of understanding and relating to self, others and God. Yet these result from the power of historical conditioning. Thus, it is argued, *feminist* theology and spirituality do not consist essentially in reflection on distinctively female ways of relating to God in contrast to male ones. That focus is more appropriately termed 'women's spirituality'. In contrast, feminist spirituality has intellectually sought to integrate a critique of patriarchal tradition and, in its application, lives out of this consciousness.[15]

In such contemporary theological approaches, a disjunction between the God who evokes a feeling response and the God of systematic theology is effectively undermined. Older styles of theology always had problems with spirituality. They were affected by limited understandings of 'scientific' truth which set great store on objective, value-free knowledge, as well as on the overwhelming importance of coherent systems. Personal experience was rejected because it was thought to have no place in the essentially rational and logical compendium of faith. Today, those who seek to trace the frontiers of theology are more likely to root themselves in a method and process that is experientially based.

THE SIGNIFICANCE OF TRINITARIAN THEOLOGY

> The doctrine of God is ultimately a practical doctrine with radical consequences for Christian [and I would add 'human'] life.[16]

We have already seen that the doctrine of the Trinity in the West became in large measure disconnected from the theology of salvation. The consequence was a separation between doctrine and what might be called 'practical' or 'applied' theology of any kind, not least spirituality. The theological frameworks employed both in post-Reformation Catholicism and, eventually, within the Churches of the Reformation suffered from the same problem. They failed until recent decades to re-envisage the doctrine of the Trinity in such a way as to re-engage the doctrine of God with Christian living.

In contrast to what might be called a Trinitarian void, the 1980s and 1990s have witnessed an extraordinary reassessment of the doctrine of the Trinity. The Trinity is once again at the centre of theological debate. In one sense this is excellent. However, the very fact that Trinitarian theology has become fashionable has its dangers. There is a tendency for some approaches to concentrate on one aspect of the doctrine while appearing to make this the whole story. Some approaches also appear to make the Trinity a way of validating contemporary cultural perspectives. This is a subtle temptation precisely because it *is* vital and valid to underline the intimate connection between Trinitarian belief, human existence and Christian practice.

The foundation for much contemporary thinking lies in some version of Karl Rahner's dictum that *'the "economic"*

Trinity is the "immanent" Trinity and the "immanent" Trinity is the "economic" Trinity'.[17] To put it more simply, the inner life of God is to be understood not as essentially other than but as inherently bound up with the whole economy of salvation. Many of the attempts to draw out the practical implications of Trinitarian belief, for example the work of Catherine LaCugna quoted above, often base themselves fairly substantially on the theology of Karl Rahner. While Rahner's approach to the Trinity has found wide acceptance, it has sometimes been criticized for appearing to suggest that there is no more to God than God's action in history. This risks a kind of reductionism that compromises God's freedom in the process of revelation.[18] Although Rahner's dictum needs to be nuanced, the phrase has the value of excluding all idle speculation about the being of God apart from God's action in salvation. It is vital to remember that the freedom of God does not imply the utter *arbitrariness* of God's action. This would imply a kind of divine dysfunctionality where there was no congruence between what God does and what God is. If the doctrine of the Trinity does truly have implications for Christian life, such an image of God would hardly do! God can only be free to do what God *is*. This, however, is not the same as to suggest that God somehow comes into being within human history or as a result of history.

Contemporary reflections on the Trinity are no longer limited to attempts to analyze the inner life of God. On the contrary. They are profoundly concerned to relate the doctrine to questions of how Christianity may be expressed in our contemporary cultures. It is nowadays more clearly understood that our images of God influence our views of reality and thus define our attitudes to the natural and social world and to what it means to live a Christian life. One only has to reflect on classic Enlightenment (or 'modern') understandings of human personhood as rational, free-standing and autonomous. This corresponds to an image of God as similarly 'objective', autonomous, disengaged and unaffected by anything outside God's own being.

If we wish to understand the riches of the doctrine of the Trinity, with its newly recovered dynamism, we need to understand it to be much more than merely one doctrine among many. In reality, to affirm God as Trinity touches every aspect of Christian belief, attitudes and living.[19] There have been a variety of proposals concerning how Trinitarian theology is now understood to have implications for Christian living. The doctrine of the Trinity matters not simply to the overall enterprise of Christian *doctrine* but equally to the life of the Christian Church and its members and even to the organization of society. The comments that follow do not pretend to be a comprehensive summary of contemporary Trinitarian thinking. They merely highlight themes in recent writing about the Trinity that appear to connect most obviously with the theory and practice of Christian spirituality. To some extent these themes group around the idea of 'relationality' and its implications for ethics as well as for a theology of the Church and for our prayer.

The concept of 'relationality' has become a popular focus for contemporary reflections on the Trinity. The problem is that such a concept is capable of being reduced to a rather simplistic equation that goes something like this. 'God is social therefore human life is social.' Despite the dangers of reductionism, the concepts of relationship and community do seem to offer especially fruitful connections between doctrine and spirituality. This shift is understandable as relatedness stands in sharp contrast to inherited images of God as essentially distinct from the world, free from the limitations imposed by change and by time and disengaged from the impact of human events.

In terms of spirituality, this view tended to reinforce individualistic, disengaged and anti-material attitudes. According to a relational model, the doctrine of the Trinity reveals a quite different understanding both of the nature of God and of human personhood in the image of God. The fundamental truth of our existence is that human beings and God are both rooted in mutual self-giving love. To exist consists of being-in-relationship.

Some modern theologians have attacked Augustine for individualism in his approach to the Trinity. Despite the evidence that may be gathered from an immediate study of his *De Trinitate* this judgement may be unfair. For one thing it is unlikely that Augustine would have understood the notion of 'individual' in our modern sense. In terms of Augustine's intellectual world, 'individuals' did not reflect the life of God in some self-contained way. On the contrary, it is 'humanity', a plurality of persons, which is in the image of God. Interestingly, Augustine's commentary on Genesis is quite clear that privacy or self-enclosure is the most insidious form of this-worldly pride which would not be reflected in the Heavenly City. This was precisely because such an attitude goes against what is public, shared, common.[20]

One approach to the implications for spirituality of a relational model of God has taken what is often called a 'social' direction. This approach has strongly political and ethical overtones but is limited by its rather functional nature. For example, Jürgen Moltmann rejects a hierarchical approach to God's nature and its implications for the ordering of human existence. The cardinal point of the doctrine of the Trinity is that no divine person is more complete or more significant than any other. The incarnate Jesus is not subordinate to the Father. Moltmann prefers the traditional image of mutual interrelationship (*perichoresis*) as more fruitful for approaching the reality of

God. He would argue that, as a consequence, 'superiority' and 'subordination' have no place in the social order either. Moltmann believes that such a view of God undermines any tendency to place our spiritual natures (soul) in a superior position over our bodies or a spiritual realm over the material world or men over women. His social theology and spirituality emphasize mutual relationships and partnership as opposed to domination and control. This applies both to interhuman relationships and to how humanity responds to the natural world.[21]

Both liberation theology and feminist theology have also contributed to the social or relational model of the Trinity. Not surprisingly, feminist theologians share with Moltmann a strong antipathy to hierarchical relationships. The equality of relations within God is the basis for non-hierarchical relationships more generally. This is not merely by way of example but also through God's concrete action within human lives.[22] Within the liberationist tradition, the Brazilian theologian Leonardo Boff also moves beyond a purely exemplary approach to God's social nature in relation to human equality. To be 'social' is the very goal of our existence, collectively as well as individually. The purpose of human history is to become 'society' in a true sense. Thus our present duty is to protest against all structures of domination, injustice and division that inhibit this fundamental vocation of humanity.[23]

Some contemporary theologians go beyond a primarily functional approach to the 'relational' Trinity. They seek to enrich the possibilities of making connections between the nature of God and the lives of Christians. For them, God's relational quality is fundamental to God's being. In other words, it is an 'ontological' category. God can only be understood as 'persons-in-communion'.[24] Attempts to develop what might be called a 'communion' model for God's nature owe a great debt to the work of the Greek

Orthodox theologian, John Zizioulas, who in turn bases himself upon the fourth-century Cappadocian Fathers.[25] According to a communion model, God is not to be thought of as absolutely simple but as 'being-in-communion'. Communion makes things be and nothing exists without it, not even God. God's unity consists in the interrelationship of persons in free and loving relationships. This understanding of God is particularly rich in possibilities for a theology and spirituality of personhood and community. 'A person' is not a self-relational category. Both particularity and relationship are structured into the very nature of all created reality including human persons.

In the course of discussions like this, we must beware of making conceptual prisons for God. 'Relationality' has its place in our thinking about God but on its own the concept cannot do justice to the full riches of Trinitarian theology. 'Relationality' can easily become yet another *conclusion* – something that we begin to say exclusively and conclusively about God. The French philosopher Jean-Luc Marion prefers the more traditional language of God as Love. This enables us to move beyond the limitations of the language of Being in reference to God. In what Marion calls the 'Trinitarian game of love', God is inherently giver. God loves by definition. 'No condition can continue to restrict his initiative, amplitude, and ecstasy. Love loves without condition, simply because it loves; he thus loves without limit or restriction.'[26] Marion's idea of God's 'ecstasy' is a reminder that the name 'Love' for God implies an overflow, an outpouring that is pure gift. This comes closer to the metaphorical language of Pseudo-Dionysius than it does to any idea of relationality as a reasonable 'definition' of the Trinity and its relevance to human existence. The outpouring of God enters human history precisely as a mysterious *God* not as an intelligible definition. This outpouring is enfleshed in Jesus of Nazareth who loved to the end, to the cross and beyond, and thereby expressed God's excessive love.

The cross carries a number of meanings that challenge the 'intelligibility' of God. First, the mode of God's revelation is, paradoxically, found in hiddenness, darkness, negativity and in the suffering of those who exist beyond the margins of public history. Further, God is experienced as a hope beyond hope whose power is often expressed within the struggle for human liberation. Finally, God provides a 'radical interruption' of human history and disrupts our self-satisfied sense of confidence in the essential continuities of history. A number of theologians, among them for example David Tracy, argue that we need to recover a far more eschatological understanding of God-as-Trinity.[27]

The contemporary emphasis on community, love and relationship at the heart of God clearly points to the practical and ethical consequences of believing in the Trinity. Yet we need to avoid the danger of reducing the Trinity to a question of relevance. The validity and strength of the doctrine does not consist simply in sanctioning contemporary social ethics or a spirituality of justice however important and admirable these may be. In the end, the doctrine of the Trinity is necessarily 'autonomous' from our needs. By this I mean that God's nature is utterly free, even if free only to be Godself – that is to say, 'Being-in-communion'. It is not the case that because we may think that democracy is a good thing we are (re)discovering that the Trinity is a *useful* idea. In the end Christians believe that the Trinitarian nature of God is a matter of revelation. In other words, it is not something we conclude by means of rational processes. Nor is it a form of extrapolation from our values such as 'community' or 'equality'. We know God as Trinity because of the life and work of Jesus Christ and the gift of the Spirit.

The Christian understanding of God, expressed in the

doctrine of the Trinity, critiques all human attempts ultimately to *conceive of God*. This is more than a question of
God being beyond our language or our definitions. To put
matters in more ethical terms, the Trinity as 'an obstinately
mobile and questioning force within [Christianity's] fundamental language'[28] undermines all attempts at idolatry.
Idolatries tend to attempt to dominate and to control not
merely the mind but also the human spirit. Spirituality and
ethics are brought radically together within the doctrine
of God as Trinity. It is valid to understand the goal of the
spiritual life as 'holiness'. However, this is not to be
attained through human effort particularly the achievement of some kind of isolated 'perfection' in which a
person comes to gaze on eternal truth! A truly Trinitarian
spirituality not only recognizes the all-embracing nature
of God's initiative as against human achievement. It also
understands that 'perfection' is to be found in an increase
of communion between persons.

Thus, a spirituality that is informed by belief in a Trinitarian God counters any tendency to reduce Christian living
to a solitary spiritual quest or to individual ethical
behaviour. Likewise such a spirituality, because it rejects
the notion of God as isolated and disengaged, excludes
any understanding of human holiness that involves being
set apart from the material world. We are called upon to
recognize and to respond to God who dwells within all
things at all moments. Several contemporary Trinitarian
writings emphasize the centrality of praise, or 'doxology',
in Christian living.[29] A Trinitarian perspective brings spirituality and theology together because doxology is central
to the doctrine. The doctrine of the Trinity does not merely
seek to speak *about* God (indeed emphasizes a certain
reticence in speaking) but underpins a *desire* for God. From
the earliest days of the Christian community, the life of
the community and of individuals within it has been under-

stood as a journey to God, through Christ and in the Spirit. Prayer does not merely express such a belief but is actually part of the process of the journey itself. Thus, praise, doxology, is not simply a way of stating things but is actually instrumental in drawing us into the relational mystery of God. Our 'end' is to be 'in God'.

The Christian life may thus be described fundamentally as a movement of deification. For Christians, this movement takes place within the life of the Church. A vital dimension of the conversion or transformation implied by deification is a new capacity for relationship. Baptism reinforced by Eucharist roots our Christian living in the Spirit of Christ that anticipates the fullness of the Kingdom of God. This is not merely an assurance of some future new life but is also a mystical participation even now in the life of God. For example, to pray the 'Our Father' is more than merely an objective statement of Christian doctrine. To pray authentically can only happen from a place that is within God. The 'end' of human existence is communion, but not purely as free-standing people with a free-standing God. Rather our purpose and our hope is a communion between human persons that is bounded by the communion that is God's own life.

HOW DO THEOLOGY AND SPIRITUALITY RELATE?

Nowadays, few people would disagree that it is important to overcome the divide between the experience of faith and intellectual reflection upon it. The serious disagreement among scholars these days is not whether spirituality and theology relate to each other but, methodologically speaking, how they do so. Basic to this issue is the question of whether we think we are bringing together two realities that do not have an inherent connection or whether we are making explicit a relationship that is always present implicitly. However this question is ultimately resolved, it is unlikely to be in simple terms where spirituality is seen as no more than the practical expression of Christian doctrine. Any description of the current debate needs to be nuanced in reference to specific writers. However, there are broadly speaking two major schools of thought. The first seeks to defend spirituality as an autonomous discipline that is distinct from theology while related to it. The second wants to avoid the development of a separate discipline and prefers to treat spirituality as a subdivision of theology.

The most significant English-speaking proponent of the first position is Sandra Schneiders. The American scholar has published several ground-breaking articles on the definition of spirituality as an academic discipline and its methodology.[30] Schneiders believes that spirituality and theology are close partners that function in mutuality but respect each other's autonomy. Spirituality should not be conceived as a subdivision of one of the traditional theological disciplines such as systematics, historical theology or moral theology. Theology cannot ultimately *contain* spirituality because the latter is essentially interdisciplinary in nature and, even in a Christian context, is no longer limited to a practical outworking of doctrines. The problem with the dominance of a theological approach is that it tends to exclude proper study of those aspects of contemporary Christian spiritualities that move beyond normal theological boundaries. Equally, this approach tends to apply dogmatic norms as the exclusive criteria of judgement. Spirituality is a particularly fruitful arena where Christian and non-Christian scholars can meet. Here, rather than in a narrowly-conceived theological context, non-Christian insights have a better chance of challenging Christian assumptions and of suggesting fruitful new lines of enquiry.

The second viewpoint is represented by the outstanding scholar of mysticism, Bernard McGinn. McGinn believes that spirituality is somehow primary in its partnership with theology. In that sense he rejects the old-fashioned view that spirituality was dependent on dogmatic theology and was exclusively theological in character. Nevertheless, he is concerned that the particularity and concrete nature of religious experience should properly be the concern of all healthy theology. Consequently, McGinn believes that spirituality is most effectively taught within a combination of theological disciplines: systematics, historical theology, ethics and the history of Christianity. Following von Balthasar, he believes that the particularity of Christian spiritual experience demands that traditions of Christian belief and practice be the primary criteria of interpretation.[31] Some scholars who start from an explicitly theological position describe 'spirituality' in terms that are closely related to the older Roman Catholic concept of 'spiritual theology'. By that I mean that spirituality can be encompassed within a purely theological framework, albeit one that is generously conceived, as a distinct area or discipline similar to systematics or Church history. Interestingly, this is true of two writers who are not Roman Catholics, the Lutheran Bradley Hanson and the Anglican Kenneth Leech.[32]

More recently, a number of British and American theologians have tried to break away from the sharp juxtaposition of the two positions just outlined.[33] It seems possible to argue for the centrality of a relationship between spirituality and theology without suggesting that spirituality should not be seen as a distinct discipline. The important word is 'distinct' rather than 'discrete' or 'autonomous'. In different ways, the new wave of writers reject any attempt by systematic or fundamental theologians to squeeze spirituality into their own tidy systems. Some speak of the need for a 'turn to spirituality' within the overall theological enterprise. Theology must come to realize more effectively its own, essential, spiritual core. It must also seek to enter into dialogue with spirituality in a way that is radically different from its more familiar conversations with philosophy or other intellectual disciplines. This involves allowing theological discourse to be questioned and even deconstructed by the deeper insight that the reality of God is beyond the 'God' of rational argument. The reality of God is more likely to be encountered by the ways of 'knowing' espoused by mystical texts that are, at the same time, ways of unknowing from the perspective of conceptual thinking.

Spirituality cannot simply be subsumed into structures determined primarily by doctrinal theology. For one thing, it is difficult to avoid the evidence of history that concrete spiritual traditions arise from Christian experiences or from the concrete realities of human existence rather than being derived from ideas and doctrines. The suggestion that experience has priority over theory needs to be nuanced. It is impossible to break open the hermeneutical circle in this way so as to establish a straightforward pattern of cause and effect. What is the first moment? Experience itself is born of assumptions, theories and reflection. Yet it is possible to say that the Christian way began with *events* rather than with a shift of theory born of intellectual speculation. The first followers of Jesus experienced their own lives and the nature of God's relationship with the world in a new way because of the impact upon them of the events of Jesus' life. In that sense experience is fundamental. We may say that Trinitarian or Unitarian understandings of God give rise to different attitudes to the Christian life. However, it is also possible to say that Trinitarian language gradually emerged over time as the

only satisfactory way of speaking about the God who had
been experienced in the Jesus events.

The classic Protestant formulae, *sola fide, sola scriptura,*
and *sola gratia* continue to offer a useful key to the process
of relating spirituality to theology. The rational discourse of
theology must be thought of as subordinate to three things:
to the original act of faith of Jesus' companions, 'You are
the Messiah, the Son of the living God' (*sola fide*); to the
fact that this faith is brought about by the action of God,
'flesh and blood has not revealed this to you but my Father
in heaven' (*sola gratia*); and to the privileged expression
of this faith in the pages of Scripture (*sola scriptura*).

I firmly believe that the relationship of spirituality and
theology is inherent and essential. They need to be reinte-
grated for the sake of each. A theology that is not related
to spirituality inevitably becomes abstract, disengaged,
rationalistic and tends towards an exclusive preference for
philosophical language. On the other hand, spirituality cut
adrift from theology not only risks becoming uncritical
devotionalism but also loses touch with the broader 'Great
Tradition' of faith that theology, at best, seeks to repre-
sent.[34] One might say that theology and spirituality are in
a dialectical relationship. Having said this, we are still left
with a difficult question concerning the precise model
for the spirituality-theology relationship. It seems easier to
describe what is *not* helpful than to provide a definitive
conclusion.

Overall, the 'spiritual theology' model nowadays appears
unsatisfactory. The contemporary study of spirituality is
inherently interdisciplinary and uses a great variety of
methodologies and genres of literature. Spirituality cannot
be fully comprehended by theology alone or be reduced
to a sector or sub-discipline within theology. Perhaps it is
more accurate to visualize the relationship in terms of
two non-concentric circles that overlap. This model would

certainly leave us free to posit a necessary relationship between the disciplines without containing spirituality exclusively within theology.

The weakness of the model, however, is that it also suggests that there may be areas of theology untouched by spirituality. We cannot separate doctrine from spirituality without actually dismembering theology through neglecting its fundamental relationships. A more fruitful model might be imaged rather like a wheel intersected by an axle. The 'wheel' of theology rotates around an axis, centre, or core of spirituality. Yet, because the image is three-dimensional, it also suggests that spirituality (the axle) points outwards beyond the constraints of purely theological definition and method into another dimension.

THEOLOGY EVALUATING SPIRITUALITY

What actual use to each other are spirituality and theology? A number of writers have reflected in interesting ways on theological criteria for evaluating spirituality. Spirituality as an area of study obviously needs tools both to analyze and to evaluate different traditions, their texts and other modes of self-communication. Given the plurality of contemporary approaches to spirituality, and the apparent novelty of some of them, the question of criteria for assessing what is 'authentic' from a Christian perspective takes on greater importance. These criteria will be based on central theological principles developed within the faith community. From a theological perspective, the process will involve addressing questions to spiritualities in order to discern theological dimensions that are often only implicit.

Some theologians have responded to the increasing appeal to experience in theology by developing criteria for evaluating religious experience. These criteria are also useful in terms of evaluating different approaches to spirituality. Theologians commonly approach the question on two levels. Prior to an examination of criteria drawn specifically from the Christian tradition, such theologians agree that it is important to show that religious experience meets the basic demands of modern 'secular' knowledge and life. This approach is conceived in terms of what are called 'criteria of adequacy'. Beyond this basic, human level lies a further level concerning issues of faithfulness to a specifically Christian understanding of existence. This approach is termed 'criteria of appropriateness'. The contemporary work of the American David Tracy may be taken as a typical example.

The application of criteria of adequacy should not be interpreted as a reduction of Christian theology and spirituality to non-religious norms. What it implies is that neither spirituality nor theology can be innocent of generally accepted developments in human knowledge. Nor can they ignore the ways in which previously overconfident views of human progress have been undermined by recent, painful historical events. To put it simply, we have to take into account the new worlds opened up by cosmology, evolutionary theory, psychology and the social and political sciences. Equally, theology and spirituality can never be the same again after the Holocaust and Hiroshima.

Tracy suggests three broad criteria of adequacy. First, every particular religious interpretation of experience needs to be meaningful. That is, it must be adequately rooted in common human experience and related to our lived experience of the self. Put another way, what aspect of ordinary human experience, shared by many or all, is expressed in any given spiritual tradition? Does it relate to reality as commonly understood? Second, the specifically religious understanding of experience should be coherent. All spiritualities make some cognitive claims in that they seek to reveal meaning. Can these claims be expressed conceptually in a coherent way? Do they also fit with the generally accepted claims of responsible scientific knowledge? Third, any given spiritual tradition needs to throw light on the underlying conditions that make existence possible. Does it have anything to say about whether our human confidence in life is actually worthwhile? Does it affirm that 'the good' will have the last word? Does it confirm the underlying conditions for the possibility of existence in the human world?[35]

When we turn to a specifically Christian perspective, David Tracy argues the need for criteria of appropriateness in general terms, while other theologians such as Dermot Lane and Walter Principe have provided useful summaries of what these criteria might be. In general terms, every particular spirituality ought to relate us to a God worthy of our complete loving involvement. It should bring about genuine conversion. Does a spirituality offer 'special' or individualistic experiences or does it offer a connection to a wider community of experience? This latter criterion seems particularly important in a world where so-called New Age practices or new religious movements appear to offer experience detached from commitment or insights that are open only to special initiates.[36]

More specifically doctrinal criteria would be as follows. Here our images of God are particularly vital. Redemption through Jesus Christ and deification through the agency of the Holy Spirit *constitute* the Christian life. Because of this, an adequate understanding of Christian spirituality must be grounded in the doctrine of the Trinity. This functions as a summary of Christian faith and critiques distorted spiritualities that are preoccupied, in a narcissistic way, with 'self-realization'.[37]

Every version of Christian spirituality can be judged in reference to belief in a Trinitarian God who is engaged with the human condition and to a belief in incarnation

and all that this implies. Does it, for example, recognize
the priority of God's grace and Jesus' saving work over the
power of unaided human effort? Is the view of God
adequately personal or is it impersonal or deist? On the
other hand, Christian spiritualities need to be adequately
transcendent and 'other'. They should avoid being excessively anthropomorphic or pantheistic. Does the spirituality
suggest a graced world or a world radically alienated from
God? Is there an adequate view of creation as God's outpouring into the cosmos? Spiritualities are ultimately
concerned with redemption. Does a spirituality portray the
created order as redeemed or is it merely that individuals
are redeemed *out of* a world that is never more than a vale
of tears? In general, the theology of grace implied in a
given spirituality needs to be examined.

Spirituality is concerned with choice or commitment. A
major question is what role is given to inspiration by the
vision and teachings of Jesus Christ. Within the limits of
legitimate diversity and of valid emphases, spiritualities
should be sufficiently 'catholic' in the sense of inclusive of
the *whole* gospel rather than selective, exclusive or unbalanced. On the other hand, spiritualities can be excessively
Christocentric by neglecting the role of the Spirit or,
indeed, of a transcendent God to whom the teachings of
Jesus point. Is the nature of the conversion described and
offered related to the dynamics of the death and resurrection of Jesus Christ? Does it not only have an individual
dimension but also a social dimension in line with Jesus'
teachings about the demands of the Kingdom of God?
How is the goal of the Christian life viewed? What models
of holiness are presented?

The role of theological anthropology is crucial to all
spirituality. Is the view of human nature excessively materi-
alistic or is it, on the contrary, dualistic with a low theology
of the human body and a detached theology of 'the spiri-

tual dimension' of human life? How are human emotions judged? Is sufficient role given to imagination as opposed to an exclusive emphasis on intellect and will? What is the understanding of sin? How is suffering viewed? How is human work viewed? Is there a balanced and healthy evaluation of sexuality?

It hardly needs to be emphasized that understandings of prayer and contemplation are presented by every spiritual tradition either explicitly or implicitly. Is the approach to mysticism elitist? Does a tradition view Christian life as essentially rooted in a common baptism, or does it tend to perpetuate a hierarchy of lifestyles? Is there a balance between contemplation and action?

Christian spirituality of its nature cannot avoid the question of 'tradition'. Does a spirituality, however radical and prophetic, exist in some kind of continuity with the experience of the Christian community across time and place? What is the role of Scripture and tradition? Is it peripheral and accidental or, on the other hand, is the approach to Scripture or tradition fundamentalist? Is the spirituality excessively individualistic or does it relate to communal activity and worship? Does it manifest a balanced approach to authority?

We are increasingly faced with spiritualities or practices of piety that seem to have an unbalanced emphasis on one aspect of Christianity to the apparent exclusion of others (for example, some versions of Charismatic renewal). Is a spirituality compatible with the hierarchy of truths and values that exists within Christianity? For example, does a spirituality focus on a specific devotion or traditional activity to such an extent that it becomes unbalanced or of no more than antiquarian interest?

Spiritualities exist on a spectrum from otherworldly in emphasis to 'secular' in tone. So, finally, an important question is whether a spirituality has a developed eschatology and specifically one that encourages an appropriate balance between 'the now' and 'the not yet'. Does a spirituality allow a proper place for the value of human history? What is its understanding of the virtue of hope?

SPIRITUALITY EVALUATING THEOLOGY

The way that spiritualities offer criteria to judge the adequacy of theology has received less attention up to this time. A fundamental question must always be borne in mind. This concerns whether a theology offers not merely some attempt at knowledge of the presence of God but a knowledge that enlivens the *practice* of the presence of God. Intellectual coherence is not enough.

> Spirituality [is] that which keeps theology to its proper vocation, that which prevents theology from evading its own real object. Spirituality does not really answer the question, Who is God? but it preserves the orientation, the perspective, within which this question remains a question that is being evaded or chided.[38]

One of the main virtues of Karl Rahner's theological method is the fact that it consistently reminds us that spirituality provides solid foundations for judging the adequacy of our theological explanations. For example, classical 'spiritual texts' can be true sources of theology. They frequently contain wisdom that theology has not taken seriously. If we were to push Rahner's basic stance (that theology arises from an experience of the Spirit) to its logical conclusion, spirituality becomes *the* way of integrating the many aspects of theology. Spirituality is the unifying factor that underlies all attempts to 'do' theology or, more properly, *be* a theologian. This is so whether the approach is dogmatic, historical, biblical or ethical. As more than one writer has noted, either implicitly or explicitly, spirituality is a kind of Ricoeurian 'field-encompassing field'. This does not simply imply that spirituality is interdisciplinary in itself but that it has the unique capacity to provide a unity and coherence to our theology as a whole.[39]

Spirituality does not merely unify our tentative attempts to approach the reality of God. It also offers a vital critique of any attempt by theology to launch itself into some stratosphere of timeless truth, abstract distinction or ungrounded definition. The way that spirituality 'speaks' of God is radically different from the approach of old-fashioned systematics. If theology turns to spirituality and allows its explanations to be questioned it will find that spirituality recognizes that what is implied by the word 'God' cannot ultimately be spoken completely. In that way 'spirituality' undermines any attempt by theology, particularly philosophical theology, to elude the elusiveness that matters most – that of God.

When the question of the evaluation of both theologies and spiritualities is discussed nowadays, traditional approaches are criticized by, for example, liberationist and feminist theories. These demand a 'hermeneutic of suspicion'. This implies that questions provoked by contemporary values and understanding will be more critical of the cultural and social assumptions behind theologies and spiritualities than used to be the case. There is a greater awareness nowadays of the conditioning that lies behind theological language and spiritual wisdom. Hidden ideologies need to be exposed to the light of day. Spirituality as well as theology as a whole, has tended to marginalize certain groups of people whether they are women or members of cultures other than dominant Euro-centric or North Atlantic ones.

As a result of these more radical perspectives, there may be a number of additional criteria that are especially

appropriate for us to apply today. We may care to ask
whether a particular theological or spiritual tradition is
open to the experience of 'the other', however that may
be conceived. Theology and spirituality also need to be
informed by human sciences that open us up to the widest
possible spectrum of reality. So many theological and spiritual traditions are uncritically Western. Or, rather, they are
uncritical in their claims to universal acceptance. Theology
and spirituality need to allow for indigenization and be
more or less critical of their own cultural conditioning and
consequent limitations. Finally, issues of justice cannot be
ignored. Many theologies and spiritualities bear noticeable
marks of patriarchy, unrestricted capitalism, racism, colonialism and individualism. Consequently the
appropriateness of the wisdom of a tradition is confronted
by the question of whether it is oppressive to any group of
people. If so, does this undermine its central values? Does
it respect the dignity and rights of the human person?
Does it foster maturity or immature dependence?

CONCLUSION

The deeply experiential character of much late-twentieth-
century theology, from Karl Rahner to liberation and feminist approaches, is a remarkable shift given centuries of
abstract theological method. Western theology and spirituality are in process of overcoming an ancient and radical
divorce that began in the late Middle Ages and was
reinforced by the Enlightenment. The last twenty years
have seen the beginnings of a serious conversation between
spirituality and theology. This is vital to both. Theology as
a whole has been increasingly able to acknowledge its roots
in human experience. Equally, spirituality has begun to re-
establish itself as an area of study that is not exclusively
theological yet is dependent on it.

PART TWO

CASE STUDIES

4

ᴏᴏᴏᴏᴏᴏᴏᴏᴏ

A Practical Theology of the Trinity: Julian of Norwich

As we have already seen, a number of contemporary theologians have become convinced that the Christian mystical tradition offers a vital source for renewing theology. However, when we approach spiritual texts with a theological frame of reference, we need to exercise some care. The great classical texts are not concerned primarily with ideas about doctrine but about the practice of the Christian life. By practice, I do not mean merely specific *practices*. For example, the writings of Julian of Norwich have remarkably little, if anything, to say about techniques of prayer or about devotional practices and ascetical disciplines. Unless, that is, the 'visions' with which Julian begins her two texts are to be understood as imaginative experiences arising from her contemplative prayer.[1] What I am implying is that it is all too easy to identify the infrastructure of theological ideas and assumptions that support the 'practice' taught by a spiritual text and yet miss its essentially religious aspect. A quite common category error is to try to explain religious experiences or teachings *merely* in terms of theological ideas. The study of spirituality must not be reduced to the theoretical ideas that people held or that we think they held.

If it is true that mysticism offers a source for the renewal of theology it will not be purely in terms of better conceptual frameworks. This is so even though certain texts, such as those by Julian, may in fact offer that as well. The writings of the great mystics introduce a *way* of knowing that is different from the way offered by traditional theological method. It is a knowledge that arises from participation and love rather than something that depends on purely rational enquiry. Mystical 'knowing' never loses sight of the essential ineffability of God and so it concentrates on seeking images to express the passionate and the poetic rather than on concepts and analysis to provide information. The mystical tradition in fact invites theologians to cultivate a degree of conceptual 'silence' and to re-engage their analysis with contemplation and the imagination.

The mystical tradition offers other possibilities for the contemporary seeker. Some people write of the contemporary 'postmodern' search for a spirituality that enables mystical union with a God who is (and who does) more than we can conceive. The contemporary parameters of spirituality also seek to cultivate an association with the suffering and abandoned Christ who is nevertheless the invincible ground of human hope and who offers a prophetic message of liberation for those who exist on the margins of human and religious life.

The writings of Julian are particularly rich from the point of view of the subject matter of this study. Her *Showings* (often called *Revelations of Divine Love*) are amongst the most theological of medieval mystical texts.[2] Julian is profoundly Trinitarian in tone. Not only that, but her approach to the Trinity echoes so many of the substantial questions raised in contemporary re-examinations of the doctrine. How does the inner relational and personal life of God connect with God's relationship with the world? How is salvation related to the inner life of God? Is the Trinity affected by creation and human history? Is the cross related only to one aspect of God, the eternal Word, or to the Trinity as such?

In one sense, Julian's 'showings' and her reflections upon them are a form of theological inquiry. She asks many questions about the nature of God, about creation and humankind, about sin and about the ultimate meaning and fulfilment of all things, or eschatology. However, at the same time, the 'showings' are an extended prayer because Julian's questions are directed to God 'not to her own ability to reason through the questions that she has asked'.[3] Julian's theology is entirely practical rather than concerned purely with the language and concepts we use concerning God. Her aim is to emphasize the love of God in such a way as to liberate her 'even [fellow or equal] Christians' from all that prevents them growing into the life of God. Our ignorance of love keeps us in sin and despair (LT73). In the end, therefore, there is only one 'showing' or 'revelation' and that is divine love. 'This is a revelation of love which Jesus Christ, our endless bliss, made in sixteen showings'(LT1). Julian is writing neither abstract theology nor as a means of self-expression – for example, a kind of spiritual diary. She wrote for others and describes the heart of her work as a 'blessed teaching' (LT73).

The basis for Julian's teachings is a series of visions of the Passion and yet in the very first 'showing' she comes to understand that 'where Jesus appears the blessed Trinity is understood, as I see it'(LT4). Two things follow from this. First, the fundamental 'showing' touches the inner reality of God in a direct way. 'And in the same revelation, suddenly the Trinity filled my heart full of the greatest joy'(LT4). The starting point of Julian's experience and theology is God the Trinity. 'For the Trinity is God, God is the Trinity.' Second, the suffering Jesus is revealed as the ground of hope. Julian experienced an inclination to 'look up to heaven to his Father' but she is drawn to say 'No, I cannot, for you are my heaven'.

> So I was taught to choose Jesus for my heaven, whom I saw only in pain at this time. No other heaven was pleasing to me than Jesus, who will be my bliss when I am there. And this has always been a comfort to me, that I chose Jesus by his grace to be my heaven in all this time of suffering and of sorrow. And that has taught me that I should always do so, to choose only Jesus to be my heaven, in well-being and in woe.(LT19)

The understanding Julian received was not only for 'the simple, unlettered creature' (LT2) who is granted the sight – a woman who was inherently on the margins of the Church without teaching authority or status. The message through Julian is for all who seek to love God, whatever their degree.

> In all this I was greatly moved in love towards my fellow Christians, that they might all see and know the same as I saw, for I wished it to be a comfort to them, for all this vision was shown for all men.(LT8)

JULIAN IN CONTEXT

Theologies and spiritual wisdom documents do not exist in a vacuum but have a context. We know very little for certain about the personal life of Julian, not even her given name. As was quite common practice among hermits, the name 'Julian' is taken from the Norwich church, St Julian's, to which her anchorhold or hermitage was attached. We do not know whether she was ever married, whether she had originally been a nun or whether she had belonged to one of the more informal women's religious groups imported from Flanders (Beguines) and which

existed in Norwich. We do not know when she became an
anchoress nor when she died. We do know from her own
writings that she received her visions in May 1373 (either
May viii or May xiii depending on the manuscript) when
she was thirty and a half. This puts her birth in 1342. In
the Long Text (51) she mentions that it was twenty years
after the visions that she fully understood the showing she
had of a 'parable' concerning the Lord and the Servant.
This would date the Long Text in its present form to about
1393. The one manuscript of the Short Text is a copy
probably dating from the middle of the fifteenth century
but its opening chapter has a scribal note that Julian was
still alive in 1413. There is also some slight external evidence concerning her dates. There is a probable reference
to a visit to Julian in the writings of Margery Kempe, a
younger contemporary spiritual figure, probably around
1413.[4] Within the period we can be sure about, extant
Norwich wills record bequests to an anchoress named
Julian in 1393/4, 1404 (the most definite evidence), 1415
and 1416.[5]

The rough parameters of 1342–1416 allow for a kaleido-
scope of events and influences within which Julian's
experience and teaching were focused. The Hundred
Years' War between England and France caused a continual death-toll from every social class and growing
taxation to pay for it. However, war also encouraged the
growth of Norwich as a port of European significance to
replace the more vulnerable towns of the south coast. At
the same time, this was the age of plague. Norwich first
succumbed to the Black Death early in 1349 and there
were two other outbreaks in the 1360s. Overall about a
third of the population died. The combination of war,
taxation and plague contributed to economic depression
and growing social instability. This culminated in the Peasants' Revolt of 1381 which was brutally suppressed, not

least by Bishop Despenser of Norwich. There was also serious instability in the Church. On the wider stage, Western Christianity was divided by the Great Schism from 1378–1414 with two and sometimes three papal claimants. In England, dissatisfaction with the Church gave rise to the anticlerical protests of John Wyclif, his departure from Oxford in disgrace in 1382 and the growth of the popular Lollard movement which, loosely speaking, drew upon some of Wyclif's ideas for reform. At the same time, the fourteenth and early fifteenth centuries saw an extraordinary flowering of spirituality in England including the writings of Walter Hilton, Richard Rolle, the anonymous author of *The Cloud of Unknowing* and related treatises and, later on, of Margery Kempe. Much of this writing was in the vernacular and paralleled the great flowering of English literature associated with Chaucer and Langland. The two texts of Julian are, in fact, the earliest extant vernacular writings by an English woman.

Julian's teaching about God and God's relationship to human beings is rich and complex. Because her *Showings* have pastoral and spiritual teaching always in mind, her approach to the doctrine of God is neither systematic nor abstract. It is woven throughout her teaching and is expressed in a variety of images that underline its practical focus. At the heart of Julian's vision of God lies the Trinity but the Trinity expressed most graphically in the suffering and humble Christ.

It is difficult to be precise or certain about connections between Julian's images and her cultural experience. Any comments must be tentative. There is no substantial evidence for Julian's sources beyond her own language. She does not explicitly quote any theological or spiritual sources nor does she make clear references to historical events. The degree to which Julian was even aware of theological influences in an explicit way is contested among scholars.[6] What is not a matter of dispute is that Julian's theological 'method' is inductive. She proceeds by reflecting on her foundational visionary experiences, rather than by using the deductive, dialectical and systematic approach of the 'schools'.

PASSION DEVOTION

A major aspect of Julian's religious culture and of her own 'showings' was the Passion of Christ. Devotion to the Passion of Jesus was widespread by the fourteenth century and so the visionary basis for Julian's teaching is not unusual. It is worth noting, however, that Julian is not unhealthily obsessed with the details of Jesus' sufferings as were some of her contemporaries.[7] The visions are simply starting points for her teaching about God's love for humanity.

We can point to a number of reasons why such devotion was common. First, it has been noted that a new kind of religious consciousness developed in the thirteenth century. Prior to that time, Western spiritual writing and art had been dominated by the image of the risen Christ or of the Logos. The humanity of Jesus, by contrast, was emphasized relatively rarely. The gradual development of a devotion to the human Jesus was fostered initially in Cistercian and then Franciscan circles. From there it passed to the broader spiritual reform movement, the *vita evangelica*, which influenced the groups of lay women known as Beguines (who were present in Norwich) and continental woman mystics more generally.[8] Artistically the thirteenth and fourteenth centuries saw an increase in crucifixes and paintings of crucifixes in churches. The affluent city of Norwich produced its own school of painting at around this time in which the humanity of Christ was significantly emphasized. The sufferings of

Christ were no longer simply formal but increasingly realistic. However it was equally the case that the theme of hope in God rather than fear of God seems to have been predominant.

These developments undoubtedly owe something to two cultural trends. Courtly or chivalrous love had its impact on spirituality particularly on the notion of spiritual love and a mysticism of intimacy with God. The joining of God to human flesh in Jesus was an increasingly powerful image. There was also a new humanism born of the long-term cultural and intellectual changes whose origins went back some one hundred and fifty years to what is rather loosely referred to as the twelfth-century Renaissance. Over the longer term this shift produced an increasing interest in individual subjectivity and in the realm of subjective feelings.[9] As well as intellectual and cultural reasons there was also the harsh fact of death produced by plague, war and famine. Julian's lifetime was dominated by these horrors. She makes no direct mention of them but she is preoccupied throughout her reflections by why suffering is permitted in a universe guided by a God whom she knows as Love.

It is worth adding that modern readers are frequently disturbed by Julian's admission (LT2) that she not only desired a vision of the Passion but also a bodily sickness that would bring her to the verge of death. Her own explanation is that the third gift she prayed for, the wounds of contrition, compassion and longing, was far more important. She only desired the vision and the sickness conditionally if it was God's will and she stated that the motive was 'because I wanted to be purged by God's mercy, and afterwards live more to his glory because of that sickness'. Strange though it may seem to us, the illness had a Christological trajectory. It was part of Julian's deep desire to participate more deeply in the Passion of Jesus. The text shows quite clearly that this was not merely a question of physical illness but of the spiritual temptation and desolation that she presumed was the experience of Jesus on the cross. This is part of the overall piety of imitation of Christ (*imitatio Christi*). It was characteristic of the great evangelical spiritual and reform movements that swept the Western Church from the twelfth century onward. The particular desire for illness as a symbol of solidarity with Jesus seems to have been more common among women than men.[10]

THE PASSION AS MEASURE OF THE TRINITY

Julian's foundational experience on which she bases her theological reflections consists of visions focused primarily upon the Passion of Jesus. Julian recognizes that everything she was taught was grounded in the first revelation (LT2-9). That is, the whole of Julian's theology finds its focus in the Passion. Her teaching on God as Trinity and on the creation and incarnation is ultimately measured by the standard of the cross. The Passion is understood fundamentally as the supreme revelation of the love of God. Love is God's nature and this love is directed outwards towards creation and humanity. Love itself, whether divine or human, is to be measured by the standard revealed in the Passion.

God's love is not an emotion. Nor is it one characteristic of God or simply related to God's external action. For Julian, Love is God's being or reality. Julian does not provide simple definitions to help us to understand what this means. Her pedagogical approach is to begin with the Passion as her foundation, expressed in visionary form, and then to proceed by means of other images and stories. In this way, Julian is able to teach a deeper wisdom beyond the language of logic. The *Showings* begin with an overwhelming image of self-giving love in the face of the crucified Jesus. Julian recognized that as she herself was, apparently, dying, she was being invited to contemplate the face of Jesus and to observe his crown of thorns and suffering. The details, while not extended or excessive compared to other contemporary piety, are none the less graphic.

> I saw his sweet face as it were dry and bloodless with the pallor of dying, and then deadly pale, languishing, and then the pallor turning blue and then blue turning brown, as death took more hold in his flesh. (LT16)

The *point* of the visions was to find in this broken figure the reality that this is God and that Julian fully experienced God's presence in Jesus. Yet, at the same time, to see God only in the flesh of Jesus or through God's 'working' also serves to preserve the otherness of God – transcendence even in the immanence.

> I perceived, truly and powerfully, that it was he who just so, both God and man, himself suffered for me, who showed it to me without any intermediary. (LT4)

Thus in Jesus Christ all humanity, creation, life and eternal future are caught up with him into the very life of God as Trinity.

> And in the same revelation, suddenly the Trinity filled my heart full of the greatest joy, and I understood that it will be so in heaven without end to all who will come there. For the Trinity is God, God is the Trinity. The Trinity is our maker, the Trinity is our protector, the Trinity is our everlasting lover, the Trinity is our endless joy and our bliss, by our Lord Jesus Christ and in our Lord Jesus Christ. (LT4)

On the cross, the relationship of God to humankind is shown to be identical with the love relationship of the

Trinity – a dynamic and mutual indwelling in which each person of the Godhead is constantly giving to and sharing with the others. This way of being is also revealed as afflicted love, united through suffering to all humanity.

> At the same time as I saw this sight of the head bleeding, our good Lord showed a spiritual sight of his familiar [or homely] love. I saw that he is to us everything which is good and comforting for our help. He is our clothing, who wraps and enfolds us for love, embraces us and shelters us, surrounds us for his love, which is so tender that he may never desert us. (LT5)

From the vision of Christ on the cross Julian learned, and teaches through a mixture of complementary images, that everything is filled with God and enclosed by God. Through the cross, God offers intimacy, 'familiar love'. Julian does not suggest directly that God suffers. Yet there are hints that God is not untouched by our condition. In the incarnation, God is indissolubly joined to the human condition and longs for us. Indeed, Julian is careful to say that,

> in his divinity he [Christ] is supreme bliss, and was from without beginning, and he will be without end, which true everlasting bliss cannot of its nature be increased or diminished.(LT31)

Julian employs paradoxical language. As second person of the Trinity, Christ is impassable as God. And yet, as united to the human condition, Christ is still said to have the thirst and longing that he had upon the cross. This will remain the case 'until the time that the last soul which will be saved has come into his bliss'. Then Julian is bolder still. There is longing and desire *in God* and this quality is part of God's everlasting goodness. Somehow, in Christ, God is touched by suffering out of love.

> For as truly as there is in God a quality of pity and com-
> passion, so truly there is in God a quality of thirst and
> longing ... And this quality of longing and thirst comes
> from God's everlasting goodness. (LT31)

Because of God's indwelling, this image of God's thirst
explains our own experience. God in Christ thirsts and
because of our union with God we also thirst. Just as
Christ's spiritual thirst is God's painful longing for us, so
the longing and yearning we feel is our unsatisfied desire
for God.

> God's thirst is to have man, generally, drawn into him, and
> in that thirst he has drawn his holy souls who are now in
> bliss. And so, getting his living members, always he draws
> and drinks, and still he thirsts and he longs. I saw three
> kinds of longing in God, and all to the same end, and we
> have the same in us, and from the same power, and for the
> same end. (LT75)

Julian is not systematic but imaginative in her theology
of God. Although she does sometimes assign traditional
'roles' to one or other of the persons of the Trinity, it is
fair to suggest that she breaches the boundaries that have
sometimes artificially separated the persons of the Trinity
in terms of their outward movement and action. Rather
than the Father being the creator, the Son the redeemer
and the Spirit the sanctifier, all persons of the Trinity
manifest creative, redemptive and sanctifying qualities.

For Julian the simple fact is that, in her understanding
of the Passion, the Trinity as a whole participate in all
activities relating to salvation even if only the 'virgin's Son'
may be said to suffer. 'All the Trinity worked in Christ's
Passion, administering abundant virtues and plentiful
grace to us by him; but only the virgin's Son suffered, in
which all the blessed Trinity rejoice' (LT23). The partici-

pation of the Trinity in salvation is also strongly implied
in the eleventh chapter of the Long Text where she sees
God 'in a poynte'.[11] Here God is seen to be in all things,
doing all things and bringing them to their ordained conclusion.

> And therefore the blessed Trinity is always wholly pleased
> with all its works; and God revealed all this most blessedly,
> as though to say: See I am God. See, I am in all things. See,
> I do all things. See, I never remove my hands from my
> works, nor ever shall without end. See, I guide all things to
> the end that I ordain them for, before time began, with the
> same power and wisdom and love with which I made them;
> how should anything be amiss?(LT 11)

The famous phrase, 'all will be well, and all will be well,
and every kind of thing will be well' is first introduced in
the Thirteenth Revelation in the context of sin and the
pain that it brings to humanity (LT27). It is in the Passion
of Jesus that the promise is made. Julian understands in
these words that this is part of the mystery at the heart of
God. This mystery of God's desire will issue in a 'deed'
and the deed that will be done to make all things well is
an action of the Trinity. In a further exposition of the
phrase the Trinitarian nature of salvation is explicitly
stated. The making well of all things relates to salvation
and all who are saved 'will be saved in the blessed
Trinity'(LT31). Julian assures her readers that on 'the last
day' the Trinity will perform a deed that will make 'all
things well'. At the same time God will reveal how this is
so. Until then it is concealed (LT32). It is clear from the
remainder of the chapter that Julian is struggling with her
sense that this may imply universal salvation and with how
this accords with the Church's teaching about the existence
of hell.[12] The central point, however, is that the ultimate
deed is the work of the Trinity. 'For just as the blessed

Trinity created all things from nothing, just so will the same blessed Trinity make everything well which is not well' (LT32).

'LOVE WAS HIS MEANING': TRINITY AND MOTHERHOOD

Julian's approach to the theology of God is performative and not simply informative. By focusing everything on the Passion (that is, on Jesus Christ) Julian is offering a strong signal that everything she has to say about God has a connection to our way of understanding human life. Thus, as we shall see, the various triads of properties that Julian uses in writing about the Trinity refer outwards to God's active being, that is, God's relationship with creation. For this reason some scholars suggest that Julian concentrates on the 'economic' Trinity.[13] It would be better to say that Julian's approach refuses to separate an economic from an immanent Trinity. For Julian, God is as God does. She is concerned to establish that the 'meaning' of God is love but this 'substantial' (i.e. natural) meaning is inherently related to God's deeds.

> Know it well, love was his meaning. Who reveals it to you? Love. What did he reveal to you? Love. Why does he reveal it to you? For love. Remain in this, and you will know more of the same. But you will never know different, without end. So I was taught that love is our Lord's meaning. And I saw very certainly in this and in everything that before God made us he loved us, which love was never abated and never will be, And in this love he has done all his works, and in this love he has made all things profitable to us, and in this love our life is everlasting. In our creation we had beginning, but the love in which he created us was in him from without beginning. (LT 86)

As we have seen, Julian is assured that God the Trinity

has the power to perform 'on the last day' a great deed whereby all that is not well will be made well (LT 32). Yet, this powerful God who can and will accomplish more than we can imagine is, for Julian, revealed totally and essentially as love. Love is not only God's meaning but the whole teaching of Julian's book. Everything else (including, for example, God's Lordship) is to be interpreted in the light of love. God may be thought of as all-powerful and all-knowing but the deepest truth about God is love. For it is love that unites the Trinity. Love is the inner life of God.

> Though the three persons of the blessed Trinity be all alike in the self, the soul received most understanding of love. Yes, and he wants us in all things to have our contemplation and delight in love. And it is about this knowledge that we are most blind, for some of us believe that God is almighty and may do everything, and that he is all wisdom and can do everything, but that he is all love and wishes to do everything, there we fail. (LT73)

Julian uses a number of triads in reference to the Trinity. These include Might, Wisdom, Love; Joy, Bliss, Delight; Maker, Keeper, Lover; Fatherhood, Motherhood, Lordship.[14] The most frequent triad is the first. Julian especially links power or might with the Father, wisdom with the Son and goodness or love with the Spirit. Yet these qualities are not to be limited strictly to specific persons of the Trinity. They are 'properties' in God. All the properties are in each of the persons. She succeeds in maintaining a delicate balance between the danger of dividing the persons of the Trinity from each other and, on the other hand, depersonalizing matters so as to deal only with abstract 'attributes'. Thus, as Julian 'contemplated the work of all the blessed Trinity' (LT58) she saw the three 'properties' of fatherhood, motherhood and lordship 'in one God'. While Julian appears later in chapter 58 to link these properties to the persons of the Trinity, she concludes the chapter by noting that our essential human nature (substance) dwells equally in each person and in all the persons together.

> And our substance is in our Father, God almighty, and our substance is in our Mother, God all wisdom, and our substance is in our Lord God, the Holy Spirit, all goodness, for our substance is whole in each person of the Trinity, who is one God.

It is generally agreed that Julian's thinking depends, whether consciously or unconsciously, on Augustine's *De Trinitate* XV. There it is the reciprocal love of each person for the others that unites the Trinity. For Julian, this love of the Trinity is never purely inward or introspective. It necessarily overflows into love for creatures or, perhaps better, it overflows itself *as creation*.

Julian is clear in her teaching about the fundamental unity of God as Trinity.

> For the Trinity is God, God is the Trinity. The Trinity is our maker, the Trinity is our protector, the Trinity is our everlasting lover, the Trinity is our endless joy and our bliss, by our Lord Jesus Christ and in our Lord Jesus Christ. (LT4)

This early statement is further underlined in chapter 23 concerning our salvation as we have seen. 'All the Trinity worked in Christ's Passion, administering abundant virtues and plentiful grace to us by him'. Again it is repeated near the beginning of the sixteenth and final revelation in reference to our creation,

> for as well as the Father could create a creature and as well as the Son could create a creature, so well did the Holy

Spirit want man's spirit to be created, and so it was done. (LT68)

The mutual indwelling of the persons of the Trinity one in the other (*perichoresis*) is affirmed at a number of points including at the end of the famous parable of the Lord and Servant.

Now the Son, true God and true man, sits in his city in rest and in peace, which his Father has prepared for him by his endless purpose, and the Father in the Son, and the Holy Spirit in the Father and in the Son. (LT51)

We are drawn into this mutual indwelling, into an intimacy with God that is Julian's version of deification. She expresses this as a mutual enclosure. We are enclosed in God and God is enclosed in us:

And I saw no difference between God and our substance, but, as it were, all God; and still my understanding accepted that our substance is in God, that is to say that God is God, and our substance is a creature in God. For the almighty truth of the Trinity is our Father, for he made us and keeps us in him. And the deep wisdom of the Trinity is our Mother, in whom we are enclosed. And the high goodness of the Trinity is our Lord, and in him we are enclosed and he in us. We are enclosed in the Father, and we are enclosed in the Son, and we are enclosed in the Holy Spirit. And the Father is enclosed in us, the Son is enclosed in us, and the Holy Spirit is enclosed in us, almighty, all wisdom and all goodness, one God, one Lord. (LT54)

All this implies, among other things, that the image of Motherhood, while used at first of Jesus Christ, is in fact a property of God as Trinity. Julian's treatment of this theme appears only in the Long Text, chapters 52-63, but then it is part of her reflections that follow on from the parable of the Lord and Servant which also appears only in the Long Text.[15] Julian is not alone among female and male writers in the Middle Ages in using the imagery of Motherhood in God.[16] She is unique however in the sophistication and complexity with which she relates the image both to the reality of God and of God's relationship to human nature. Julian's thought has been compared, unhelpfully, with the use of Motherhood imagery in the prayers of Anselm of Canterbury and in the *Ancrene Riwle* written in the thirteenth century for female hermits like Julian.[17] The comparison is inaccurate because both Anselm and the hermit rule portray the Motherhood of Jesus as standing between us and the righteous anger of God.

It is interesting to note that Julian does not suggest that God is *like* a mother but that God *is* mother. The choice of metaphor over simile is important because Julian does not wish simply to project conventional notions of human motherhood onto God. Rather the contrary. The motherhood of God is the measure of true human motherhood: ' . . . it is not that God is like a mother, but mothers make visible a function and relationship that is first and foremost in God'.[18] Thus Jesus Christ is 'where the foundation of motherhood begins' (LT59).

> This fair lovely word 'mother' is so sweet and so kind in itself that it cannot truly be said of anyone or to anyone except of him [Jesus] and to him who is the true Mother of life and of all things. (LT 60)

Of course the additional effect of suggesting that true motherhood *begins* in God is to underline that the 'being' and work of women are as much in the image of God as men are.

Julian may begin her reflections on motherhood with conventional human images such as nurturing and sustaining but she quickly moves divine motherhood onto another plane (e.g. in LT60). If the human mother feeds a child with milk, Jesus feeds the Christian with his very life in the Eucharist. The wound in Christ's side is a kind of parallel to the human mother's breast but in this case it nurtures us to the 'inner certainty of endless bliss'.

Julian's image of mothering is not passive but is seen as a work. She highlights the process of giving birth in both our natural creation and in the rebirth of salvation (e.g. LT57,60,63,64). The Passion is a labour and is compared to the pains of birth labour (60). There is nurturing (LT 60 and 63) and nursing (LT 43, 57 and 60) as dimensions of God's loving. But motherhood is not merely a matter of loving protection. There is also a motherhood of wisdom and knowing. 'To the property of motherhood belong nature, love, wisdom and knowledge' (LT60). This guiding role brings the human soul to its proper fulfilment.

Interestingly one of the most common images Julian uses for Jesus Christ throughout the 'showings' is 'teacher'. Thus: 'This is a revelation of love which Jesus Christ, our endless bliss, made in sixteen showings ... with many fair revelations and teachings of endless wisdom and love'(LT1). She is always being gently taught the truth of God's love, often in answer to her questions or worries. This is part of Christ's Motherhood and intimacy. God in Christ is not a remote pedagogue. Teaching is yet another aspect of love and has as its purpose not more abstract knowledge but a deepening of that kind of knowing that is founded on love. 'Our precious lover helps us with spiritual light and true teaching, in various ways from within and from without, by which we may know him' (LT71). Given that Julian presents her teaching about God as Trinity within such a strongly Christological framework, 'teacher' must be deemed one of her strongest images for God. Sometimes this is quite explicit. 'He [God] is the foundation, he is the substance, he is the teacher, he is the end, he is the reward for which every loving soul labours' (LT34).

In the first place to image God as teacher serves Julian's purpose to turn attention away from herself to the source of the teaching which is God. The purpose, no doubt, is to encourage all those who desire to be Christ's lovers to be drawn into a situation where they may be taught spiritually as she has been taught. Teaching and learning are presented as something that takes time. Psychic experiences such as visions (if that is what Julian experienced) are not what counts. The true teaching and the deep learning involved years of contemplation, reflection and thinking. However, another purpose of writing of God as the teacher is to deflect any suggestion that Julian herself claims to be a teacher at a time when lay people and women in particular were not accorded that role in the Church. Julian's 'showings' offer a message for all her fellow Christians. She is compelled to teach and yet the Church says that she cannot. So she is able to use the image of Christ/God as teacher as a rhetorical device to communicate the message without fear. In the meantime she safely remains the one who is simply *taught*, not least by Holy Church! She frequently uses the device of 'as Holy Church teaches me to believe' (e.g. LT32).

LORDSHIP AND FAMILIARITY

The image of the Lordship of God appears throughout Julian's writings. Sometimes the word 'lord' refers to God, at other times to Jesus Christ. On the other hand, one of Julian's most fundamental insights is that the mystery of the Trinitarian Godhead is located in the crucified Christ. Lordship is not merely a scriptural image but, for Julian, undoubtedly reflects the experience of feudal and hierarchical relations, albeit in an unusual and challenging way. It is not too far-fetched to suggest that Julian's challenge to traditional concepts of Lordship may encapsulate the serious questions being raised concerning the established social order in the fourteenth century. The rapid growth of cities like Norwich and the expansion of urban industry and trade was in one sense a symbol of the new world that was coming to birth. Feudalism, based on land ownership and the obligations of military service, was essentially a rural concept and it was on the decline. This was further exacerbated by the decimation of the traditional peasantry by the Black Death and famine as well as by a growing cynicism with the system as a result of the interminable wars with France. The impact of both was sharply expressed in the Peasants' Revolt of 1381.

We might logically expect an image of Lordship based on the world of feudalism to have produced an understanding of God as dominating or even domineering. This is not the case in Julian. Overall, her dynamic and life-giving experience of the Trinity is immensely attractive and convincing. It challenges both the tendency to posit a distant, hierarchical relationship between the persons and between the Trinity and creation and the classic image of a wrathful God generating a fear of damnation. One aspect of the teaching that 'all shall be well' is shown to Julian as an indication of God's homeliness and humility: 'he wants us to know that he takes heed not only of things which are noble and great, but also of those which are little and small, of humble men and simple, of this man and that man' (LT32).

Early in her text (LT7) Julian anticipates the parable of the Lord and the Servant. God shows her the example of 'a majestic king or a great lord' welcoming a poor servant into his presence with familiarity (another of Julian's favourite images for God's way of action) and in front of others. Julian contrasts this with merely showering a person with material gifts while remaining personally distant. Later, Julian is 'lifted up into heaven'. There, God is imaged as the lord who entertains all his friends to a great feast (LT14). The language Julian uses is almost lyrical:

> I saw him reign in his house as a king and fill it all full of joy and mirth, gladdening and consoling his dear friends with himself, very familiarly and courteously, with wonderful melody in endless love in his own fair blissful countenance, which glorious countenance fills all heaven full of the joy and bliss of the divinity.

The allegory or parable of the Lord and the Servant in the Long Text (51) is central to Julian's teaching. It provides a key to understanding the nature of God's faithful love and God's union with humanity through suffering. While the language reflects feudal hierarchies, the context and dynamic of the story and its teaching contrast sharply with social realities. For one thing, God is not simply the lord but also the servant who is identified not only with Adam and humankind but with Christ, second person of the Trinity and equal to the Father. Then again, the explanation of the parable in the Long Text, chapters 52-63, is dominated by Julian's feminine imagery for God – God as Mother. This not only redefines our images of God but also our notions of 'lordship' or authority.[19]

The language of 'courtesy' is chivalrous and courtly. The humility and reverent fear of 'our Lady St Mary' before God are commended (LT7). But 'our good Lord, who is so to be revered and feared, is also familiar and courteous'. The image of Jesus Christ as 'courteous Lord' is regularly repeated throughout the text. God's 'royal dominion' is closely linked to his 'wonderful courtesy' (for example, LT48). 'Courtesy' was an important attribute in the society of Julian's day. It involved polite behaviour in which one deferred to another – in other words, put the convenience or desires of another person before one's own.[20] So God defers to us and finds pleasure especially in giving pleasure. So courtesy implies familiarity but it is an unexpected (and unearned) familiarity that implies the crossing of conventional boundaries.

> So it is with our Lord Jesus and us, for truly it is the greatest possible joy, as I see it, that he who is highest and mightiest, noblest and most honourable, is lowest and humblest, most familiar and courteous. (LT7)

GOD AND PLACE

There can be no more striking image of God's courtesy and familiarity than to see the Lord and King dwelling in the humble state of the human soul. That is what Julian does. God's home, God's place, God's heaven is imaged as within us.

> For I saw very surely that our substance is in God, and I also saw that God is in our sensuality, for in the same instant and place in which our soul is made sensual, in that same instant and place exists the city of God, ordained for him from without beginning. He comes into this city and will never depart from it, for God is never out of the soul, in which he will dwell blessedly without end. (LT55, see also LT68)

There is a tension in Julian between her sense that God is 'in place' within created reality and a sense that her experience drew her beyond the limits of physical space. Her 'place' was with God. God was within her soul and God was within the created world. Yet, at the same time, God transcends the limits of the physical and material and so the Christian must not believe that contingent reality can satisfy human desires. This tension is perhaps most sharply expressed in Chapter 5 of the Long Text. The image of 'something small, no bigger than a hazelnut' affirms God's creation in love and continual preservation of all things. Yet Julian goes on to suggest that humans should 'despise as nothing everything created'. In the full context of Julian's teaching this is not a rejection of created reality but an affirmation that humans will not ultimately be satisfied if they mistakenly think of creation as ultimate reality.

In the very first revelation, Julian was astonished that God could be 'at home' (or 'familiar') with a sinful creature.[21] She initially interpreted the great joy that she was given as a form of temporary spiritual consolation because 'our Lord Jesus wanted, out of his courteous love, to show me comfort before my temptations began'(LT4). In a way this was true yet she came to see that it also revealed a teaching about the humility of God. Because God is humble, Julian's perfectly conventional desire to be with God in *heaven* (LT19) was converted. This was a defining moment in the teaching. She found that she did not need to go to a heaven elsewhere to be with God, for God was already 'at home' in the flesh of Jesus Christ and therefore with us in this life. God's 'homeliness' towards us is an extension of 'being at home'. The divine love was revealed to Julian not simply as willing to suffer on the cross but as at home in the human condition.

THE STABILITY OF GOD

The word 'homely' also has linguistic resonances of 'permanent' or 'habitual'. There is, therefore, an interesting connection between God's 'homeliness' and the Benedictine vow and virtue of 'stability'. This not only implies a commitment to make one's home permanently in a physical place but the virtue of *staying* or *sticking at it* 'for richer and for poorer'. This is the quality of God's dwelling among us. In the historical context of the late fourteenth century, the quality of permanence and stability has a particular force and poignancy. Not only was the Church and civil society racked by instability and insecurity but there was a widespread failure of trust in the social structures that should have provided an image of faithfulness. Bishops such as Henry Despenser of Norwich spent little time in their dioceses preferring London and service to the crown. Feudal lordship, based originally on a stable relationship not only with a place but with a group of dependent people, was in serious decline. In this sense the 'stability of God' filled the gap as a model both of true lordship and of real *episcope*.[22]

The stability that Julian formulated in terms of the economy of God's relationship to created reality reflects God's inner stability. Julian's Trinity is supremely active in creation and in human lives. The inner life of the Trinity involves a constant motion of relationships. Yet the Trinity also dwells in peace and stillness. 'Now the Son, true God and true man, sits in his city in rest and in peace' (LT51).

REALITY SEEN THROUGH GOD'S EYES

Mystics make truth claims in the sense that their writings attempt to express what they have come to know inwardly about God. In quite singular ways, a mystic such as Julian embodies God's presence. What she seeks to articulate from her experience is not only something of what God is but also something of how God sees. Because of this, she offers a radically alternative vision of created reality, including human existence. We might think of this as 'the world seen through God's eyes'.

123

It is this perspective, amongst other things, that differentiates Julian's approach to the Passion from the more common expression of Passion devotion. Essentially her experience of God is centred on the cross of Jesus. However, she does not simply see the Trinity through the cross. She also sees the cross through the eyes of the Trinity. For this reason she can write of the cross as the Trinity's joy or bliss. The most concise statement is in the first chapter of the Long Text in which Julian summarizes all the revelations. 'The ninth revelation is of the delight which the blessed Trinity has in the cruel Passion of Christ, once his sorrowful death was accomplished . . .' Interestingly it is while Julian contemplates the blood running down Jesus' face (LT4) that '*in the same revelation* [italics mine], suddenly the Trinity filled my heart full of the greatest joy'. It was precisely in 'this sight of his blessed Passion' that Julian understood the ultimate comfort that was God's desire for all humanity.

Julian's view of the world and especially human nature is also through God's eyes.[23] This results in two striking assertions. First, there is neither blame nor wrath in God (LT45-9). Second, and related to it, sin is 'nothing' (ST viii) or 'no deed' (LT11). In seeing God in everything (LT11) Julian also sees all things in God and therefore 'in all this sin was not shown to me'. Later, as she considers how sin hinders her longing for God (LT27) she is taught that she could not see sin as she contemplated the Passion because 'it has no kind of substance, no share in being, nor can it be recognized except by the pain caused by it'. Sin is the cause both of human pain and of the Passion and yet 'sin is necessary'. In an echo of the Easter Vigil, sin is the *felix culpa* that reveals so great a redeemer or, in Julian's teaching, enables us to experience the depths of God's being as love.

In the end, God does not 'see' sin but only the bliss that

will be ours. In God's vision this is the ultimate truth and so Julian, in her God's eye view, cannot see sin even though humanly she knows its effects. This is not to deny the reality of sin in the world of human actions and experiences. However, it is to say that the centrality of sin in human experience and theology is not reproduced on the level of God's essential relationship with humanity. Julian expresses this in terms of paradox at the end of chapter 34: 'When I saw that God does everything which is done, I did not see sin, and then I saw that all *is* well. But when God did show me about sin, then he said: All *will* be well' [italics mine]. One might say that in her God's eye view Julian has a realized eschatology but that from the point of view of human experience she necessarily has a proleptic eschatology. This is what saves her teaching from the accusation that it is unrealistic about the reality of sin and evil.

The two assertions are based on God's 'great endless love' (LT45). 'God is that goodness which cannot be angry, for God is nothing but goodness' (LT46). However, as the famous parable of the Lord and the Servant makes clear (LT51), it all depends on a difference of seeing. The parable is really a response to Julian's questions and concerns about sin and why she cannot see it when she contemplates all reality in God. God looks on human beings and their failings with compassion and not with blame. Interestingly, the only time that Julian suggests that God acts strongly seems to be in reference to the tribulations of Holy Church (LT28). In order to combat the dangers of 'the pomps and pride and the vainglory of this wretched life' God says 'I shall completely break down in you your empty affections and your vicious pride'. This is likely to be a contemporary reference to divisions in the Church – probably to controversies surrounding the papacy and perhaps to the fears of heresy.[24]

In the parable, the fallen servant sees neither his loving

lord 'nor does he truly see what he himself is in the sight
of his loving lord'. We do not see ourselves truly. Indeed,
as Julian suggests in the next chapter (52) 'God sees one
way and man sees another way'. Essentially God cannot
but see humanity in the light of his Son. 'When Adam fell,
God's son fell [into Mary's womb]; because of the true
union which was made in heaven, God's Son could not
be separated from Adam, for by Adam I understand all
mankind'(LT51). Julian finally understands the parable
when she begins to see matters from God's perspective.
From this standpoint, the story of Adam (the Fall) and
of Christ (the incarnation) are somehow the same. The
moment of Adam's fall becomes the moment of salvation
as well. The parable is an exposition of salvation history
from God's viewpoint. God looks upon us as we are in
Christ and sees us in our final integrity: healed, sinless and
glorified. In the light of eternity we are ever in union with
God and always have been. This has already been implied
in the phrase, 'I saw God in a point [or instant of time]'
(LT11). All that is in both time and place is but a single
'point' to God. 'And for the great endless love that God
has for all mankind, he makes no distinction in love
between the blessed soul of Christ and the least soul that
will be saved' (LT54).[25]

Julian's anthropology is complex and depends on understanding two dimensions to human existence, 'substance'
and 'sensuality' (especially LT54-9). These are not easy
to define as the words have a number of implications.[26]
However, one aspect of them is to describe 'substance' not
simply as that dimension of ourselves that is by nature
united to God but also as the self that God sees. 'Sensuality', therefore, may stand for the self that we see. Neither
is exclusively true and neither is untrue. The paradox of
the self is somehow caught in the image of 'the crown'.
We are God's crown. That is a crown of thorns as Jesus

Christ suffers for our sins (LT4) and a crown of glory 'which crown is the Father's joy, the Son's honour, the Holy Spirit's delight, and endless marvellous bliss to all who are in heaven' (LT51).

CONCLUSION

Julian's theology of the Trinity is entirely 'practical' as is the whole of her theological perspective. The Trinity, as it were, is the 'answer' to the question of whether and how God is engaged with the world. The God of Julian's *Showings* is joyfully and purposefully involved in human history, in the smallest of human events and in the lives of all of her 'even Christians'. While the freedom of God demands that this involvement be by choice, it is nevertheless, for Julian, God's happiness and fulfilment. In that sense, God's salvific action in the world is not simply a *revelation* of God's inner nature as community of persons. It is also the *vehicle* for mutual Trinitarian interaction. In this way, Julian draws together the immanent Trinity and the economic Trinity. God's action *is* God's Trinitarian way of being.

A final question remains. Is the purpose of the 'showings' merely to convince Julian's fellow Christians that their own, individual status before God is assured? Interestingly, the image of God (in Jesus Christ) dwelling in the human soul may be interpreted as encouraging a self-absorbed interiority. It is generally accepted that Julian's theology of God owes something to Augustine. As we have seen in an earlier chapter, Augustine focused on the traces of the Trinity (*vestigia Trinitatis*) particularly in the soul of the individual human being. The question is whether this interiorization effectively undermines a spirituality of engagement with the outer world. Yet this is not the tenor of the 'showings'. Throughout, Julian is moved by compassion for her 'even' or fellow Christians. The effect on

127

her own sensibilities, therefore, of her theology of God is not to drive her into self-indulgent reverie but to empower her with an urgency to pass on the teachings. The compassion of God for us in Christ will surely lead to our compassion as we are caught up ever more deeply into the life of the Trinity.[27] By implication we can assume that the impact on Christians touched by Julian's teaching will be a similar deepening of compassion for God's creation and for our fellow humans within each of whom dwells the divine presence.

5

∞∞∞∞∞∞∞∞∞

Spiritual Freedom in Ignatius Loyola and George Herbert

It may seem odd to relate Ignatius Loyola (1491–1556) and George Herbert (1593–1633) in the same chapter. To begin with, a leading Spanish figure of sixteenth-century Catholic reform and a seventeenth-century Anglican are surely separated both by culture and by the great divide of the Reformation. It might be presumed that their theological presuppositions, not least about God, would be so fundamentally opposed that their spiritualities would scarcely resemble each other. Then again, Herbert is an exquisite poet and Loyola is no literary stylist. Herbert is evocative; the Ignatius Loyola of *The Spiritual Exercises* is a kind of technician of the spiritual life. Despite these differences, the approaches to the spiritual life according to Herbert and Loyola have a surprising amount in common. Even the contrasts serve to throw an interesting light on each of these spiritual teachers and their sense of God.

Anglican spirituality as it began to emerge in the early part of the seventeenth-century was not simply rooted in *The Book of Common Prayer* although this is undoubtedly its most fundamental feature.[1] All the major Reformation traditions had significant continuities with the pre-Reformation Church and with medieval spirituality – far more than was admitted to later in history.[2] There were also varying degrees of influence by post-Tridentine Roman Catholicism on the Churches of the Reformation. The

129

Church of England, because of its ethos as a reformed Church with particularly strong Catholic continuities, was especially susceptible to such influences. Ignatian spirituality, sometimes in mediated forms (for example in the popular writings of Francis de Sales), had a considerable impact in the seventeenth century. The degree to which Ignatian approaches to prayer or the spiritual life directly influenced specific figures among the so-called Caroline Divines, not least George Herbert, has been contested in recent years.[3] It is probably invalid to argue for any direct connections between Herbert and Loyola. There is a probable allusion to the devotional practice of 'examination of conscience' in the poem 'The Church-Porch' (verse 76). Yet even this proves little as the practice had become widespread beyond Ignatian circles by the early seventeenth century.

THE LATE MEDIEVAL DILEMMA

One obvious fact that united all the spiritualities of the Reformation, Catholic and Reformed, is that they were a response to the failures of late medieval theology and devotion.[4] In summary, there was widespread anxiety about the worth of human effort in search for holiness. In many respects, the struggles of Martin Luther as an Augustinian friar are a paradigm of the basic dilemma. He strove to observe his community's rule with great strictness, had a longing to imitate the desert fathers of the early Church and tried to combat his moral scruples with frequent sacramental confession. Subjectively the traditional means of asceticism and religious practice failed to assuage his sense of guilt and spiritual inadequacy. More objectively, Luther came to see that even if he was theoretically capable of earning salvation by intense effort there were no experiential criteria by which to know whether he was justified or not. God demanded perfection but the problem was how anyone could know whether they had reached it or fallen short. The result in Luther was a sense of futility and near-despair from which he was liberated by the realization of justification by faith alone. In a very general sense, George Herbert is in a line of descent from Luther's 'solution'.

A similar futility, despair (even to the point of suicide), tested Ignatius Loyola during his immediate post-conversion experiences.[5] The *Spiritual Exercises* are, if you like, the fruits of his own liberation from late-medieval excesses. They formalized Ignatius' experience of spiritual conversion and spiritual freedom into a systematic framework. There are those who see Loyola, with Luther, as part of a common stream of Pauline and Augustinian thought that dominated post-Reformation spirituality on both sides of the divide. There is a drive towards interiority and experience rather than external devotions and duty. Apart from this, the *Spiritual Exercises* emphasize attentiveness to God's activity in the person rather than human actions as a means of *earning* God's love and favour. The Ignatian Exercises show more attention to individual holiness or sanctification than George Herbert. Both Ignatius Loyola and George Herbert are Christocentric. However, Herbert is also far more explicitly ecclesiocentric in his spirituality in the sense of focused on the life and prayer *of the Church*. Both Herbert and Loyola may be understood in terms of a movement towards spiritual freedom brought about by the action of Christ. It is within this framework of understanding that this chapter will examine each in turn and offer some comparisons.

IGNATIUS AND FREEDOM

Spiritual freedom is a major theme in Ignatian spirituality. However, Ignatius' own journey of conversion, and the kind of language he uses about spiritual freedom in the Exercises, clearly concern more than a straightforward response to the classic late-medieval spiritual dilemma. Ignatius' life story is well known and it would be tedious to repeat it in detail here. For our purposes one or two points are particularly worthy of note.

Ignatius was born in 1491 at Loyola into a family of Basque nobility. His early life was directed towards a military and courtly career as well as towards marrying well. This part of his life reached a climax in the service of the Viceroy of Navarre. He was severely wounded in 1521 at the siege of Pamplona by the French and his military career ended. His painful convalescence from 1521-2 and a subsequent period as a hermit at Manresa and Montserrat near Barcelona were an extended conversion experience. The text of *The Spiritual Exercises* arose from this experience and from Ignatius' attempts to accompany other people in their spiritual search. Eventually Ignatius studied at the Universities of Alcalá, Salamanca and Paris between about 1526-35, was ordained and founded the Society of Jesus with a group of companions in 1540. The point of rehearsing these few biographical details is to underline that Ignatius came from a background steeped in the aristocratic and military tradition of *hidalguía* in which status, class pride and courtly formality played a major role. He was also born into a Spain that was still steeped in the tradition of crusade and *Reconquista*. The last Arab city, Granada, fell in 1492, the year after his birth.

When Ignatius himself mentions freedom in *The Spiritual Exercises* an important aspect is 'disordered attachments'.[6] To be freed from these is stated to be a fundamental purpose of the Exercises (Exx 1). Later, in an opening 'Principle and Foundation' (Exx 23) prior to the prayer exercises of the retreat, Ignatius wrote of our need for indifference or detachment in relation to all that inhibits our relationship with God. Interestingly he cites health, wealth, honour and a long life. In Ignatius' consideration of sin and our need for liberation, the fundamental concept of sin is pride. Later still when retreatants are invited to make a choice for Christ the movement is away from coveting riches, empty honours and unbounded pride (Exx 142). God is characterized as Lord and Christ as King but God chooses powerlessness in the incarnation and Christ's way is that of poverty and humility and, ultimately, the cross. Freedom, therefore, in Ignatius' writings also concerns a reversal of the prevailing attitudes of his class and culture. *Hidalguía*, to be literally 'the son of a someone', was no longer to be the status that mattered. True status was to have been called by God while yet an unworthy sinner and made dependent solely on the will of God.

STRUCTURE OF THE SPIRITUAL EXERCISES

The book of the *Spiritual Exercises* was intended to be a handbook for a month-long retreat rather than a book of spiritual devotion. Apart from copious notes of advice, the main body of the work is a series of carefully-ordered biblical meditations or contemplations. Broadly speaking, the purpose of the Exercises was to aid the growth of inner freedom so that a person could respond to the personal call of Christ. The retreat is divided into four phases which Ignatius refers to as 'Weeks'. Each of these have a specific focus through which (in his experience) a retreatant might be expected to pass. How each person moves through each phase and how long it is useful to remain in each will in practice be different. If the text itself has a dynamic this is meant to assist the spiritual dynamic within each person rather than to constrain it.

In very simplistic terms, the first 'week' focuses on sin

and the acknowledgement of sinfulness and yet the call to discipleship by God even within human weakness. The second 'week' invites the retreatant to be and work with Christ. This call is deepened throughout the week in contemplations on the life and ministry of the human Jesus. The retreatant is gradually faced with a choice – for or against Christ. This in turn leads naturally into the third 'week', the Passion. Those who elect to follow the way of Jesus are inevitably drawn into a participation in the Passion. Beyond this is the fourth and final 'week' in which the retreatant is finally drawn to share in Jesus' own hope, joy and glory in resurrection. The summit of the process is a final contemplation on finding God present in all things. This acts as a bridge from the retreat back into everyday life and to a spirituality suited to intense engagement with the ordinary.

THE GOD AND CHRIST OF THE EXERCISES

After his conversion, Ignatius initially manifested a rather uncritical and not particularly healthy piety. His devotions were centred on Christ but this was fairly confused and unbalanced. He was ardent in devotion to the Passion but in the morbid late medieval way that Julian of Norwich managed to avoid. This was actually a version of what Schillebeeckx refers to as 'Jesusolatry' in which the suffering humanity of Jesus took priority over the divinity of Christ and sadness over hope. His excessive penances while living as a hermit at Manresa must be interpreted as a temptation to rely on rigour to please God (the merit of works) rather than on God's gift of grace. The underlying image of God emphasized justice that needed placating rather than love that sought a response.

The *Spiritual Exercises*, however, show quite different spiritual emphases. Ignatius emphasized the importance of experience, particularly the inner movements of the soul. The stress on 'feeling and tasting things internally' (Exx 2) implicitly points to an understanding of God as dwelling and working within each person. This is likely to have Augustinian overtones as does his related stress on inner movements as the basis for discernment and on attentiveness to our desires as a means of spiritual growth. The experience of 'movements', not unlike Herbert's struggle with contrary feelings, is central to the spiritual journey. They are signs of God's activity within the person. In the Exercises, God's action is central. God is the guide and the teacher (Exx 15) and it is God's will that is to be sought.[7] The purpose of acting according to God's will is not to earn favour but to respond to God's loving action in our lives.

The 'Annotations' (or introductory remarks) at the beginning of the Exercises insist that the one who gives the Exercises to another must not interfere with the inner relationship between God and the person who makes the retreat. On the contrary, the spiritual director should 'leave the Creator to work directly with the creature and the creature with the Creator and Lord' (Exx 15). At the heart of the teaching of the Exercises lies the gift and art of discernment. The retreatant is invited throughout the experience to understand how both God and other forces work within to lead the person in the direction of life or of disharmony (Exx 313-36). The true giver of the retreat is God. The human guide should avoid getting in the way so that

> the Creator and Lord communicate himself to the faithful soul in search for the will of God as he inflames her in his love and praise, disposing her towards the way in which she will be better able to serve him in the future. (Exx 15)

For Ignatius, God is the one who deals immediately with humans (Exx 15 and 89).

In the first Principle and Foundation, before the start of the Exercises proper, Ignatius points to the fundamental importance of how the retreatant understands the nature of God and why God has created us (Exx 23). God is creator and has made humanity 'to praise, reverence and serve God'. The soteriology is excessively private ('to save our souls') from a contemporary perspective. While the Christian tradition has usually spoken in terms of the salvation of individuals rather than of humanity as a whole, in reality God does not save people in isolation from their relationships with others. Ignatius' culture treated the rest of creation as 'things'. Humans were isolated agents created by God to use these 'things' for their own ends. Such an attitude, of course, suggests that God also had a hierarchical relationship with creation. Within medieval scholastic theology a sharp distinction emerged between spirit and matter. The word 'spiritual' came to be applied only to intelligent creatures (that is, human beings) in contrast to non-rational creation (that is, animals and nature). As 'spirit', God related in a unique way to human beings. There was no real mutuality between God and natural creation nor was there mutuality between nature and humankind.

The very first instruction about prayer in the first exercise of the First Week (Exx 46) reminds the retreatant 'to ask God our Lord for grace that all my intentions, actions, and operations may be directed purely to the service and praise of his Divine Majesty'. Later in the third of Ignatius' 'Additional Directions' to help the retreatant benefit more from prayer, he suggests 'I shall stand . . . with my mind raised up to consider how God our Lord looks at me' (Exx 75). Taken together these suggestions clearly remind us of the sovereign freedom and initiative of God in the

Christian spiritual life. In the First Week, God is revealed as loving and forgiving in the face of our sinfulness. However the First Week also reveals a God who loves unconditionally and who therefore calls human beings to discipleship *even though they are not worthy* and are unable to respond purely of their own volition.

In the Second Week, God is revealed again as a loving God whose love expresses itself especially in the life and actions of Jesus. This incarnational bent is underlined as something inherent in God first of all by the first contemplation of the Second Week, the incarnation. Here the Trinity 'in their eternity' decide that the Second Person should take flesh (Exx 102).

At the heart of our human motivation is what Ignatius refers to as our desires. At the beginning of prayer Ignatius recommended that the one who prayed should ask for 'what I want and desire' (e.g. Exx 48). Fundamentally this was to ask God for the grace that was needed at that moment. However one thinks of this, it is certainly an indication that God's initiative and guidance were paramount throughout. True desires, the ones that lead us towards life, are God's gifts to us.

In the contemplation on the incarnation the recommendation is to ask for 'an interior knowledge of Our Lord, who became human for me' (Exx 104). For Ignatius this means the intimate loving knowledge of the heart. The desire is ever to know God better as God most truly is and this 'truth' of God is expressed for Ignatius most substantially in the person of Jesus. We are invited to open ourselves in response to this God who loved us so much. This response reaches its climax in making a choice, or 'election', for Christ (Exx 169-89). If one is truly able to make this choice it is a gift. The gift consists of the freedom that Jesus Christ had to be available to the Father. Then, in that freedom, God can truly make the divine will known.

In the Third Week, God is revealed especially in the suffering of Jesus. The balance is different from the treatment of the Passion in the mysticism of Julian of Norwich. The Passion is a natural and inevitable consequence of Jesus' life and mission. The cross does not stand for arbitrary suffering but is to be understood as the inevitable consequence of God's engagement with a world that is sinful and marred by conflict. In that sense it is the totality of Jesus' *life* rather than simply his death that is the measure of God's reality. Ignatius' spirituality (and thus implied theology of God) is thoroughly incarnational rather than narrowly defined by the suffering Jesus on the cross.

To put this specifically in terms of the Exercises, we cannot understand the purpose of the Third Week (the cross) except in relation to the Second (the following of Christ). The theme of the vulnerable God who becomes a crucified God is implicit throughout the Exercises from the moment Ignatius invites the retreatant to contemplate the incarnation (Exx 101-9). The option of God in Jesus for the suffering and sinful world is made in the incarnation. This option to enter the powerlessness of the human condition is expressed in cumulative terms throughout the Second Week in focusing on the life and mission of Jesus. Even in the Second Week the self-emptying quality of God in Christ is expressed by Ignatius when he offers a contemplation on the Kingdom. For Ignatius Christ invites all those throughout time who seek to be his disciples to follow him 'in suffering' or in pain (Exx 95). This is reinforced later in the Second Week when in the classic meditation on the Two Standards (of Christ and of Lucifer or 'the World') the retreatant is brought to realize that to choose Christ means travelling by his way of poverty, contempt and humility (Exx 146). Thus when the retreatant reaches the stage of explicitly contemplating the Passion, it is the fundamental option of God in Christ for powerlessness that reaches a climax in the first contemplation of the Third Week. 'Consider how the divine nature goes into hiding, i.e. how Christ as divine does not destroy his enemies although he could do so' (Exx 196).

For Ignatius, the divinity of Christ is hidden in the Passion and only manifested in the resurrection on which the Fourth Week focuses (Exx 223). Once again the Fourth Week can only be understood in terms of the Third. Spiritually and theologically, the 'moment' of the cross moves into the moment of the resurrection. The cross becomes the sign not only of God's utter engagement with human ambiguity but also the sign that disharmony can be overcome in the power of the redemptive love of God.

The very last contemplation of the Exercises, the Contemplation to Attain Love (Exx 230-7), even more graphically focuses on how God loves through action towards us. God is presented as the fount and source of all things. God lives in all creatures (but labours *for humans* in this indwelling) and lives in humans in a special way. In the rest of creation, God dwells in things to give them 'existence' or 'life' or 'sensation'. Only humans are said to be 'created in the likeness and image of his Divine Majesty' (Exx 235). This contemplation at the end of the Exercises acts as a bridge into a spirituality of finding God in all things in the midst of everyday life. There are great similarities between Ignatius' own experience and that of the seventeenth-century Anglican mystic Thomas Traherne who had a similar sense of the way that even the small grain of sand revealed a transcendent God.

> We often saw how even the smallest things could make his spirit soar upwards to God, who even in the smallest things is Greatest. At the sight of a little plant, a leaf, a flower or a fruit, an insignificant worm or a tiny animal Ignatius could

soar free above the heavens and reach through into things which lie beyond the senses.[8]

The dynamic of the Exercises or, perhaps more accurately, the dynamic behind the process of the Exercises involves an interplay between God's initiative and human response. For Ignatius, there is a reciprocity between God and the human person. God's action is always primary and yet, within a dynamic relationship, God invites, illuminates and graces but then awaits a response.

> It becomes clear that it is God who is the giver of growth, the energizer of the process, the one who first lovingly gives the spontaneous desire of the human heart for himself, who caringly invites and entices it into the open and watches over its unfolding, who himself strengthens it through the pain and darkness, the hesitations and the taking heart, the struggles and surrenders, the angers and fears, the alternations of repugnance and joy.[9]

THE GOD WHO IS ALWAYS GREATER

Hugo Rahner summarizes the God who appears in the pages of *The Spiritual Exercises* as 'the God who is always greater'. The God of Ignatius could both possess a person at depth and at the same time evoke a sense of respectful distance.[10] This may be thought of as a paradox: Ignatius' God was essentially above and comes down from above (*desde arriba*) and yet is to be found as 'the within' of all things, especially in the heart of the believer. A case can be made that this Ignatian paradox is played out in the very different approaches of two of the greatest twentieth-century Roman Catholic theologians, Karl Rahner and von Balthasar. Both were formed in the Ignatian tradition and both looked to it as a major source of their theology. The different theological methods, von Balthasar's 'theology from above' and Rahner's emphasis on the believing subject, may be thought of partly in terms of a disagreement about how to interpret Ignatian spirituality.

In a sense, God's movement is a permanent *descent* into the heart of all things. The measure of God's relationship to humanity is in Ignatius' contemplation on the incarnation (Exx 101-9). Here the Trinity 'were looking [or, "looked down"] at all the flatness or roundness of the whole world'. The heart of the spirituality of the Exercises is *not* human action even though there is great emphasis on human response. Both structurally and dynamically the Exercises begin, continue and end with God's action and initiative in creation, incarnation-redemption and indwelling in all things.

Ignatius' own experience was to be drawn to contemplate a God who is above. The phrase he used in his *Spiritual Diary* was that he is permitted 'to look upwards'. This appears to contrast with Julian of Norwich's perception that she felt drawn to look up to heaven away from the suffering Jesus on the cross but came to realize that Jesus was her heaven.[11] Yet in Ignatius' sense of the 'liberality' of God, God dwells in all things and all creatures exist in God. God is the source of grace and of all good things on the earth. All that exists, exists only in God. In some ways this echoes Julian of Norwich. However Ignatius' emphasis is fundamentally different. He is not reflecting about the ontology of created things but about how humans may perceive and relate to them. As the opening Principle and Foundation of *The Spiritual Exercises* reminds us (Exx 23), the only way to engage with the 'reality' of created things is to see and relate to them 'in God'. In order truly to find God in all things below, we must have encountered the God who is 'above'.

Ignatius' approach to the nature of God raises questions that are difficult for some contemporary readers. As a number of sympathetic feminist interpreters of the Exercises have noted, the understanding of God and of God's relationship to creation is culturally-conditioned and may be unbalanced in some of its elements.[12] Ignatius Loyola not surprisingly uses male metaphors for God such as King and Lord. Ignatius' famous meditation on 'The Two Standards' (Exx 136-48) is one of the lynch-pins of the process of the 'election' in the Second Week. It portrays two military leaders, Christ and Satan, about to do battle and calling their followers together. This has obvious connections with the crusade mentality that still permeated Spain after seven centuries of combat with the occupying Arabs. It suggests a world dominated by a fundamental division between good and evil. The Kingdom of God is advanced by combat, courage, struggle and obedience as well as the renunciation of security, tranquillity and domesticity. If God is imaged primarily in the figure of Jesus, the Christology of the Two Standards portrays Jesus as a confident and inspiring leader. The Ignatian portrayal of Jesus, with the invitation to be with and work with him, is instructive in what it includes and what it excludes. The latter part of the Second Week which covers the public ministry of Jesus emphasizes authority and control. There is no reference to those Gospel passages that speak of healing or forgiveness, to parables or reference to the Jesus who prefers the companionship of the vulnerable, the marginal and the sinner (Exx 158-61). Ignatius' God comes close to us in Jesus but is never really intimate. This is not the 'courteous', 'homely' and 'familiar' God of Julian of Norwich who takes pity and where 'love was his meaning' rather than power. Rather, Ignatius' God is deadly serious in his very male relationship with the retreatant.[13]

THE TRINITY IN IGNATIUS LOYOLA'S WRITINGS

The mysticism of Ignatius' *Spiritual Diary,* including its visionary experience, is much more explicitly Trinitarian than *The Spiritual Exercises.* The Diary records a period in 1544 when Ignatius was struggling with the rules for poverty that would appear in the Jesuit *Constitutions* he was composing. As part of an intense process of discernment, Ignatius wrote down his experiences during the regular celebration of Mass. He often used the votive liturgy of the Trinity and it is not surprising that references to the Trinity are scattered throughout the entries. Interestingly, of the passages Ignatius himself marked as important, the majority concerned visions of the Trinity.

Ignatius experienced that prayer to any person of the Trinity brought with it a sense of their mutual indwelling and unity and therefore deepened his love for the Trinity as a whole. 'When I felt consolation I was delighted with any one of them, and I rejoiced in acknowledging it as coming from all three.'[14] Although in other contexts, Ignatian spirituality is very Christocentric, Ignatius indicates clearly in his diary that Jesus is in some sense a gift to him by the Trinity. 'It seemed in some way to be from the Blessed Trinity that Jesus was shown or felt, and I remembered the time when the Father put me with the Son.'[15] In a later entry there are almost echoes of Julian's sense (LT4 and 19) that in Jesus is the Trinity and that she need not look beyond the suffering Jesus. Ignatius was seeking confirmation of his choices by the Trinity but instead experienced feelings that had Jesus as their object. 'I could not turn myself to the other Persons, except in so far as the First Person was Father of such a Son ... I had desired confirmation by the Blessed Trinity, and now I felt it was communicated to me through Jesus.'[16] Interestingly on two occasions, once in his Reminiscences (or 'Autobiography') and once in his Diary, Ignatius records visionary experiences of the Trinity as a whole. In the Reminiscences while living as a hermit at Manresa shortly after his conversion he was praying the daily Office and he 'saw' the Trinity as three keys on a keyboard – presumably referring to three individual notes making a single chord. In the Diary, during and after Mass, Ignatius,

> felt and saw, not obscurely but brightly, in full light, the very Being or Essence of God, appearing as a sphere . . . in some way I saw all three Persons as I had seen the first, viz., the Father in one part, the Son in another and the Holy Spirit in another, all three coming forth or having their derivation from the Divine Essence, without leaving the spherical vision.[17]

When we turn to the more familiar text, *The Spiritual Exercises*, the expressions that Ignatius most frequently used for God are much more ambiguous. 'God our Lord' (*Dios Nuestro Señor*) and 'Creator and Lord' (*Criador y Señor*). He also used the phrase 'His Divine Majesty' (*Su Divina Majestad*). In contrast to Julian of Norwich, Ignatius' continual instinct was to think of God in reverential terms rather than in terms of familiarity or endearment. Both Julian and Ignatius regularly employ the term 'lordship' which they no doubt drew from the feudal or military hierarchies of their day. However, Ignatius' usage is far more deferential. This may reflect his maleness, his military background or the Iberian knightly tradition of *hidalguía* – that is, aristocratic concern for status or social formality. The titles for God are ambiguous because they may be Trinitarian or Christological. 'God our Lord' frequently means Christ, or at least includes Christ, and the famous colloquy at the end of the first exercise of the First Week (Exx 53) calls Christ 'the Creator'.[18]

> The authentic theology of Ignatius [in the Exercises] is centred around a Christology of the historical Jesus and the following of that Jesus. Imbedded in that theology, then, is a certain understanding of God . . .[19]

The eternal Trinity is uniquely expressed in Jesus. For Ignatius it is not possible to bypass Jesus Christ in our search for God. All immediate contact with God is eternally mediated through him.

The spirituality of the Ignatian Exercises has sometimes been criticized as excessively based on human effort. However all the activities or methods that the text offers by way of aid to retreatants must be placed firmly within a context of God's sole initiative. Indeed, the contemporary Uruguayan theologian Juan Luis Segundo is actually critical of Ignatius' approach because his 'theology of a test' accords too little space for genuine human collaboration. The Kingdom of God is completely God's doing and our test is simply whether we will choose this.[20] This judgement may be too harsh but it is certainly true that the will of God and our response to it is absolutely central to the Exercises.

Finally, Ignatius was not a deist. At the heart of his vision of God is God's nearness to us and involvement in the world. The underlying theological presupposition is that God is dynamically active. The climax of the Exercises is the Contemplation to Attain Love (Exx 230-7). In it God is described as the one who continually 'works' for us, who gives not merely gifts but wishes 'to give me himself'. The Trinity freely chooses to enter into the fullness of the human condition in all its weakness. We cannot separate the inner nature of God from God's action and self-revelation. Ignatius portrays the incarnation as the outflowing of a conversation within God the Trinity. Thus 'the dialogue on the royal throne ends in the room at Nazareth'.[21]

GEORGE HERBERT AND THE TEMPLE

George Herbert is best known for two of his works, *The Country Parson* and the collection of poems known as *The Temple* published in 1633 shortly after Herbert's death. The latter are the most revealing with regard to his inner spiritual struggle.[22] It is widely agreed that within *The Temple* there is a conscious movement, a process or a dynamic. Some authorities have assumed that their purpose is primarily didactic and explain the dynamic in terms of assumptions about Herbert's theology. For example the 164 poems are said to be 'arranged in an order that traces the Christian pilgrimage from "imputed righteousness" (justification) to holiness (sanctification), which is achieved only after this life'.[23] The context of Herbert's time suggests that he accepted the classic Protestant understanding of justification by faith. However, it is not easy to reduce the complexity of the spiritual struggle expressed in his poems to a simple theological structure.

The poems are gathered into a three-part structure, 'The Church Porch', 'The Church' and 'The Church Militant' of which the middle part is both the largest and spiritually the richest and most dynamic. The titles of the three sections reveal the different layers of meaning of 'Temple' or 'Church'. It is a physical building, the architectural space within which God is praised in the liturgy. It is also the Body of Christ, the Christian community. Finally it is the individual human soul, the 'temple of the Holy Spirit'. There are poems that express the Church's year or liturgical structure (for example, 'Evensong', 'Mattins', 'Lent'). There are poems, too, that use the features of a religious building as their framework ('The Altar', 'The Church Floor', 'The Windows'). However the thread that runs through all the poems is a personal relationship with

146

God, and a relationship that is characterized by struggle both on the side of God and on that of the human heart.

The intensity of the poems suggests that the struggle they describe was a real and personal one rather than something contrived for catechetical purposes. It may be that Isaak Walton, the seventeenth-century author of Herbert's life, was more of a hagiographer than a biographer in the modern sense. However, the words he attributes to Herbert concerning his writings accord well with the substance of the poems themselves. Herbert sent the poems from his deathbed to Nicholas Ferrar, a friend and founder of the experimental community at Little Gidding. The message he apparently sent to Ferrar suggested that the poems were 'a picture of the many spiritual conflicts that have passed betwixt God and my soul before I could subject mine to the will of Jesus my Master: in whose service I have now found perfect freedom'.[24] The poems themselves, however, do not chart a simple spiritual chronology – from purgative to unitive way or some equivalent process. Complexity and simplicity, doubt and faith vie with each other throughout. Even the final poem of 'The Church', 'Love III', continues to express a deep spiritual struggle. One suspects that its resolution through surrender expressed in the last line is not conclusive for it is only the latest of several such surrenders throughout the poems.

> Love bade me welcome: yet my soul drew back,
>> Guilty of dust and sin.
> But quick-ey'd Love, observing me grow slack
>> From my first entrance in,
> Drew near to me, sweetly questioning,
>> If I lacked anything.
>
> A guest, I answer'd, worthy to be here:
>> Love said, You shall be he.

147

I the unkind, ungrateful? Ah my dear,
    I cannot look on thee.
Love took my hand, and smiling did reply,
    Who made the eyes but I?

Truth Lord, but I have marr'd them: let my shame
    Go where it doth deserve.
And know you not, says Love, who bore the blame?
    My dear, then I will serve.
You must sit down says Love, and taste my meat:
    So I did sit and eat.

Thus each of the poems in the middle section, 'The Church', charts a fluctuating relationship with God in which God struggles with Herbert's 'peevish heart' ('Sion' line 13). The poems are devotional. Indeed they are conversations of great intensity between Herbert and God. As his poem 'The Quiddity' makes clear, Herbert understood poetry itself as a form of prayer. 'My God, a verse is not a crown/...But it is that which while I use/ I am with thee, and *Most take all*.' The conversational poems of 'The Church' are similar to the kind of intimate prayer Ignatius Loyola recommends in *The Spiritual Exercises* and describes as 'Colloquies'.

> A colloquy, properly so-called, means speaking as one friend speaks with another, or a servant with a master, at times asking for some favour, at other times accusing oneself of something badly done, or telling the other about one's concerns and asking for advice about them. (Exx 54)

HERBERT'S CONTEXT

Before we examine Herbert's vision of God in more detail, we need to consider a further question. This concerns George Herbert's context, both the situation of the Church of England in the early part of the seventeenth century and Herbert's own background and life. Because George Herbert stood on the other side of the Reformation divide from Ignatius Loyola, it may be assumed that his understanding of God's grace and spiritual freedom would have a different resonance.

There has been a major difference of interpretation among scholars concerning George Herbert's theology and how this affects our understanding of his poetry. This has frequently been framed in terms of the question: was George Herbert essentially a Catholic or a Protestant in his theology? On the one hand, some scholars have emphasized Herbert's place within the predominantly Catholic nature of the structure and liturgy of the Church of England. This approach tended to concentrate on medieval allusions or references in Herbert's works and on his undoubtedly liturgical and sacramental spirituality. The 'Catholic' school of interpretation often drew attention to the influences of Catholic Reformation spiritual writers (such as Ignatius Loyola or Francis de Sales) on seventeenth-century Anglicans.[25]

For many years this 'Catholic' interpretation held the field. Because it was a one-sided viewpoint, it was inevitable that it would be corrected eventually by a 'Protestant' revisionism. This viewpoint emphasized that the Church of England was essentially a Reformed Church for all its continuities with the medieval past. In this context, Herbert's understanding of God, human nature and redemption must have been unequivocally Protestant and specifically Calvinist.[26]

More recently there has been some attempt to mediate between the 'Catholic' and 'Protestant' interpretations of Herbert. First, there is the obvious fact that the two traditions were and are not as mutually exclusive as has sometimes been thought. There is also a question of the particularity of Anglicanism which scholars are nowadays more inclined to acknowledge.[27] It is true that members of the Church of England in Herbert's time considered themselves Protestant whatever party they belonged to. To identify oneself as Protestant at this stage did not mean that there was no sense of continuity with a Western Catholic past. The term 'Anglican' is of much later provenance. However there was a sense that the English Church was distinctive and that, in its ambiguities, it mediated in some way between the two 'extremes' of Geneva and Rome. This sentiment is clearly expressed in Herbert's poem 'The British Church'.

There were strict Calvinists within the Church of England during Herbert's period and the Church was committed to a Calvinist doctrine of predestination, described as 'full of sweet, pleasant and unspeakable comfort' in Article 17 of the Thirty-Nine Articles of Religion. However, it is not accurate to describe the Church overall simply as Calvinist. Even Article 17 is ambiguous about the stricter Calvinist doctrine of double predestination. That is, whether God elects all to salvation or actually predestines some to damnation. Leaving this aside, the Calvinist tradition Herbert inherited certainly affirmed that God gives sinners salvation as an entirely free gift and that Christ's death was only efficacious for those whom God freely elects.

George Herbert seems to have been typical of most non-Puritan divines of his time in that he accepted elements of Calvinist doctrine but was not a strict or straightforward Calvinist. He was a friend of other contemporary spiritual figures such as Bishop Lancelot Andrewes and Nicholas Ferrar (to whom he bequeathed his poetry) whose theologies and spiritualities were complex. These connections as well as his defence of elements of the Prayer Book rejected by Puritans (such as the use of the sign of the cross) suggest that Herbert had no sympathy with Puritanism. There is also some evidence in Herbert's poetry of a tension between the classical reformed doctrines of predestination and justification and a sense of people's freedom and responsibility. Herbert clearly believed that the Church to which he gave his loyalty made it possible to hold together a Protestant doctrine of grace, redemption and faith and a Catholic stress on the centrality of liturgy, the importance of a sacramental life and personal holiness.

On a personal level, Herbert like Ignatius Loyola came from an aristocratic background and had ambitions of preferment at court. Like Ignatius he changed his course but for reasons that are unclear. Somehow and somewhere in the early 1620s Herbert moved from a successful university career at Cambridge and life as a Member of Parliament to ordination as a deacon in 1624 and eventually as priest in 1630. Although this was not always the case for aristocratic clergy, Herbert actually chose to live in the vicarage alongside his parishioners of the village of Bemerton outside Salisbury. During his brief ministry until his death in 1633 he concentrated his energies on the daily round of worship and on pastoral care. It is perhaps not too fanciful to interpret elements of Herbert's inner struggle as related to this radical change of direction and to its consequences. Perhaps there are hints of past struggles (even continuing ones) in one of Herbert's poems about prayer, 'Prayer II'.

> I value prayer so,
> That were I to leave all but one,
> Wealth, fame, endowments, virtues, all should go;
> I and dear prayer would together dwell,
> And quickly gain, for each inch lost, an ell.

THE NATURE OF GOD

The central focuses of Herbert's poetry are the nature of God, the journey of the Christian person and the relationship between the two. If we return to the poem 'Love III' which is the climax of the main section of *The Temple*, two important aspects of Herbert's understanding of God stand out. First, God is a lover who woos the Christian soul rather than an impersonal power that seeks to impose an imperious will. Second, the figure of Love is explicitly both creator ('Who made the eyes but I?') and redeemer ('who bore the blame?'). As we shall see, Herbert is, like Ignatius Loyola, profoundly Christocentric. While Herbert's God is infinitely varied, the nature of God is most clearly revealed in and through the life and death of Jesus Christ. Arguably, too, the Spirit is at least implicitly present in the poem. 'Love' is one of the Spirit's traditional designations and the Spirit's gift of sanctification, in which one is made a 'guest... worthy to be here', is clearly the overall dynamism of the poem.

The God of Herbert's poetry is free and active – indeed the idea of God as, predominantly, the active partner in the divine-human relationship runs throughout the poems. Yet God's freedom and action are most powerfully expressed as love. 'My God, thou art all love' ('Evensong'). Even though God's action is always at the heart of things for Herbert, human beings are not purely passive. They are creatures of desire who (as Herbert does in his poetry) struggle to reach out to God in response.

> For my heart's desire
> Unto thine is bent:
> I aspire
> To a full consent.
>
> ('Discipline')

152

God woos the human soul delicately rather than over-powers it. This enables Herbert to allow for a certain reciprocity between God and human creatures.

> My God, what is a heart,
> That thou shouldst it so eye, and woo,
> Pouring upon it all thy art,
> As if that thou hadst nothing else to do? ('Mattins')

An interesting study that compares the poetry of George Herbert and Gerard Manley Hopkins notes that Herbert's image of God is to some degree the opposite of Hopkins'. For Herbert, as opposed to Hopkins, God is not terrible, overwhelming, dominating – the awesome transcendent Other.[28] Interestingly, Hopkins is never able to be angry or 'peevish' with God in the way Herbert feels free to be. Although God is utterly holy ('I cannot look on thee' in 'Love III') Herbert's conflicts are within a context of intimacy and his starting point is always God's love rather than God's judgement or wrath. The poem 'Sacrifice' vividly portrays the fickleness and sinfulness of humanity even in face of the cross but, as in the First Week of the Ignatian *Spiritual Exercises*, God's sole response is one of generosity rather than judgement. Even the poem 'Discipline' which speaks of God's wrath, invites God to 'Throw away thy rod,/ Throw away thy wrath'. Indeed in the final stanza Herbert seems to suggest that because God is God wrath is unnecessary, even inappropriate 'Though man frailties hath'. God's love is actually more powerful and effective. 'Love will do the deed:/ For with love/ Stony hearts will bleed'.

Herbert's sense of God's presence and intimacy is focused less on nature or landscape (compared, say, to Thomas Traherne) than on everyday events and action.[29] Apart from finding God in the everyday round (for example 'The Elixir'), Herbert experiences the divine within himself and in the celebration of the Eucharist. One of the most important images of *The Temple* is God dwelling and working within the heart (for example, 'The Altar' and 'The Church Floor'). The sacramental theme is so pervasive that it would be tedious to list all the poems where the Eucharist is mentioned or implied. Indeed, intimacy with God is often expressed eucharistically in Herbert. In 'The Agony' the association between the experience of God as Love, the cross and reception of Communion is tightly drawn.

> Who knows not Love, let him assay
> And taste that juice, which on the cross a pike
> Did set again abroach; then let him say
> If ever he did taste the like.
> Love is that liquor sweet and most divine,
> Which my God feels as blood; but I, as wine.
> (Lines 13–18)

The particular intimacy between God and those who preside at the Eucharist, and the burden this lays upon them, is mentioned in *The Country Parson* (Chapter XXII) and in the poem 'The Priesthood'.

> But th'holy men of God such vessels are,
> As serve him up, who all the world commands:
> When God vouchsafeth to become our fare,
> Their hands convey him, who conveys their hands.
> Oh what pure things, most pure must those things be,
> Who bring my God to me! (Lines 25–30)

In tension with this strong sense of presence and God's loving intimacy, is a sense of God's absence. This common spiritual experience appears in a number of Herbert's poems. 'The Search' expresses how profoundly painful this is.

> Whither, Oh, whither art thou fled,
> My Lord, my Love?
> My searches are my daily bread;
> Yet never prove.

Faithfulness and discipline in prayer cannot on their own assuage the sense of bemusement at God's apparent absence but rather deepen it.

> My knees pierce th'earth, mine eyes the sky;
> And yet the sphere
> And centre both to me deny
> That thou art there.

Sometimes, as the poem 'Denial' suggests, it is easier to give up the struggle when God does not seem to hear and there is no feeling apart from a vague discontent.

> Oh cheer and tune my heartless breast,
> Defer no time;
> That so thy favours granting my request,
> They and my mind may chime,
> And mend my rhyme.

Somehow a deepening of faith is implied. As 'The Search' suggests, we struggle to touch God and yet much of the time we are called to walk by faith alone and not by sight or sense. Another poem 'Longing' implies a sense that God sometimes deliberately withholds consolation for reasons that are impossible to fathom. Ultimately, God's way of seeing and acting is inscrutable. Perhaps Herbert's way of expressing the experience hints at specifically Protestant sensibilities – the hidden God (*deus absconditus*) of Luther and the sovereign will of the God of Calvin. However the experience that Herbert describes is the common currency of all Christians who struggle with God. In *The Spiritual Exercises* Ignatius Loyola places a similar emphasis on seeking the will of God and on the struggle to surrender to it. The sense of feeling forsaken is clearly described in the 'Rules for the Discernment of Spirits' (Exx 313-36). Sometimes God withdraws 'to test us' (Exx 320). Yet, even if fervour is absent God 'still supplies sufficient grace for our salvation'. One of the reasons for spiritual desolation may be

> to give us true information and understanding, so that we may perceive through experience that we cannot ourselves arouse or sustain overflowing devotion, intense love, tears or any other spiritual consolation, but that everything is a gracious gift from God our Lord. (Exx 322)

THE TRINITY

There are not many direct allusions to the Trinity in *The Temple*. There is a possible musical image in the 'three parts' of the final stanza of 'Easter'. There is a clear reference in the poem 'Trinity Sunday'. The first stanza suggests the classic threefold titles of creator, redeemer and sanctifier.

> Lord, thou has form'd me out of mud,
> And hast redeem'd me through thy blood,
> And sanctifi'd me to do good . . .

There also seem to be three triads in the final stanza which, as it were, express the desired impact or reflection of the Trinity in Herbert's life.

> Enrich my heart, mouth, hands in me,
> With Faith, with hope, with charity;
> That I may run, rise, rest with thee.

Herbert's relative reticence about God as Trinity is perhaps explained in the poem 'Ungratefulness'. Here Herbert suggests that God 'hast but two rare cabinets full of trea-sure/ The *Trinity* and *Incarnation*'.

> The statelier cabinet is the *Trinity*,
> Whose sparking light access denies:
> Therefore thou dost not show
> This fully to us, till death blow
> The dust into our eyes:
> For by that powder thou wilt make us see.

However it is the incarnation that can 'allure us' at this point. This is the more immediate and attractive treasure.

Certainly it is difficult to discover evidence of sharp distinctions between the traditional attributes of the persons. Herbert regularly changes focus from God as creator to God as redeemer. The Lord of the poem 'Longing' is 'Lord JESU' (l. 73) and the one who 'didst bow/ Thy dying head upon the tree' (ll. 31-2). Yet the Lord is also, implicitly, the God who has created ('Indeed the world's thy book' l. 49) and whose 'duty' is to continue to sustain ('To thee help appertains./ Hast thou left all things to their course,/ And laid the reins/ Upon the horse?' ll. 42-6). Once again, in the poem 'Redemption' it is the rich Lord of heaven who goes to earth as Son. One of the central poems of the collection, 'The Sacrifice', uses the structure of the Reproaches from the Western Catholic liturgy for Good Friday to express the grief of Christ on the cross. Yet the figure who grieves on the cross is also the maker (l. 6), 'he that built the world' (l. 67), the one who gives breath (l. 70), the Lord of hosts (l. 79) and the one who lives eternally (l. 99).

In 'The Church', the central portion of *The Temple* (and the 'temple' is, partly, Christ), nearly all Herbert's poems concern Christ or are directly addressed to him. Yet Herbert's Christology is not greatly concerned with the life of the human Jesus compared to the Catholic Reformation

157

spirituality of Ignatius Loyola. Herbert's emphasis is strongly on the cross. Our way to holiness is not Christ-focused devotion or 'imitation of Christ' in mission but to accept God's grace in Christ and to trust in it. Throughout all our struggles and uncertainties, our ultimate assurance is the triumph of Christ expressed in the poem 'Easter'.

Herbert blends together the eternal creator God and the suffering Christ on the cross. This tends to outweigh any sense of a harsh version of the 'penal substitution' theory of the Passion. God is revealed as love rather than as a judge and this love is known especially in Christ. The lesson of 'The Sacrifice' is that we cannot finally defeat God's love. Even our refusals of love merely serve to reveal further depths of love in God's patient endurance. Herbert's frequent use of the title 'Lord' for God is not, therefore, a matter of power. Indeed God seems closest when met precisely as the Lord who is courteous or who, for example in 'Redemption', does a favour or 'grants a suit'. There is even a modest hint of a feminine image for God in the poem 'Longing' where, as in Julian of Norwich, human motherhood is a reflection of God.

> From thee all pity flows.
> Mothers are kind, because thou art,
> And dost dispose
> To them a part:
> Their infants, them; and they suck thee
> More free.

For Herbert, the nature of God is ultimately beyond the power of words to express. This is another aspect of the elusive and hidden quality of God. Words serve to describe and to praise but if we rely on them too much (as noted in the poem 'Jordan II') they merely shut off the source of light and life. Herbert possessed a high view of preaching but a still higher view of prayer. Even in *The*

Country Parson, where there is a fairly didactic model of
ministry, 'the Country Parson preacheth constantly' but
not primarily in a catechetical way. He is to choose 'texts of
Devotion, not Controversy, moving and ravishing texts,
whereof the Scriptures are full' (Chapter VII). The
purpose of preaching is to lead people to prayer for
'Praying's the end of preaching' ('Perirrhanterium' 410).
And if prayer for Herbert is above all 'the Church's
banquet', the prayer of the Church, the daily Offices and
the Eucharist, there is beyond those structures and set
formulae a promise of something ultimately intangible; a
way of knowing that is perhaps mystical. This is expressed
beautifully yet allusively in the accumulated images of
'Prayer I'.

> Prayer the Church's banquet, Angel's age,
> God's breath in man returning to his birth,
> The soul in paraphrase, heart in pilgrimage,
> The Christian plummet sounding heav'n and earth;
>
> Engine against th'Almighty, sinners' tower,
> Reversèd thunder, Christ-side-piercing spear,
> The six-days world transposing in an hour,
> A kind of tune, which all things hear and fear;
>
> Softness, and peace, and joy and love, and bliss,
> Exalted Manna, gladness of the best,
> Heaven in ordinary, man well drest,
> The milky way, the bird of Paradise,
>
> Church-bells beyond the stars heard, the soul's blood,
> The land of spices; something understood.

INNER STRUGGLE

It is impossible to reduce the nature of Herbert's inner
struggle towards spiritual freedom to one thing only. Struc-

turally, the poems seem to offer a sense of movement from a more moral, active, meditative stance in 'The Church Porch' to a more God-centred, contemplative and passive mood at the end of 'The Church'.[30] However, if there is a movement towards contemplative experience it involves much more complex spiritual movements within Herbert. Herbert's theology of the human person suggests that humanity is both the meeting place of heaven and earth and a place of conflict, 'A wonder tortur'd in the space/ Betwixt this world and that of grace' ('Affliction IV').

If we say that Herbert's struggle can be summarized as a battle to accept God's love this covers a variety of sub-plots. In *The Spiritual Exercises* Ignatius Loyola suggests that the fundamental sin that separates humanity from God is pride and that spiritual freedom, therefore, consists in knowing one's sinfulness and accepting the way of humility and poverty, whether spiritual or material. By contrast, Herbert appears to portray his basic problem as a more 'Protestant' sense of unworthiness and therefore an inability to cope with the purity of God's love. On further reflection, however, pride is clearly part of Herbert's struggle as well.

Herbert wants to be worthy even in the final poem of 'The Church', 'Love III'. What is lacking at Love's feast? 'A guest, I answer'd, worthy to be here.' The fundamental question throughout the central section of *The Temple* is how is the writer to allow God to love and serve him? How is he to surrender his own standards? This is a subtle form of pride but pride none the less.

Such difficulties would be a good subject for Ignatius Loyola's set of 'Rules for the Discernment of Spirits' aimed at the spiritually more advanced. Here temptations are not crude but masquerade 'under the guise of good' (Exx 328-36). It seems good to be worthy but in the end that is to put at the heart of things the human capacity to respond

appropriately to God rather than God's gift of love.
Herbert does not deny that human beings are called to
respond to God but the response is, paradoxically, to
accept an inability to offer true love in return for true love.

It would be strange if Herbert's aristocratic sensibilities
had no further impact after his conversion. It is one thing
to renounce a career in public life and quite another to
accept the full consequences. A number of poems express
frustration and the temptation to give up. 'Affliction I'
suggests the writer can see no sense in what is happening
in his relationship with God. 'Well, I will change the
service, and go seek/ Some other master out.' As if to
underline that there is no simple progression in our spiritual pilgrimage (any more than in the collection of poems
themselves), a much later poem 'The Collar' has similar
sentiments. Its dramatic form indicates the continuing
temptation to rebellion.

> I struck the board, and cried, No more.
> I will abroad.
> What? shall I ever sigh and pine?

Herbert seems to be raging against his own imperfections
but behind this lies a degree of self-serving. The initial
response is not surrender but revolt against the ultimate
renunciation of self that seems to be asked for.

The endings of both 'Affliction' and 'The Collar' suggest
that nothing more is asked of us than a simple acceptance
of God's love. This battle to accept that God is love rather
than more logically a judge is another dimension of Herbert's struggle throughout *The Temple*. Even in this God
confounds our reasonable expectations. We are sinners, we
are utterly unworthy; logically we should be condemned.

> Oh dreadful Justice, what a fright and terror
> Wast thou of old,

> When sin and error
> Did show and shape thy looks to me,
> And through their glass discolour thee!

No doubt the poem 'Justice II' expresses both the contrast between the Old Law and the New Law of Christ and Herbert's own experience. The point is that fear belongs to the past and it is broadly true that Herbert does not appear to battle with an existential fear of God even while he struggles to accept that God *ought* not to be feared.

Herbert's struggle with God and the movement towards spiritual freedom is just as real as it is, in a somewhat different guise, in Ignatius Loyola. Although the will of God is central to Herbert, the dominant image for God's way of being and acting is Love. The spiritual dynamic, therefore, cannot be one of a conclusion (salvation) imposed on human beings. God's love is conclusively and freely offered, not provisionally on offer depending on our capacity to earn it. There is nothing more to be achieved or completed in salvation and that is equally true of the 'Protestant' Herbert and the 'Catholic' Ignatius Loyola. Yet, equally, both recognize that God's love has to be truly received.

In the poem 'Redemption' the writer as 'tenant' seeks to 'make a suit' to God in heaven as the 'rich Lord' that he be given a new lease as the old was no longer satisfactory. When he finds the Lord, strangely on earth amidst thieves and murderers, the suit is immediately granted on sight without more ado or discussion. This has sometimes been read as indicating that the human experience of searching for God is ultimately meaningless and pointless from the point of view of Reformed theology. This appears to mistake the poem's own dynamism. The point is not that seeking God is valueless but that God in Christ is not to be found in the expected place. The writer 'knowing his great birth' sought God 'in great resorts;/ In cities, theatres, gardens, parks and courts'. In fact God is found among the unworthy and powerless thus providing an object lesson to the writer who, it seems, struggles with such things. It is from the midst of the messiness of the human condition, not from the safety of power and invulnerability, that God grants the suit.

It is the case in 'Redemption' as it is in the poem 'Love' at the climax of the main part of *The Temple* that nothing is imposed but all is granted. God is revealed as the one who respects the human person. The final submission in the poem 'Love' – 'You must sit down, says Love, and taste my meat:/ So I did sit and eat' – is neither hopeless resignation nor the act of someone who obeys an order. It is the acceptance of an invitation. In that acceptance is freedom. This is because it involves, too, the realization that in the invitation to eat Love's meat 'I the unkind, ungrateful' have been granted a true vision of my real value before God.

Both Ignatius Loyola in *The Spiritual Exercises* and George Herbert in *The Temple* begin with human unworthiness. Although they approach matters from different angles, and sometimes use different language, both of them map out a pilgrimage of the human spirit. This journey involves a realization that human beings do not cease to be unworthy but are actually loved by God *as sinners*. Any true response, any authentic following of Christ starts from that realization and acceptance. Interestingly, both spiritual teachers bring the movement to a climax with a contemplation of God's love and with a realization and acceptance that it is God who gives all and achieves all. In that is truth and freedom.

Take, Lord, and receive all my liberty, my memory, my understanding and my entire will, all that I have and

possess. You gave it all to me; to you Lord I give it all back.
All is yours, dispose of it entirely according to your will.
Give me the grace to love you, for that is enough for me.
(Exx 235)

164

6

'Place' and Human Identity

In Cambridge it is possible to stand inside one of the
wonders of the Christian world – King's College Chapel.
This is a rich example of late-Gothic architecture with a
stone-vaulted roof fanning out like the branches of a tree
and creating an ethereal acoustic for its world-famous
choir. Most of all, however, King's is noted for its exceptional fifteenth-century stained glass windows. These vast
expanses of colour run the full length of the chapel, illustrate the history of salvation and bathe the building in
extraordinary patterns of light.

Interestingly, the permanent display that introduces visitors to the chapel begins with the sentence: 'We exist not
only in the world but in an image or picture of the world'.
In other words, people in any given society exist within a
general system of signs by which they identify themselves
and see their world. This world view is conditioned by
many different experiences and assumptions (including
beliefs about God) and, in turn, determines their
behaviour.[1] Concretely, King's College Chapel expresses in
its architecture and decoration a quite specific image of
the cosmos. The 'world' is not simply a neutral collection
of raw data but is something we experience as having
meaning. From a Christian perspective, 'meaning' implies
that the world has theological significance and therefore
implications for spirituality – the way people seek to live
their beliefs. At a more basic level, to say that the world

165

has 'meaning' makes it a 'place' rather than a neutral space.

HUMAN EXPERIENCE OF PLACE

It is important to distinguish between 'space' and 'place' for the purposes of this essay. 'Space' is our experience of three-dimensional extension or the linear distance between a number of fixed points. This does not make space a completely empty or meaningless void but, on its own, mere extension has no specific definition. On the other hand, 'place', while certainly involving 'space', implies a great deal more than mere extension or distance. It is a *location*, a portion of space with particular significance. 'Places' are connected with people, either because they are occupied by them or because they reflect something with human significance. This is especially true of sacred places.

Places have a position in the sense both of location and of moral value. To 'know your place' implies a sense of identity within a wider framework of people, values or structures. 'Place' also carries a sense of appropriateness. To be 'in the right place' is to be at home or to be encompassed by what is natural or fitting and to be 'out of place' signifies the opposite.

Walter Brueggemann in his bold and controversial work on 'the Land' as a central theme of biblical faith underscores this attempt to distinguish 'space' and 'place'. 'Place is space which has historical meanings, where some things have happened which are now remembered and which provide continuity and identity across generations.'[2] The meaning of place is humanly constructed or, in other words, place is interpreted space. In the last analysis, place (including its sacredness) is internal to us rather than external despite our tendency to objectify the environment. It is 'a complex network of relationships, connections and continuities ... of physical, social and cultural conditions that describe my actions, my responses, my awareness and that give shape and content to the very life that is me'.[3] The outside world and our inner world form a continuum.

Apart from our own embodied selves, our most common experience of place, or being placed, is familiar landscapes. Any analysis of place inevitably has a subjective element. We learn to be who we are by 'being in place', by relating to the foundational landscapes of childhood or to adopted landscapes that became significant because of later events and associations. A sense of 'continuities' is also important. Where we are placed, as opposed to merely situated, involves more than personal belonging. Our presence, our *present*, in any given place is also connected to a myriad other presences in its past. Such a sense of place marks us for life. Landscapes are more than physical features. They are the geography of our imagination. Their power concerns more than beauty for landscapes are not necessarily inherently romantic or awe-inspiring.

We cannot but be culturally conditioned in terms of the kinds of landscape that exercise power over us. This can be detected in the distinctive approach to landscape painting in different countries. For example, the English live in a small country with very few 'grand' landscapes (and changeable weather). They tend to be struck by a combination of small natural features and the subtle play of light and shadow cast by clouds. Clearly England is not alone in idealizing landscape in art. However, there is a sense in which English landscape painting has a unique quality because it became a particular vehicle for a kind of nostalgia for 'the spiritual'. The essence of Englishness was to be found in an idealized image of a rural past which made the natural world a kind of enclosed garden created by God as both a shelter and an inspiration. In contrast, the American Rockies and plains are overwhelming in their vastness and the desert at the heart of Australia is disconcerting in its emptiness.[4]

The central point, however, is that the power of place in general stems more from cultural factors or human associations than it does from something inherent in the landscape itself. Whatever they are, our personal landscapes seem to have a dual quality. On the one hand they evoke a profound sense of being rooted – not simply *there* in the specific place but also in ourselves, in life, in the *saeculum*, the here and now. Kathleen Norris in an essay on 'spiritual geography' writes of 'the place where I've wrestled my story out of the circumstances of landscape and inheritance'.[5] On the other hand, and at the same time, landscapes frequently have a capacity to carry us beyond ourselves and beyond the immediate. They are often our first intimations of the sacred.[6] This dual experience both of 'here and now' and of transcendence suggests that the distinction often made between sacred places and other, 'secular', places is difficult to sustain.

'Place' has something to do with accepting our contexts and being accepted. If we are placeless people without roots we are not only insecure but also in danger of abusing the world and people around us in a vain attempt to create an artificial identity we do not naturally experience. Cultural historians agree that place is a universal human category (though not with a universal definition) without which human groups cannot exist because it is a fundamental framework for the human experience of relating to self, other people and the world. As the philosopher Heidegger suggests, 'Place is the house of being'.[7] 'Place' is not merely a spiritual issue but also a political one because, for example, colonialism undermined the identity of local peoples precisely by defining them in Eurocentric terms.

Place also has the capacity to reveal and evoke the sacred or the deepest meaning of existence. This transcends what can be uttered or ultimately known. It has a transformative effect because at that moment and in that place our inmost selves stand exposed and naked. Sacred place or, better, the sacred quality of place, is where the timeless and the deep can be found and in this is both grace and revelation. Because of this, place needs to be a fundamental category of theology and spirituality.

Unfortunately, the meaning of places is not always self-evident. Places, particularly those that are directly human constructions, are 'texts' in the broad sense implied by semiotics. We need to have a key in order to 'read' their sign systems and thus interpret their meaning. King's College Chapel, for example, was constructed in the fifteenth century with certain levels of 'meaning' built into the stonework as it were. Because a medieval religious building may be understood as an act of worship in itself, as well as a space for liturgy, it is not unreasonable to say that its art and architecture are directly at the service of theology. The Gothic style of architecture represented by King's chapel is a bearer of quite specific religious ideas – not least about the nature of God.

Gothic 'space' has been characterized as, among other things, dematerialized and spiritualized. It thereby expressed the limitless quality of an infinite God through the soaring verticality of arches and vaults which were a deliberate antithesis to human scale. The medieval fascination with the symbolism of numbers cannot be ignored either. The basic three-storey elevation of Gothic form (main arcade, triforium and clerestory) cannot be explained purely by progress in engineering. Both Rupert of Deutz and Abbot Suger in the twelfth century drew explicit attention to the Trinitarian symbolism of three-storey elevation. However, King's is notable for another typically Gothic characteristic. The stone walls that support the chapel have been pared down to a minimum and replaced by vast expanses of glass. The stories in the windows might teach the worshipper much about the doctrine of God and of salvation but there was also a sense in which glass expressed what might be called a 'metaphysics of light'. God was increasingly proclaimed as the one who dwelt in inaccessible light yet whose salvific light illuminated the world.[8]

Today's visitor to King's chapel may just as easily be a tourist as a worshipper and may have no sense at all of how churches are built, what they express and how they are used. If we understand medieval church buildings as expressions in stone of a particular world view, microcosms of the cosmos, both the language of the stones and the image of the world to which the building points are completely alien to many contemporary visitors. The cosmic view is even strange (though less unintelligible) to a twentieth-century Christian brought up with a different theology and different knowledge about the material world. This does not mean that somewhere like King's cannot be decoded by the modern person although it is difficult to see how someone who is detached entirely from religious sensibilities could enter into meaningful conversation with the givenness of the building. Such reflections also lead us on to consider the fact that all places – not least those that have been considered in some way sacred – do not have a single, fundamental 'meaning'. Places have many different layers of meaning beyond the immediately obvious.

Historians of religion and religious anthropologists such as Mircea Eliade and Victor and Edith Turner (strongly influenced by Eliade's ideas) have dominated the field of studies about sacred place and sacred journey until fairly recently. They tended to assume that there was a single category for understanding both places and pilgrimage. For Eliade, a sacred place was an *axis mundi*, the centre of the world, with boundaries separating it from all surrounding space which was secular and profane. Such places were a kind of Jacob's ladder linking heaven and earth. This approximates to what can be said about *some* religious traditions (for example, the Celtic Christian one) but is simply inaccurate as a generalization. For the Turners, in their discussions of pilgrimages to sacred places, the operative paradigm is the creation of what they call 'communitas' or a special temporary state in which conventional social or other distinctions are transcended in favour of a spontaneous sharing of experience. However, more recent reflections on the subject tend to note the *plurality* of meanings given to particular places by those who relate to them. Places, whether generally considered as sacred or not, do not have a single 'given' significance but are perceived quite differently by people. Indeed, as the very title of one recent volume of essays on pilgrimage suggests (*Contesting the Sacred*), place and the sacred are just as likely to cause divisions as provoke a consensus of interpretation. The classic example would be Jerusalem and the Holy Land in which no less than three major world faiths contest the meaning of sacred sites.[9]

PLACE AND CONFLICT: AUSCHWITZ

A disturbing example of how places do not have a single, ultimate meaning but radically different meanings for people is the former Auschwitz-Birkenau extermination camp in Poland. The fiftieth anniversary of its liberation was marked in 1995. Auschwitz brings into sharp and, for Christians, painful focus the intimate connection between the meaning of place and the quality of human relationships associated with it. If 'place' is fundamentally relational it inevitably has an ethical dimension. Indeed, 'place' may be said to be ethically constructed. There has been intense conflict about the site of Auschwitz and how it should be treated. This reminds us how powerful and emotionally engaging the question of place is.

The tragedy is that Christian attempts to remember Auschwitz by erecting a Carmelite monastery on the edge of the camp and a church somewhat further away have simply become a cause of misunderstanding and hurt. Much of the conflict has to do with mutual preconceptions inherited from a past history of unhappy Jewish-Christian relationships in Poland. Sadly, Polish Christians failed to acknowledge the presence of two different Auschwitz camps. Between 1940-2, Auschwitz I eliminated some 270,000 of the Polish leadership and intelligentsia and unknown thousands of Russian POWs in a forced labour camp. Auschwitz II (or Auschwitz-Birkenau) two miles away was purely an extermination camp. The 1,500,000 victims between 1942-5 were 90 per cent Jewish.

This place of death is now itself dying as the barbed wire rusts and the concrete crumbles. There are agonizing questions. Should Auschwitz be left to decay because of what humans did to other humans in the place or should it be continuously maintained in order to deliver a particular and powerful message? Can we find a language of meaning for a place like Auschwitz and for the Holocaust in general? Specifically, is it appropriate to use Christian terms of reference to interpret a Jewish tragedy – for example the cross and resurrection of Jesus? And, even if theoretically legitimate, are the terms humanly sufficient? Even Jürgen Moltmann's popular 'theology after Auschwitz' is open to the criticism that it is ultimately another version of Christian superiority – the Crucified One is the 'answer' to the horrors of the camps.[10]

There is a profound conflict concerning place expressed

in the religious attitudes of Christians and Jews. For Jews, Auschwitz can never be sacred – not even, as on gravestones, 'sacred to the memory' of so many people. It is desolate morally and philosophically and so it is only appropriate to leave it so physically. 'All culture after Auschwitz, including the penetrating critique of it, is garbage.'[11] It is hard to imagine a more forceful expression of moral revulsion than this.

For many Polish Christians Auschwitz is profaned but the profanity can be reversed. After all, Christians have always reconsecrated desecrated churches and built shrines where martyrdom occurred. This is the reverse side, as it were, of the fact that the Christian tradition also feels it possible ritually to deconsecrate sacred places so that they become once again 'secular' or 'ordinary'. This easy-going attitude to the sacredness of specific places is not typical among the religions of the world and, for example, explains why people from western, Christian-based, cultures find it hard to grasp the intense reactions of other cultures to the desecration of places.[12]

Do these conflicting attitudes reflect different emphases in the doctrine of God? For some Christians, it is axiomatic that Jesus' teaching about God contrasted with conventional Jewish, especially pharisaical, approaches. Thus, Jesus rejected belief in God's punitive justice in favour of mercy and love. Yet it can be shown quite clearly that such a view (often allied to a notion of Judaism as a religion of works) is quite invalid. Equally, Jesus' references to God as *Abba*, Father, have often been thought of as unique. However rabbis in the pharisaical tradition did adopt a similar approach when they addressed God as 'my father'.[13]

Clearly it is invalid to contrast 'the God of Jesus' crudely with 'the God of the Jews' for Jesus was nothing if not a faithful Jew. Nevertheless, there may be a key to important differences of emphasis about God in the later Christian proclamation of resurrection. Does this imply that the world *is* redeemed despite the visible evils? To most Jews the Christian belief that inner change effected by God in Jesus will eventually result in a changed world does not accord with experience. Jewish scepticism is a salutary warning against any tendency to spiritualize redemption. An overbalanced 'realized eschatology' that emphasizes too strongly that eternal life is already won may, in practical terms, produce a certain lack of care about actual life here and now. Unless we are to ignore the real evil in the place Auschwitz, we need to place much more emphasis on a proleptic theology of Easter. That is, that God in the death and resurrection of Jesus affirms that self-giving love *will* be, is bound to be, eventually victorious.

Many Polish Christians believe that it is possible, and necessary, to recreate the sacredness of place in the remains of Auschwitz. This suggests that forgiveness *of the place*, as well as of the people who perpetrated the horrors, is vital lest the sum of evil be added to. Are there different concepts of forgiveness involved and do these reveal different notions of God? The Christian view would tend to emphasize the possibility of the healing of divisions because Christ took the sin of the world upon himself and brought about reconciliation between God and the world (2 Cor. 5:19). Equally, traditional Christian approaches to sin and grace appear to suggest that all people are in some sense equally sinners who may be forgiven by a gratuitous act of God and equally precious however much they defile the image of God within. For Jews, forgiveness is the prerogative of God alone and is closely related to a concept of restitution to victims – impossible in the case of 1,500,000 dead. The Jewish image of God is subtly different too. It is not only the love of God that is emphasized. There is, if you like, more struggle at the heart of God.

Mercy and justice contend together and achieve something like a balance.[14]

Perhaps we are simply left with the thought that the only truth to be asserted about Auschwitz is that there can never be answers about the use of its ruins. Auschwitz has too many symbolisms for mutually suspicious groups of people. In that sense even Christian spirituality (or perhaps *particularly* Christian spirituality) needs to learn something from postmodernism. Auschwitz is visible as the place where God is not. This is true at least of what some call the 'God of the philosophers' or others call the God of systems and 'isms'. If God is somehow to be discerned in Auschwitz, it can only be a paradoxical presence-in-absence.

PLACE AND THE DEVELOPMENT OF CHRISTIAN TRADITION

Before attempting to reflect on 'place' from a perspective of theology and spirituality, we need to ask how Christianity, from its origins, has tended to respond to place. In the Hebrew Scriptures there was what we might call a tension between two different theologies regarding the sacredness of place. Jewish (and Christian) theologies contrast the freedom of a transcendent God of history with the limited, static or 'placed' deities of the soil. A God of freedom could never comfortably be contained in one place. The Mosaic tradition was born of the experience of exodus and wilderness. There was always the question of whether the faithfulness of the people of Israel to God's covenant implied being continually in transit, spiritually if not actually, because they were to find their place in God alone. Prophetic theology continued to emphasize the hidden God (*deus absconditus*) whose home is nowhere and who is therefore experienced as both boundless and elusive.

Yet the God who can be located by no one is nevertheless made known by acts of self-placement (the burning bush of Moses, Mount Sinai, the holy places of Bethel, Shiloh and eventually the Jerusalem Temple). And so God is also the one who is revealed, accessible through Israel's various cultic centres. The story of Moses' encounter with God in the burning bush (Exod. 3) is interesting in a number of respects. For example, it reminds us of important aspects of the Hebrew understanding of the sacredness of place. Although it is a burning bush that draws Moses aside and it is from the midst of the fire that God speaks, the message is that it is precisely where Moses stands that is to be thought of as holy ground (v. 5). Wherever we stand is a place of encounter, epiphany and, ultimately, commitment. There is also an interesting ambiguity in the story of the burning bush. The ambiguity concerns the nature of the God who is encountered. Holy ground reveals God, yet reveals God as the one who cannot be named (Exod. 3:13-15). The recognition of divine presence that places may evoke for us must give way to the realization that where God is, is at the same time not God.

The covenant between God and the people of Israel dominates much of the Hebrew Scriptures. This assured the people of a land of their own and this Promised Land as a whole was a privileged 'place' for the active remembering of God's faithfulness. Thus, the Davidic tradition was grounded in the settled experience of the land and the building of a temple as cultic centre on a site with ancient religious antecedents. The throne of David would never fail, the land was a possession forever (albeit not by right but only by divine gift) and the power of the king was linked to the dwelling of God's power in some special way on Mount Zion.

Given the importance of place in human culture overall, as well as the central significance of 'land' in the theological dialectic of the Hebrew Scriptures, it may seem strange that the Christian Scriptures make little direct reference to either. The fact is that the Christian Scriptures were to a great extent born in the late Jewish urban diaspora around the Graeco-Roman world. They also reflect an atmosphere of apocalyptic. The Promised Land had become largely symbolic and the focus was on the impending overthrow of all earthly conditions as a prelude to the establishment of the true Kingdom of God. So, Christianity came into being in the context of intense future-directed expectations. The power of the gospel for Christians lay in a belief that the 'event' of Jesus Christ represented the beginning of God's definitive act of intervention – a new creation.

Yet placement could not be avoided entirely because the incarnational character of Christian faith meant that the scandal of particularity, that God became flesh in a specific time and place, was intrinsic. For Gentile Christians, the central concern, however, was to move out into the whole world in advance of the rapidly approaching last days. Indeed, Acts 1:8 has Jesus himself exhort his disciples to move beyond the city of Jerusalem to the ends of the earth in their mission of witness. Largely because of the successes of the Pauline mission, Hellenistic Christianity came to overshadow Jewish Christianity. For Christians, God was increasingly to be worshipped in whatever place they found themselves. The first martyr, Stephen, is described as dying precisely for questioning the supreme sacredness of the Temple and for reminding people that 'God does not dwell in houses made of hands' (Acts 7:48).

The Christian situation is complicated by a powerful belief that revelation is focused not on a place but on a person, Jesus Christ, and on a text, the New Testament. Although the Holy Land and traditional Jewish sacred places continued to have some importance and appeal, this was primarily as places where Jesus, the source of meaning and the focus of hope, lived, died and was resurrected. So place became a spatial or geographical expression of a life, a teaching and a theology. The itinerary of pilgrimage, for example, is governed by the texts of the Gospels. What matters is not the places themselves (indeed the 'holy places' have moved around in the course of history!) but what happened there and how, in a quasi-sacramental way, the pilgrim may be brought into contact with the saving events.

Perhaps this explains the intensity of the sixteenth-century founder of the Jesuits, St Ignatius Loyola, on his visit to the Holy Land. According to his *Autobiography*, he paid someone to be allowed back to the Mount of Olives because he could not remember the precise details of the supposed footmarks of Jesus imprinted in a stone while ascending to heaven! Later, in his *Spiritual Exercises*, St Ignatius adopted a form of Gospel contemplation as a significant medium for retreatants to open themselves to personal transformation. Here, in what was traditionally called 'composition of place' in English, the person praying is invited to enter imaginatively into a Gospel scene. Actually the Spanish phrase (*composición viendo el lugar*) is better translated as 'composition, seeing the place'.[15] This captures the different levels that are implied. Certainly St Ignatius intended an imaginative exercise in relation to the Gospel scene. But 'composition' also implies a centring 'of myself' in this place. The 'place' in the sight of which one is to be composed includes the scriptural scene but also the present situation – the total context of the person praying.

In a more general way, the developing Christian tradition substituted the holiness of persons for the idea of holiness associated essentially with 'the land'. Places were sacred by association with human holiness. The rise to prominence of the Christian Church throughout the Mediterranean world between the late-third and the mid-fourth centuries caused the location of the sacred to shift. People increasingly came to believe that the supernatural was represented on earth by a limited number of exceptional human beings. The primary examples were the Apostles – and the places where they were supposed to have worked, died and been buried. But there were also the martyrs of the second- and third-century persecutions, some theologically formidable early fourth-century bishops and the great men and women ascetics who lived around the eastern Mediterranean in Syria, Palestine and Egypt.

The result of focusing the sacred on people was shown especially in the physical contours and piety of the Christian Church. Among the abiding monuments to the sacred were the 'living saints' who gathered in organized communities. So, one of the earliest recorded pilgrimages was specifically to visit the *monks* as much as the Holy Places. The pilgrim Egeria probably came from Spain and her endearing account was written in the late-fourth century probably for a community of dedicated women. She recorded,

> We had the unexpected pleasure of seeing there the holy and truly dedicated monks of Mesopotamia, including some of whose reputation and holy life we had heard long before we got there. I certainly never thought I would actually see them.[16]

The celibate ascetics showed that the era of apostles and martyrs was not over and became star attractions in themselves. They incarnated the power of faith to control nature and to witness to the presence of God. One young pilgrim Daniel set out for the Holy Land but reached no further than Simeon Stylites on his pillar near Antioch. Apparently this confrontation was quite startling enough for Daniel. People were fascinated with the prodigious behaviour of the living saints. It was recorded that Simeon Stylites used

179

to touch his toes 1244 times in bowing before God. Presumably there were witnesses obsessed enough to count![17] Simeon built his pillar near a major highway. The same ambiguity about solitude and accessibility to visitors characterizes the places chosen by early medieval Celtic ascetics. In a context of waterlogged landscape with few tracks, the wild headlands and rocky islands where they lived were not always places of separation but places of connection. At any rate, a genre of literary portraiture, known as hagiography, was born where from Late Antiquity through the Middle Ages the values of religion were summed up and made effective by outstanding individuals.

Ascetics eventually died and it was their tombs, along with those of martyrs and apostles, that became the other abiding monument of a changed understanding of the sacred. The monastery of St Simeon Stylites built towards the end of the fifth century had one of the largest churches in the eastern Mediterranean to mark the spot of the saint's various progressively higher pillars. The ruins are still visible. In a certain sense as well, shrines did refocus the sacred on place when Christianity moved its centre of gravity from missionary journeys to settled urban communities around the Roman Empire.

With the legalization of Christianity under the Emperor Constantine came the building of basilicas, the creation of public liturgy and the growth of artistic decoration. The sites of major churches were often associated with holy people and their tombs. The primacy of the Roman Church was built upon the tombs of the apostles both literally and symbolically. Reversing the older Roman imperial tradition of placing tombs outside cities, the saintly dead were now either moved into cities, or their burial places became themselves the focus of new centres of habitation.

It is also worth recalling that churches were built for rituals, such as baptism and the Eucharist. These symbolized the incorporation of the believer into the death and resurrection of Jesus Christ. Thus the sacredness of church buildings cannot be separated from their role in facilitating the union between the Christian and Jesus Christ as saviour.

Nevertheless there was some debate about the value of special places and of the growing habit of pilgrimage to them as a spiritual discipline and means of personal transformation. In the late fourth century, St Gregory of Nyssa launched his attack. A 'change of place does not effect any drawing nearer to God'. St Gregory was particularly concerned to contrast Christian attitudes with pagan visits to temple shrines. In one sense he was defending the ubiquity of God's presence. In another sense he was defending the apophatic pole of Eastern theology – that God is not only beyond human language but essentially inaccessible.[18]

Such a view was reinforced from a more practical point of view by many of the famous sayings of the desert ascetics of the fourth century.

> An old man said, 'Just as a tree cannot bring forth fruit if it is always being transplanted, so the monk who is always going from one place to another is not able to bring forth virtue'.

And again,

> The old man said, 'Sit in your cell and do the little you can untroubled. For I think the little you can do now is of equal value to the great deeds which Abba Anthony accomplished on the mountain, and I believe that by remaining sitting in your cell for the name of God, and guarding your conscience, you also will find the place where Abba Anthony is'.

What mattered spiritually was the individual's heart rather than the place where he or she happened to be or to visit.

God could not be confined to any specific place. Equally, a change of place on its own would not liberate one from negative forces.

> The Fathers used to say, 'If a temptation comes to you in the place you live, do not leave the place at the time of temptation, for wherever you go you will find that which you fled from there before you'.[19]

Even in the heyday of the Celtic ascetic wanderers, there was a deep suspicion of pilgrims who did not already carry with them the God whom they sought in their journeying. 'Coming to Rome, much labour and little profit! The King whom you seek here, unless you bring Him with you you will not find Him.'[20]

Despite this ambivalent attitude, tombs, cults and pilgrimages played an important role throughout the Middle Ages in the religious experience of the majority of Western Christians and continue to have significance today. It was the virtue of the holy person, and divine power acting through human agency, that mattered more than the place itself. Bodies of saints were moved, stolen, and even broken up in attempts to benefit from their virtue. If a holy person lived and worked in a particular area, that created an indissoluble bond and gave the place and its inhabitants certain rights even after the saint's death. In the case of a certain St Lupacinus, there was a competition between two places for his body once he died. The deciding argument was 'This man belongs to our people. He drew water from our river. Our land transferred him to heaven'.[21]

Interestingly, beyond Europe, this classically Christian approach to place was challenged. Major work has been done by anthropologists on the religion of the Andes after the Spanish conquest in the sixteenth century. The invaders sought to impose a 'pure' faith on what they saw as spiritually primitive people. However, what they could not control, and often did not even notice, was how Christian approaches to place combined with indigenous beliefs in a dynamic syncretism that continues today. Thus, images of Mary and the saints were deliberately installed in or near traditional sacred sites as a way of supplanting loyalties to local gods. No doubt the 'personalities' associated with place did get translated. However, what missionaries did not understand was that traditional local cosmology put place, or an animate landscape, above personalities – even gods. So, paradoxically, by planting a statue of the Virgin Mary in a pre-Christian site, Spanish missionaries merely confirmed these places as special instances of the sacred power of the land.[22]

A THEOLOGICAL PERSPECTIVE

Western theology and spirituality have traditionally had a great deal more to say about time (and eternity) than about place. So, is the sacredness of place really a *theological* question? Roman Catholic and Anglican considerations have generally limited themselves to space in reference to liturgy, sacraments and architecture.[23] Classical Protestantism has often been less than happy with the sacredness of place. It believed, first, in the unbridgeable gulf between the holiness of God and sinful creatures. Second, it concentrated with Luther on the *sacred community* of the Church, constituted by the Word being proclaimed and the sacraments celebrated in the assembly of believers. Remarks by the German Protestant theologian Rudolph Bultmann are revealing of this ambivalent attitude.

> Luther has taught us that there are no holy places in the world, that the world as a whole is indeed a profane place. This is true in spite of Luther's 'the earth everywhere is the

183

Lord's' (*terra ubique Domini*) for this, too, can be believed only in spite of all the evidence.

In the same way the whole of nature and history is profane. It is only in the light of the proclaimed word that what has happened or what is happening here and there assumes the character of God's action for the believer...Nevertheless the world is God's world and the sphere of God as acting. Therefore our relation to the world as believers is paradoxical.[24]

This view tends to encourage a strong moral emphasis in any theological reflection on the sacredness of place. This may lead to a suspicion of any suggestion that the sacredness of 'place' is a given irrespective of how people behave there. The ethical dimension is vital to any theology or spirituality of place. Nor is this view limited to Christians. A sacred place in all cultures carries with it all kinds of rules governing people's behaviour in relation to it.

The classical Protestant difficulty with the sacramentality of place is a significant reminder to all Christians of two things. First it undermines any tendency to build a sacramental spirituality on what Rowan Williams criticizes as 'the rather bland appeal to the natural sacredness of things'. It is possible to declare that the world is charged with the grandeur of God in a naive way when the world of actual events is palpably not like that. A true sense of the sacred in the place that is our world has to be carved out of a process of estrangement, surrender and then re-creation. A sacramental perspective on reality demands more than a simple recognition of a sacredness that is 'there'. There must also be a reordering of the situation in which we are. To live sacramentally involves setting aside a damaged condition in favour of something that is offered to us through sacramental actions for 'where we habitually are is not, after all, a neutral place but a place of loss and need'.[25]

Second, we are reminded that the crucial question behind everything is a *God* question. This in fact increases rather than diminishes the possibilities of talking about the sacredness of place. As we have already discussed, theologians more generally are rediscovering that the God question, particularly the Trinity question, is vital to the way humans actually operate in the world. Christianity has always understood God to be other than contingent creation. The question with which Christianity has therefore had to tussle is how, if at all, God and created reality are related. Can the world of places be in any sense where God dwells and acts? Much of our contemporary attitude to this question goes back to a major shift in imagination in the seventeenth century dubbed 'the spatialization of knowledge'.[26] This had a profound effect not only on our language about the sacred but on our conception of it. 'The supernatural' came to mean somewhere outside the world we know inhabited by various spiritual beings and by God.

'And by God'. Using place language such as 'heaven' to describe where God 'dwells' seemed to imply that it is only the human dead as well as, of course, a mysterious spirit world of angels who are 'in God's dwelling place'. This does not help people to think of God as present in more down to earth 'places'. If God is essentially 'elsewhere', as it were, then at best certain special places may enable us to pass beyond the material world to a spiritual world.

If we take seriously the implications of classical Trinitarian and incarnational theology, an ethical approach to 'place' cannot be the only valid one. The problem with a purely ethical approach is that it has generally been limited to interpersonal relations or divine-human ones. This connects with the tendency we have already noted in Christianity for holiness and 'the sacred' to be focused primarily on people rather than on location. An exclusive emphasis on the holiness of persons tends to lead to what might be called a desacralization of place and of nature. The natural world is subordinated to human need and to human priorities. For example, in his *Spiritual Exercises*, St Ignatius Loyola could write that:

> The human person is created to praise, reverence and serve God Our Lord and by so doing to save his or her soul. The other things on the face of the earth are created for human beings in order to help them pursue the end for which they are created. It follows from this that one must use other created things in so far as they help towards one's end, and free oneself from them in so far as they are obstacles to one's end. (Exx 23)

The doctrines of Trinity and incarnation do not simply have implications for human identity. They imply a divine indwelling in all material reality and a revelation of God through the created order.[27] For the Christian, truth is not an abstract to be found in some dimension that is 'no place' in particular. Incarnation concerns the particular. Truth must be sought paradoxically in the particularities of time and place that have the capacity to speak to us sacramentally, beyond themselves, of God's presence and promise.

As Augustine and the best of the Augustinian tradition remind us, the Trinity images God essentially as Love – the most self-giving of categories. A Trinitarian theology of God affirms a real connection between God and the world and yet that God is not the world and the world is not God. This central doctrine frees us from the unhelpful position of attempting to say the most important things about God in terms of otherness, and then trying to find ways of establishing a real connection between this essentially detached God and creation in time and space. The fundamental theological insight is that God is inherently oriented outward as Trinity into an ecstasy of creation, incarnation and indwelling.

Two English spiritual classics from very different periods relate a strongly Trinitarian emphasis to a positive view of the created order as the 'place' where God dwells. The recently rediscovered writings of the seventeenth-century Anglican mystic Thomas Traherne richly affirm God-in-Trinity's essential relationship to creation.

> The Lord God of Israel, the Living and True God, was from all Eternity, and from all Eternity wanted like a God. He wanted the communication of His divine essence, and persons to enjoy it. He wanted Worlds, He wanted Spectators, He wanted Joys, He wanted Treasures. He wanted yet He wanted not, for He had them. (*Centuries* 1.41)[28]

> O Adorable Trinity! What has Thou done for me? Thou has made me the end of all things, and all the end of me. I in all, and all in me. In every soul whom Thou hast created, Thou hast given me the Similitude of Thyself to enjoy! (1.69)

For Traherne, it was the whole world that was sacred, 'charged with the grandeur of God' as Gerard Manley Hopkins described it.

> The world is a mirror of infinite beauty, yet no man sees it. It is the Temple of Majesty, yet no man regards it. It is the Paradise of God. It is more to man since he is fallen than it was before. It is the place of Angels and the Gate of Heaven. When Jacob walked out of his dream, he said '*God is here, and I wist it not. How dreadful is this place! This is none other than the House of God and the Gate of Heaven.*' (1.31)

While God is not the world and the world is not God, God might be said to be the 'within-ness' of all things and all places.

It seems that Julian of Norwich, a highly original theologian as well as mystic, also understood this well. For Julian there was no division between God's inner reality, God incarnate in Jesus and God in relationship to creation and humankind.

> For the Trinity is God, God is the Trinity. The Trinity is our maker, the Trinity is our protector, the Trinity is our everlasting lover, the Trinity is our endless joy and our bliss, by our Lord Jesus Christ and in our Lord Jesus Christ . . . For where Jesus appears the blessed Trinity is understood as I see it. (Long Text, Chapter 4)

When in her eighth revelation Julian is tempted to look beyond the suffering Christ to the transcendent Father, she responds, 'No I cannot, for you are my heaven' (Chapter 19). All that we need to know of God is in the suffering Christ. In another place Julian speaks of the Trinity as 'comprehended in Christ' (Chapter 57) who is also united to us. Julian's theology of human nature and personhood is closely allied to her profound Trinitarian theology. God as Trinity dwells in us essentially and from the beginning. 'Our soul is a created trinity like the uncreated blessed Trinity, known and loved from without beginning, and in the creation united to the Creator (Chapter 55). Julian describes the human person in terms of place – and, importantly, God's place.

> For I saw very surely that our substance is in God, and I also saw that God is in our sensuality [i.e. that aspect of ourselves that makes us distinct persons in time and space], for in the same instant and place in which our soul is made sensual in that same instant and place exists the city of God,

ordained for him from without beginning. He comes into this city and will never depart from it, for God is never out of the soul, in which he will dwell blessedly without end. (Chapter 55)

This motif is repeated in the sixteenth revelation when God showed Julian her soul. This place at the heart of a person is not only sacred but is 'as if' it were infinite.

I saw the soul as if it were an endless citadel, and also as if it were a blessed Kingdom, and from the state which I saw in it, I understood that it is a fine city. In the midst of that city sits our Lord Jesus, true God and true man . . . The place which Jesus takes in our soul he will nevermore vacate, for in us is his home of homes and his everlasting dwelling (Chapter 68).

THE CRISIS OF PLACE

We have discussed 'place' as a fundamental category of human experience, reflected on how it has been generally viewed in the Judaeo-Christian tradition and examined some theological boundaries within which to view the subject. It is appropriate to conclude this case study by examining how reflections on place and human identity can throw light on our contemporary spiritual climate.

It seems that contemporary Western cultures are experiencing a crisis of place. In this context, it would be possible to address a number of issues. For example, the advance of information technology and the so-called 'information superhighway' has already provoked serious reflection on the reality or otherwise of 'virtual place'. Is it a place of isolation or community? Do ethical questions apply, and if so, how? Can we speak about a theology or spirituality of place in relation to cyberspace?

Other issues about place are raised by contemporary

postmodernists, both theologians and others. Postmodernist theory, with its inherent intellectual hesitation (and spiritual nihilism, some critics would say), seems to suggest 'that there is now no other place to think than amidst the dereliction of former ideas'. In our long-drawn-out moment of Western cultural decline, we now appear to exist in a wasteland. The question is whether it is a place of transition towards some form of future renewal. Some would suggest that with the post-Marxist death of teleological views of history we stand in an 'unspecific intellectual location' that leads precisely 'nowhere'.[29]

However, in this final section I wish to highlight another element of the contemporary crisis: the fragmentation and privatization of physical space. Firstly, Westerners are increasingly an exiled and uprooted people, living 'out of place'. The social geographer Anne Buttimer suggests that it is essential to have 'place identity' but that since the Second World War we have de-emphasized place for the sake of economic values such as mobility, centralization or rationalization. The global relativity of space dissolves the reality of place. 'The skyscrapers, airports, freeways and other stereotypical components of modern landscapes – are they not the sacred symbols of a civilisation that has deified reach and derided home?'[30]

Similar sentiments are expressed by the theologian Michael Northcott. 'The modern city celebrates and facilitates mobility at the expense of settlement, movement at the expense of place.'[31] This is not simply a social issue but a spiritual and theological one. Without a sense of place there is no centring of the human spirit. When human conditions undermine this, the consequent displacement is striking in its effects on individuals and societies. In hardly more than a century, we have moved from a pre-modern, predominantly rural society through an industrial revolution and urban society into what many people call a post-modern, post-industrial world. In an increasingly placeless culture we have become 'standardised, removable, replaceable, easily transported and transferred from one location to another'.[32] If there is a sense of place, it is predominantly a private one in the face of cynicism about the outer, public world.

The privatization of place is also bound up with how we construct our built environments. Architecture and cities are the monuments of our collective consciousness, living symbols of our ideals. When towns began to revive from approximately 1000 onwards, as a result largely of a developing economic role and the growing social importance of the urban mercantile class, two things stand out. First, the urban population continued to need a favourable rural environment because they were great consumers. Medieval cities were still inextricably part of their surrounding landscapes and the division between urban and rural life was not hard and fast. It is not therefore surprising that in the decoration of medieval cathedrals, for example Chartres, the images of rural life such as the seasons, harvesting and vine-growing still predominate. 'The countryside' was not objectified as a place for leisure. In contrast, today's city is essentially disconnected from surrounding place and food production. Citizens are nowadays global consumers and the supposed limitations of seasonal foods are a thing of the past. Urban growth in the High Middle Ages also led to the development of the notion that 'the city' could be understood as a holy place. Sometimes this was because of the concentration of religious buildings and artifacts. Italy also preserved the ideal that civic life in itself, with its organized community of people living in concord, could be just as much a way to God as monastic life.[33]

On the other hand, the monumental architecture that still characterizes much of today's cities stands neither for

the value of individual people, nor for intimate relationships, nor again for focused community. Rather, it speaks
the language of size, money and power. Commercial com-
plexes such as Canary Wharf tower in London's Docklands
exist in brooding isolation rather than in relationship to
anywhere else. Our cities frequently lack proper centres
that express the whole life of a complete community. The
effect of such designs forces us back into our own worlds
behind defences (physical or spiritual) rather than invite
us out into shared, humane meeting places. New domestic
ghettoes are increasingly protected against sterile public
space that is no longer respected but abandoned to violence and vandalism.

There are a number of different responses to the crisis of
place. One Christian philosopher of the American political
Right, Michael Novak, actually suggests a theological justification for the kind of uncentred culture that produces
sterile cities. The virtue of pluralism that characterizes
Western 'democratic capitalism' demands that each of us
be our own centre in a world of private preference – if we
have that luxury! Conscience must be free and so there
can be no agreed spiritual core or imposed notion of
'God'. For Novak, the central Christian doctrine of incarnation implies merely that we must respect the world as it
is rather than preach some kind of eschatological transformation of the *outer* world. In fact this is a theology of
the incarnation that is emptied of its redemptive heart.
Such a society, empty of conviction and prey to the power
of those who are materially rich, merely produces urban
deserts from which are absent 'all shared narratives of
human hope'.[34]

The British theologian John Milbank has a Christian
vision of the city but unfortunately his position appears to
perpetuate rather than heal the division between an outer
(material) and inner (spiritual) city. Milbank writes of the

Christian vision of a society of peace rather than of violence. Milbank would have no sympathy for Novak's
defence of a contemporary 'wasteland' in which the fit
survive and the remainder are casualties but the question
is whether Milbank's vision is too idealized and too otherworldly to be redemptive in the actual world of events.
Milbank's vision is Augustinian. For him the outer city is
'secular' and is to be rejected because, built on human
reason, it is inherently involved in a culture of violence.
This vision does not seem capable of *redeeming* time and
place and of saving the 'secular city'. The life of the
Christian community seems too sharply set apart from
the everyday world. God in a foreshadowing of the Heavenly Jerusalem sends into the secular sphere 'the City of
God'. This appears to be already complete in relation to
the world rather than to grow within it. The danger is that
Milbank's vision 'effectively destroys the idea of a city'.[35]

Because Augustine's *City of God* was more concerned
with the city as community (*civitas*) rather than physical
place (*urbs*), people have been able to draw from it a
radical distinction between the earthly and heavenly cities.
This aspect of Augustine's legacy tends to disable Christianity from offering positive visions for reconstructing
public places as sacred. This is a legacy that Christianity
still struggles to overcome.[36] However, in fact the individualism that permeates so much of Western culture would
have been alien to Augustine. For Augustine it is humanity,
rather than autonomous individuals, that is created in the
image of God. Virtue consists of defending what is public
or held in common. There will be no room in the Kingdom
of God for a self-enclosed and protected privacy.[37]

Cities reflect and affect the quality of human relationships. The fact is that in the context of urban environments
we cannot separate functional, ethical and spiritual questions. If place is to be sacred, places must affirm the

sacredness of people, community and the human capacity for transcendence. It could be argued that in the medieval city the cathedral fulfilled that function. It was at the same time an image of God and a symbol of the ideals of the citizens.[38]

Too often our contemporary urban places are not like this because we have built nothing into them that is really precious to us. In the past material places had a clear and recognizable order. Buildings were so organized that they were both significantly differentiated from each other and, at the same time, sufficiently related to each other. 'Place' is space that has the capacity to be remembered and to evoke our attention and care. We need this if life is to be conducted well. 'We need to think about where we are and what is unique and special about our surroundings so that we can better understand ourselves and how we relate to others'.[39]

We could turn our backs on the city in pursuit of a rural idyll. However, apart from the logistical impossibility for the majority of such a massive social reversal, the danger is that unless we solve the problem of alienation at some other level we simply carry it with us to another place. The early desert ascetics quoted earlier knew this full well. The city is pre-eminently human in conception and construction. It both represents and creates a climate of values that define how we gather together and shape our sensibilities and ways of seeing. We need not so much to flee the city as to repossess it for people, all people, by day and by night. The state of our urban environment highlights again the importance of ethics to any reflection on place. Whose place is it? Who owns it? Who is kept out or marginalized? Who is not made to feel at home? In our Western cities doorways are increasingly filled with the homeless and women particularly feel unsafe on the streets. In Britain there has been some attempt to achieve a 're-enchantment' of the city by creating pedestrianized precincts and even a café culture. The problem is that the model used still marginalizes and excludes a significant number of people. The culturally, if not materially, rich are protected from the poor. We can no longer afford to ignore the urgency of recreating built environments that nurture community rather than alienation.

CONCLUSION

There are serious theological questions which we must reflect upon if our built environments are to support the kind of relationships that will enable humans, individually and collectively, to achieve their deepest identity. Culturally speaking, places are constructed by the people that inhabit, use or relate to them. From a Christian standpoint, people are created in the image of a *Trinitarian* God. Trinitarian faith has a particular capacity to hold unity and multiplicity together. This offers a way beyond the contemporary tendency (reflected in much postmodern writing) for community and indeed the individual 'self' to fragment into a 'pastiche of personalities'. The Christian story unequivocally relates that we come to be as people in and through communities of reciprocal and equal relationships. These relationships both reflect and deepen our contact with the 'community' that is God. In terms of this theological vision, our built environments can be either sacraments or anti-sacraments. They may be revelations of God or denials of God. As such they also reveal what it is to be human or become false 'revelations' of the underlying meaninglessness of human existence. If what we build is an antithesis of human proportion, we should not be surprised that the lack of either intimacy or glory radically undermines the image of the divine at the heart of human living.

Conclusion
ooooooooooo

Two related beliefs about a Christian approach to spirituality are outlined throughout this book. In the first place,
the prolonged separation of spirituality and theology has
been profoundly unhelpful to both. Contemporary
attempts to encourage a conversation between them are
therefore vital. This conversation is potentially a rich
source for the renewal of theology. It also guarantees the
continued development of spiritualities that are rich in
tradition while fully attentive to contemporary questions,
values and experiences.

The second belief is that the most fundamental question
underlying all spiritualities is the nature of 'the sacred'.
Every spirituality encapsulates a world view and, in
Christian terms, this view includes an understanding of the
kind of God humans are dealing with. Who is the God to
whom we pray and with whom we struggle?

The problem for Christian spiritualities is that we exist
in a difficult and confusing period of cultural and religious
transition. In the West, pre-modern religion was essentially
a collective reality that was variously thought of as 'the
Church' or 'Christendom'. At least on the face of it,
the nature of God and God's dealings with humanity was
a matter of widespread, if mainly implicit, agreement. The
sweeping intellectual, religious and social changes of
Renaissance and Reformation across some two centuries,
later reinforced by the Enlightenment, gave birth to an

196

emphasis on individuality and individual responsibility. In terms of religion, this 'modern' era produced competing denominations and traditions. To a degree their theological horizons and religious practices expressed significantly different understandings of God. Yet the question of God continued to be important overall and, indeed, to be fought over. In our own times, this world of certainties, even competing ones, has passed away. 'God' seems to have evaporated into a rather vague, diffuse and immaterial reality that exists behind a bewildering variety of visions of the world and spirituality. On the whole, the nature of God is no longer a major preoccupation nor, it seems, are the various religious institutions that claim to speak with authority for or about God. Vast crowds, including many young people, still turn out for papal visits. However, people's respect appears to be more for a significant spiritual icon than for an authoritative leader to whom obedience is given or who speaks for specific beliefs.

There appears to be a variety of evidence for the existence of 'spirituality' in the West. However it is a spirituality that is increasingly disassociated from clearly-defined belief systems or corporate loyalties. The stable social and family structures that served to pass on the traditions and sense of history of community religion are no longer the force they were. In the market place of contemporary spiritual seeking, many of the teachings on offer are explicitly alternatives to traditional Western Christian (and, indeed, Jewish) belief. Other teachings are somewhat ambiguously connected to the Christian tradition (for example, New Age versions of Hildegard of Bingen or Meister Eckhart). We now inhabit a world of options, preferences, and concern for 'meaningful' as well as effective lifestyles. In this world, spiritualities are freely chosen not inherited.

'Spirituality' has now become a buzzword. Alongside individual spiritual hunger, the word is even creeping back

197

into the public arena. It appears in discussions about the renewal of organizations and social sectors that seem to have lost their souls – such as the media, education, health care or politics. In one sense, from a Christian perspective, all this seems encouraging because it may indicate a post-secularist rediscovery of the sacred. However, it is possible to diagnose some quite serious problems. These questions matter profoundly because they are not simply issues of language or definition but have an impact on our attitudes and behaviour.[1]

Despite the frequent use of the word, there is a great deal of confusion about the exact definition of 'spirituality' as well as about the fundamental questions concerning human nature and God which lie behind it. The modern taste for optional 'spiritualities' detached from faith traditions tends to bypass issues of commitment. Such spiritualities do not readily help us to distinguish between different versions of 'the sacred' or 'God' and their implications for good or for ill. Another serious question is how far this approach to spirituality can challenge our uncritical desire for human fulfilment. Many of the great Christian spiritual teachers such as Augustine, Julian of Norwich, Ignatius Loyola and many others saw *desire* as the key to spiritual growth. However, not all immediate yearnings unambiguously point to our deepest desires. One task of spirituality is to teach discernment. It also needs to offer a language to identify an object of desire that draws us beyond the superficial, the immediate and the self-absorbed.

Many contemporary Western versions of 'spirituality' offer personal practices to assuage our inner hunger. Even those that derive from some of the great world faiths such as Buddhism can too easily be converted into another version of Western consumerism. Because such consumerism is insidiously individualistic, modern Western spiritualities do not necessarily have a language or practices that facilitate true communion between persons in and through communion with the sacred or the divine. For much the same reason, such spirituality is not particularly well equipped to offer a vision of public values or to make a substantial social or political impact. It seems to lack a capacity to address the major building blocks of human existence, beyond personal experience, and thus to reshape worlds. In a sense this kind of spirituality shares in the most unconstructive aspects of postmodern fragmentation.

Are the theologically rich traditions of Christian spirituality capable of stepping into the vacuum? It is certainly important for Christianity to find a voice within the conversation that is beginning to take place about the spiritual renewal of society. There is no question that the Christian tradition of belief and practice has the potential to offer a vocabulary of the human spirit that is missing in so many of the contemporary debates. However, it is no longer self-evident that Christianity will be allowed a significant voice. Many people assume that traditional religion is out of date and cannot offer us wisdom for today. 'Spirituality' in its modern idiosyncratic sense seems better suited to serve people's subjective experiences and feelings. 'Religion in the...popular mind is still that other thing, that thing with doors and windows, clergy and tax-exempt status, moral expectations and social implications'.[2]

The task of making the Christian tradition a convincing conversation partner in the reshaping of society is not the same as an old-fashioned search for 'relevance'. This tended towards reductionism or the dilution of Christian beliefs. Such an approach does not ultimately serve anyone well. However Christianity has to face a problem of conviction and a complex matter of translation. It may have a great deal to share but ways must be found of expressing its riches that are engaging and make sense.

First of all, we have to begin with a certain modesty. We cannot assume that Christian traditions have a permanent right to dominate in Western culture or that the new pluralism is eventually going to go away. We need to accept that the language of Christian belief is no longer immediately recognizable by a majority of people or obviously helpful to them. We also need to recognize that Christianity has often emphasized less important or even completely outdated aspects of its life at the cost of what is most central.

In other words, part of the problem lies within the various Church communities rather than solely with a set of intellectual or socio-cultural forces 'out there'. For example it is not self-evident to many people why belief, or non-belief, in the Trinity should have an impact on how we understand and pursue spiritual development, how we engage with the natural world or create social structures. This gap needs to be addressed urgently. Sadly, the Churches have often done remarkably little to provide adequate catechesis or religious and theological education for adult members and to link this to spiritual formation. Equally, some Christian traditions have been profoundly suspicious of what seems to be implied by 'spirituality'. As a consequence they have offered virtually nothing by way of teaching or practices focused explicitly on communion with God. Even Christian communities that have espoused spirituality in theory have sometimes limited its impact to special groups within the Church or have felt more comfortable with a kind of moralism than with mysticism.

Christianity has become a religion of too many words – especially in its Western forms. The explosion of the modern media and the new technology forcefully underlines how important it is to expand beyond the use of words alone to employ image and evoke imagination. Often it is image rather than word that has the more powerful impact on the way people see the world and operate within it. Equally, in the face of mystery and in the service of wonder, word must ultimately give way to silence. Words are only useful in so far as they create space for transcendence and communion. The Christian treasure house contains a rich array of resources that speak to the imagination. Liturgy and spirituality have always known this. Sadly this has often been forgotten in an over-emphasis in theology and preaching on definition and rationality.

One only has to look at the extraordinary impact on our contemporaries of religious music or the way in which religious sensibilities are touched upon, sometimes indirectly or allusively, in poetry and art. Music, art, ritual, the poetic and the mystical are not merely incidental but central to our expressions of the Christian tradition. This does not have to be elitist. The currents of contemporary culture suggest that all that has the power to evoke imagination may offer a particularly powerful means of commending and communicating the Christian tradition.

The Christian tradition has to learn a new language. It must be able to speak in a world in which lifestyle and immediacy of experience are the central features of the spiritual quest. This does not mean that the Churches should forget about doctrine and reintroduce a separation between spirituality and theology. It may be valid to respond critically to some contemporary spiritual preoccupations, such as a tendency to become overly concerned with self-improvement, rather than simply to take them at face value. Being prophetic, however, does not mean clinging to patterns of thought or ways of speaking that have become eccentric. It will not help Christianity or society at large if, under the guise of purity and tradition, it in fact retreats from a public role to reinvent itself as another privatized option.

We need to begin with the human and spiritual questions that preoccupy our culture and to make them our own. We must rediscover for ourselves within this culture the Christian vision of God and the values of the gospel before we speak to others. It will only be if we learn how to speak from within the experience of the majority rather than as disengaged and superior observers that we will be able to show how the particular riches of Christian theology and spirituality relate to and expand that experience. Even in our privatized culture, people still seek moments and places to celebrate a sense of human solidarity. We also come together to mark moments of great collective joy or sorrow and their spiritual dimension even if in a rather inchoate sense. The challenge to Christian spirituality is to show how its vision of God may contribute powerfully to the desire to find communion with others, express compassion for others and transform the world.

Notes

ooooooooo

Introduction

1. See David Tracy, *On Naming The Present: God, Hermeneutics and Church* (New York: Orbis Books/London: SCM Press, 1994), pp. 42–5.

CHAPTER 1: Living Our Theology

1. Abraham Heschel, *Man's Quest for God* (New York, 1954), p. 87.
2. The modern translation is from Julian of Norwich, *The Showings*, Long Text Chapter 56, edited by Edmund Colledge and James Walsh (New York: Paulist Press, 1978).
3. See, for example, the 'non-realist' position of Don Cupitt, *Taking Leave of God* (London, 1980), especially Chapter 8. Also the critical response by Professor Keith Ward, *Holding Fast to God* (London, 1982).
4. This would be true of some aspects of what is popularly but misleadingly known as the 'New Age' movement. For some sophisticated and balanced assessments from a Christian standpoint, see David Toolan, *Facing West From California's Shores: A Jesuit's Journey into New Age Consciousness* (New York, 1987); also Richard Woods, 'What is New Age Spirituality?' and John Saliba, 'A Christian Response to the New Age' both in *The Way*, July 1993, *New Age Spirituality*, pp. 176–88 and 222–32 respectively.
5. See for example Philip Sheldrake, *Spirituality and History: Questions of Interpretation and Method* (London: SPCK, Revised Edition 1996), pp. 2–3, and Ann W. Astell (ed.), *Divine Representations: Postmodernism and Spirituality* (New York: Paulist Press, 1994), pp. 2–3.
6. For example, Jean-François Lyotard, *The Postmodern Condition: A*

Notes

Report on Knowledge, ET (Minneapolis: University of Minnesota Press, 1984), p. xxiv.

7. In practice theological responses to postmodernism are varied. For a helpful overview of theology and postmodernity, see Paul Lakeland, *Postmodernity: Christian Identity in a Fragmented Age* (Minneapolis: Fortress Press, 1997).

8. Nicholas Lash, *The Beginning and The End of Religion* (Cambridge: Cambridge University Press, 1996), p. 187.

9. David Tracy, *On Naming The Present: God, Hermeneutics and Church* (Maryknoll: Orbis Books/London: SCM Press, 1994), p. 17.

10. For example, Thomas Guarino, 'Between Foundations and Nihilism: Is *Phronesis* the *Via Media* for Theology?' in *Theological Studies*, 54/1, March 1993, pp. 37–54. The opposing viewpoint is expressed by Jack Bonsor in 'History, Dogma and Nature: Further Reflections on Postmodernism and Theology' in *Theological Studies*, 55/2, June 1994, pp. 295–313.

11. See Veronica Brady, 'Postmodernism and the Spiritual Life', pp. 179–87, and Max Charlesworth, 'Postmodernism and Theology', pp. 188–202, in *The Way*, July 1996.

12. See, for example, Geraldine Finn, 'The Politics of Spirituality: The Spirituality of Politics' in Philippa Berry and Andrew Wernick (eds.), *Shadow of Spirit: Postmodernism and Religion* (London/New York: Routledge, 1992), especially pp. 116–18.

13. See Astell, *Divine Representations*, Introduction, pp. 3–12 and her essay 'Postmodern Christian Spirituality: A *Coincidentia Oppositorum?*' in *Christian Spirituality Bulletin*, 4/1, Summer 1996, p. 3. See also Edith Wyschogrod, *Spirit in Ashes: Hegel, Heidegger and Man-Made Mass Death* (New Haven: Yale University Press, 1985), pp. 15–16, and Jean-François Lyotard, *The Postmodern Explained*, ET (Minneapolis: University of Minnesota Press, 1993), pp. 18, 19, 28–9, 78.

14. See for example, David Tracy, 'Theology and the Many Faces of Postmodernity', in Robin Gill (ed.), *Readings in Modern Theology* (London, 1995), p. 228.

15. Tracy, 'Theology and the Many Faces of Postmodernity', p. 229.

16. See for example the interesting typology of Christian world views in H. Richard Niebuhr, *Christ and Culture* (New York: Harper & Row, 1975).

17. Tracy, *On Naming the Present*, p. 16.

Notes

18. Rowan Williams, *Resurrection* (London: Darton, Longman & Todd, 1982), p. 29.

19. Theodore Jennings, 'Making Sense of God', in Peter Byrne and Leslie Houlden (eds.), *Companion Encyclopedia of Theology* (London/New York: Routledge, 1995), p. 911.

20. See, for example, Anthony Meredith, 'Patristic Spirituality' in Byrne and Houlden, pp. 536–57.

21. Catherine LaCugna, 'Trinitarian Spirituality' in Michael Downey (ed.), *The New Dictionary of Catholic Spirituality* (Collegeville: The Liturgical Press, 1993), p. 968. The late Professor LaCugna, in several important works, brilliantly summarized the contemporary 'rediscovery' of Trinitarian theology and particularly its role in the reintegration of theology and spirituality.

22. See Thomas Merton, *Sign of Jonah* (New York: Doubleday, 1953), pp. 8–9. Merton had attempted to use contemporary theological categories to approach the teachings of John of the Cross in his rather unsuccessful book, *The Ascent to Truth*. See also Sandra Schneiders, 'A Hermeneutical Approach to the Study of Christian Spirituality' in *Christian Spirituality Bulletin*, Spring 1994, p. 11.

23. John Milbank, *Theology and Social Theory: Beyond Secular Reason* (Oxford/Cambridge, Mass.: Blackwell, 1990), especially Introduction and Chapter 12 'The Other City'.

24. Milbank, p. 1.

25. For an interesting critique of Milbank's theories, see Gillian Rose, 'Diremption of Spirit' in Berry and Wernick, pp. 45–56. For specifically theological reflections on Milbank, see Gregory Baum, *Essays in Critical Theology* (Kansas City: Sheed & Ward, 1994), Chapter 3 'For and Against John Milbank'. Also Lakeland, pp. 68–76.

26. See Schneiders, 'A Hermeneutical Approach to the Study of Christian Spirituality', p. 11.

27. See, for example, George A. Lindbeck, *The Nature of Doctrine: Religion and Theology in a Postliberal Age* (London: SPCK, 1984).

28. On the relation of practice to the theological enterprise, see for example, David Tracy, *The Analogical Imagination: Christian Theology and The Culture of Pluralism* (New York: Crossroad Publishing, 1991 edition), Chapter 2 'A Theological Portrait of the Theologian'.

29. See John Meyendorff, *Byzantine Theology* (New York: St Vladimir's

205

Seminary Press, 1974), Introduction; also Vladimir Lossky, *The Mystical Theology of the Eastern Church* (London, 1973), Chapter 1.

30. Tracy, *Analogical Imagination*, pp. 77–8.

31. An important response to this dilemma is offered by Professor Edward Farley, the author of a number of major works on theological education. See, for example, his 'The Structure of Theological Study' in Gill, pp. 255–66, reprinted from his highly influential book, *The Fragility of Knowledge: Theological Education in The Church and The University* (Philadelphia, 1988).

32. On the broader context of patristic theology, see Jaroslav Pelikan, *Christianity and Classical Culture* (New Haven: Yale University Press, 1993), Chapter 4 'God and the Ways of Knowing'. The complete works of Dionysius are now available in reliable English translation. See Colm Luibheid and Paul Rorem (eds.), *Pseudo-Dionysius: The Complete Works* (London/New York: Paulist Press, 1987). For useful studies of Dionysius see Andrew Louth, *The Origins of the Christian Mystical Tradition* (Oxford: Oxford University Press, 1981), Chapter VIII and his *Denys the Areopagite* (London: Chapman, 1989); also Denys Turner, *The Darkness of God: Negativity in Christian Mysticism* (Cambridge: Cambridge University Press, 1995), Chapter 2.

33. See Rowan Williams, 'The Via Negativa and The Foundations of Theology: An Introduction to the Thought of V.N. Lossky' in Stephen Sykes and Derek Holmes (eds.), *New Studies in Theology, 1* (London, 1980), p. 96. Italics are in the original.

34. Rowan Williams, 'Hegel and the gods of postmodernity' in Berry and Wernick, pp. 73–80.

35. From 'Via Negativa' in R.S. Thomas, *Later Poems* (London: Macmillan, 1983).

36. Michel de Certeau, *The Mystic Fable*, vol. 1 ET (Chicago: University of Chicago Press, 1992), p. 299. The emphases are the author's.

37. *Mystic Fable*, especially 'Introduction', pp. 1–26.

38. Tracy, *On Naming The Present*, pp. 3–6.

39. See *The Mystic Fable*, passim but especially chapter 7, 'The Enlightened Illiterate'. De Certeau also edited the work of Surin: *Jean-Joseph Surin: Correspondence* (Paris: Desclee, 1963) and *Jean-Joseph Surin: Guide Spirituel pour La Perfection* (Paris: Desclee, 1963).

40. See, for example, Carlo Carozza, 'Mysticism and the Crisis of Religious Institutions' in Christian Duquoc and Gustavo Gutierrez (eds.), *Mysticism and the Institutional Crisis, Concilium* 1994/4, pp.

17–26. However, in an important and complex study, Denys Turner questions the modern concept of 'mysticism' which refers to a certain kind of *experience* and is the creation of nineteenth and twentieth-century theorists. He suggests that the apophatic tradition did not expound subjective mysticism in this sense. See Turner's *The Darkness of God*, especially the Introduction and Chapter 11 'From mystical theology to mysticism'.

41. John of the Cross, *The Ascent of Mount Carmel*, Book 1, Chapter 13, no. 11, translated in Kieran Kavanaugh and Otilio Rodriguez (eds.), *The Collected Works of St John of the Cross* (Washington, DC: Institute of Carmelite Studies, 1979).

42. On God and the category of 'Being' see Jean-Luc Marion, *God without Being*, ET (Chicago: University of Chicago Press, 1995), especially Chapter 3.

43. See James Walsh (ed.), *The Cloud of Unknowing* (New York: Paulist Press, 1981), Chapter IV and Chapter VI.

44. Thomas Traherne, *Centuries* (Leighton Buzzard: Faith Press, 1975), 1st Century, 42. Traherne was one of the so-called 'Caroline Divines' living in the mid-seventeenth century. An Anglican priest and arguably a mystic, many of his most striking spiritual works have only been recovered in recent decades.

45. *The Analogical Imagination*, p. 360.

46. *Analogical Imagination*, p. 385.

47. See, for example, Karl Rahner, 'The Theology of Mysticism' in K. Lehmann and L. Raffelt (eds.), *The Practice of Faith: A Handbook of Contemporary Spirituality* (New York: Crossroad Publishing, 1986), pp. 70–7. Also Rowan Williams, *Teresa of Avila* (London: Geoffrey Chapman, 1991), Chapter 5 'Mysticism and Incarnation'.

48. See the modern English translation of Gregory of Nyssa, *The Life of Moses* (New York: Paulist Press, 1978), Book 2.239.

CHAPTER 2: The Divorce of Spirituality and Theology

1. For example: Bradley Hanson (ed.), *Modern Christian Spirituality: Methodological and Historical Essays* (Atlanta: Scholars Press, 1990), Part One: What is Spirituality? and 'Theological Approaches to Spirituality: A Lutheran Perspective' in *Christian Spirituality Bulletin*, Spring 1994, pp. 5–8; Edward Kinerk, 'Towards a Method for the Study of Spirituality' in *Review for Religious*, 1981, 40/1, pp. 3–19;

Bernard McGinn, 'The Letter and The Spirit: Spirituality as an Academic Discipline' in *Christian Spirituality Bulletin*, Fall 1993, pp. 1–10; Walter Principe, 'Towards Defining Spirituality' in *Sciences Religieuses*, 1983, 12/2, pp. 127–141; Sandra Schneiders, 'Theology and Spirituality: Strangers, Rivals or Partners?' in *Horizons*, 1986, 13/2, pp. 253–74, also 'Spirituality in the Academy' in *Theological Studies*, 1989, 50, pp. 676–97, 'A Hermeneutical Approach to the Study of Christian Spirituality' in *Christian Spirituality Bulletin*, Spring 1994, pp. 9–14, and 'Spirituality as an Academic Discipline: Reflections from Experience' in *Christian Spirituality Bulletin*, Fall 1993, pp. 10–15; Philip Sheldrake, *Spirituality and History: Questions of Interpretation and Method* (New York, 1992/ London: SPCK, revised edition 1996), Chapter 2; Otto Steggink, 'Study in Spirituality in Retrospect' in *Studies in Spirituality*, 1991, 1, pp. 5–23; Kees Waaijman, 'Toward a Phenomenological Definition of Spirituality' in *Studies in Spirituality*, 1993, 3, pp. 5–57.

2. There are few overall historical surveys of the relationship between theology and spirituality. Some pointers are provided in two recent articles. See, Steggink, 'Study in Spirituality in Retrospect', especially pp. 5–10, and Waaijman, 'Toward a Phenomenological Definition of Spirituality' especially pp. 5–37. See also Sheldrake, *Spirituality and History*, pp. 36–49, and Eugene Megyer, 'Spiritual Theology Today' in *The Way* 21/1 January 1981, pp. 55–67.

3. For an excellent summary of patristic and medieval exegesis, see the essay by Sandra Schneiders, 'Scripture and Spirituality' in Bernard McGinn, John Meyendorff and Jean Leclercq (eds.), *Christian Spirituality: Origins to the Twelfth Century* (New York: Crossroad/London: Routledge, 1986), pp. 1–20. On monastic exegesis, the classic study remains the four volumes of Henri de Lubac, *Exégese Médiévale: Les Quatres Sens de L'écriture* (Paris: Aubier, 1959–63).

4. See Louis Bouyer, 'Mysticism: An Essay on The History of the Word' in R. Woods (ed.), *Understanding Mysticism* (London: The Athlone Press, 1981). Also Paul Rorem, 'The Uplifting Spirituality of Pseudo-Dionysius' in McGinn, Meyendorff and Leclercq (eds.), *Christian Spirituality, 1: Origins to the Twelfth Century.*

5. See Vladimir Lossky, *The Mystical Tradition of the Eastern Church* (London, 1973).

6. See the classic study of monastic theology, Jean Leclercq, *The Love*

of Learning and Desire for God, ET (London: SPCK, 1978), especially Chapter 9.

7. For a critical study of the relationship in the twelfth century between traditional monastic theology and the new 'theology of the schools' see Jean Leclercq, 'The Renewal of Theology' in Robert Benson, Giles Constable and Carol Lanham (eds.), *Renaissance and Renewal in the Twelfth Century* (Toronto, 1991 edition), pp. 68–87. For a pioneering study of the creation of the universities and the origin of 'the intellectual', see Jacques Le Goff, *Intellectuals in the Middle Ages,* ET (Oxford: Oxford University Press, 1993).

8. Hans Urs von Balthasar, 'Theology and Sanctity' in his *Word and Redemption: Essays in Theology* (New York, 1965), p. 57.

9. See Caroline Walker Bynum, *Jesus as Mother: Studies in the Spirituality of the High Middle Ages* (Berkeley: University of California Press, 1982), pp. 82–109.

10. Guigo II, *The Ladder of Monks,* ET (Cistercian Studies 48, Kalamazoo: Cistercian Publications, 1981), especially Chapter 2.

11. On Gerson, see Alois Maria Haas, 'Schools of Late Medieval Mysticism' in Jill Raitt (ed.), *Christian Spirituality: High Middle Ages and Reformation* (London: Routledge/New York: Crossroads, 1987), pp. 169–171. On Nicholas of Cusa, see Lawrence Bond (ed.), *Nicholas of Cusa: Selected Spiritual Writings,* Classics of Western Spirituality (New York: Paulist Press, 1997).

12. See the treatment of these issues by John O'Malley in 'Early Jesuit Spirituality: Spain and Italy' in Louis Dupré and Don Saliers (eds.), *Christian Spirituality: Post-Reformation and Modern* (London: SCM Press, 1990), pp. 3–27; also Joseph Veale, 'Ignatian Prayer or Jesuit Spirituality' in Philip Sheldrake (ed.), *The Way of Ignatius Loyola: Contemporary Approaches to the Spiritual Exercises* (London/St Louis, 1991), pp. 248–60.

13. See Andrew Louth, *Discerning the Mystery: An Essay on the Nature of Theology* (Oxford: Oxford University Press, 1983), chapters 1 and 6.

14. On Protestant spirituality, see for example: Frank C. Senn (ed.), *Protestant Spiritual Traditions* (New York: Paulist Press, 1986); various essays in Dupré and Saliers.

15. See for example Wolfhart Pannenberg, *Christian Spirituality and Sacramental Community* (London: Darton, Longman & Todd, 1984), Chapter 1 'Protestant Piety and Guilt Consciousness'.

16. For recent summaries of the Anglican spiritual tradition, see

Notes

Gordon Wakefield, 'Anglican Spirituality' in Dupré and Saliers; A. M. Allchin, 'Anglican Spirituality' in Stephen Sykes and John Booty (eds.), *The Study of Anglicanism* (London: SPCK,1988/Minneapolis: Fortress, 1988); Paul Marshall, 'Anglican Spirituality' in Senn.

17. Catherine LaCugna, *God For Us: The Trinity and Christian Life* (San Francisco: HarperCollins,1993), p. 1.

18. Christoph Schwöbel (ed.), *Trinitarian Theology Today* (Edinburgh: T & T Clark, 1995), his Introduction 'The Renaissance of Trinitarian Theology: Reasons, Problems and Tasks', pp. 4–5.

19. For example, Michel René Barnes, 'Augustine in Contemporary Trinitarian Theology', *Theological Studies* 56 (1995), pp. 237–50. The argument is that the polarization is a simplistic assumption among modern systematic theologians based on an uncritical acceptance of the work of the late-nineteenth-century French Jesuit, Theodore de Regnon. See *Etudes de théologie positive sur la Sainte Trinité* (Paris: Victor Retaux, 1892–8). However, at least one of the modern Trinitarian theologians Barnes criticizes, the late Catherine LaCugna, does *not* accuse Augustine of sacrificing an economic understanding of the Trinity. See LaCugna, *God For Us*, pp. 10–11 and Chapter 3, also 'God in Communion With Us' in Catherine LaCugna (ed.), *Freeing Theology: The Essentials of Theology in Feminist Perspective* (San Francisco: Harper, 1993), pp. 88–9. Equally, LaCugna is actually highly critical of de Regnon's typology in *God For Us*, pp. 11–12.

20. See *De Trinitate*, v-vii, for example in *Corpus Christianorum, Series Latina*, L, *Aurelii Augustini Opera*, Pars XVI, i (Turnholt: Brepols, 1968) and an English translation in Philip Schaff (ed.), *The Nicene and Post-Nicene Fathers*, vol. III, St Augustine (Grand Rapids: W.B. Eerdmans, 1956).

21. See *The Happy Life* 1.4.35 and *Commentary on the First Letter of John* 5.7 and *Commentary on the Epistle to the Galatians* 4.5.

22. Translation by James Wiseman (ed.), *John Ruusbroec: The Spiritual Espousals and Other Works* (New York: Paulist Press, 1985), 'The Spiritual Espousals' Book 2, Part 4, p. 128.

23. 'Selections from the Commentary on John', 82 in Edmund Colledge and Bernard McGinn (eds.), *Meister Eckhart: The Essential Sermons etc* (New York: Paulist Press, 1981), p. 153. 'Books of Parables of Genesis' in *Essential Sermons*, pp. 97–8.

24. See Steggink, 'Study in Spirituality in Retrospect', pp. 6–9, and

Notes

Sheldrake, *Spirituality and History*, pp. 44–7, new edition pp. 52–5. For the manuals, see A.A. Tanquerey, *The Spiritual Life* (Tournai: Desclee, 1930); also R. Garrigou-Lagrange, *Christian Perfection and Contemplation* (St Louis: Desclee, 1937). For an Anglican work see F. P. Harton, *The Elements of the Spiritual Life* (London: SPCK,1932).

25. Pierre Pourrat, *Christian Spirituality*, Volume 1, ET (London: Burns & Oates, 1922), Preface, p. v. The original appeared as *La Spiritualité Chrétienne* (Paris, 1921–30).

26. See Louis Bouyer, *An Introduction to Spirituality* (New York, 1961). For Bouyer's vision of the relation of spirituality to other theological disciplines, see his *A History of Christian Spirituality*, Volume 1 'The Spirituality of the New Testament and the Fathers', ET (London: Burns & Oates, 1963), Preface, pp. vii-ix.

27. Schneiders, 'Theology and Spirituality', pp. 253–74; 'Spirituality in the Academy', pp. 687–97; Also Peter Van Ness, 'Spirituality and Secularity', *The Way Supplement* 73, 1992, pp. 68–79.

28. For an overall connection between ethics and spirituality, see a recent collection of essays, *Spirituality and Ethics*, edited Michael Barnes, published as *The Way Supplement*, 88, Spring 1997. Also Keith Egan, 'The Divorce of Spirituality From Theology' in Patrick Carey and Earl Muller (eds.), *Theological Education in the Catholic Tradition* (New York: Crossroad, 1997), pp. 296–307, especially 301–4. An accessible liberal Roman Catholic overview of these shifts of perspective in moral theology is Kevin Kelly, *New Directions in Moral Theology: The Challenge of Being Human* (London: Geoffrey Chapman, 1992), *passim* but especially Chapter 2. For a Protestant perspective see James M. Gustafson, 'The Idea of Christian Ethics' in Peter Byrne and Leslie Houlden (eds.), *Companion Encyclopedia of Theology* (London: Routledge, 1995), pp. 691–715. For a feminist perspective see the work of Anne E. Patrick, *Liberating Conscience: Feminist Explorations in Catholic Moral Theology* (New York: Continuum, 1996), Chapter 6 'Toward Liberating Conscience: Spirituality and Moral Responsibility', and 'Ethics and Spirituality: The Social Justice Connection' in *The Way Supplement*, 63, 1988, pp. 103–16. Also Anne E. Carr, *Transforming Grace* (San Francisco: Harper, 1988), Chapter 10.

29. Williams, *The Wound of Knowledge: Christian Spirituality from the New Testament to St John of the Cross* (London: Darton, Longman & Todd, 1990), p. 2.

30. See Walter Principe, 'Pluralism in Christian Spirituality' in *The Way*, 1992, 32/1, pp. 54–61.

31. On the contextual nature of the contemporary study of spirituality, see Steegink, 'Study in Spirituality in Retrospect', pp. 12–14, Waaijman, 'Toward a Phenomenological Definition of Spirituality', pp. 39–42, and Sheldrake, *Spirituality and History*, pp. 58, 84–6, 167–8. See also Michel de Certeau, 'Culture and Spiritual Experience' in *Concilium* vol. 19, 1966, *Spirituality in the Secular City*, pp. 3–31. While written thirty years ago, this remains one of the most sophisticated approaches to the issue.

32. On the value and limits of a cultural approach to spirituality see Caroline Walker Bynum, *Jesus as Mother: Studies in the Spirituality of the High Middle Ages*, pp. 3–6. On context and asceticism see Columba Stewart, 'Asceticism and Spirituality in Late Antiquity: New Vision, Impasse or Hiatus?' in *Christian Spirituality Bulletin*, 4/1, Summer 1996, pp. 11–15. This is a review article of Vincent Wimbush and Richard Valantasis (eds.), *Asceticism* (New York: Oxford University Press, 1995).

33. Raimundo Pannikar, *Myth, Faith and Hermeneutics* (New York: Paulist Press, 1979), pp. 241–5.

34. See Jamie Scott and Paul Simpson-Housley (eds.), *Sacred Places and Profane Spaces: Essays in the Geographics of Judaism, Christianity and Islam* (Westport CT: Greenwood, 1991), p. 178.

35. See, for example, the collection of essays published by *The Way Supplement*, 81, Autumn 1994, *Spirituality, Imagination and Contemporary Literature*.

36. The dialogue between spirituality and science has been pursued most strongly in relation to the 'new' cosmology and quantum mechanics. See, for example, *The Way*, 32/4, October 1992, 'Mysticism, Spirituality and Science'.

37. The relationship between spirituality and psychology was examined more critically in a series of essays published by *The Way Supplement*, 69, Autumn 1990, *Spirituality and Psychology*.

CHAPTER 3: Partners in Conversation

1. On the relationship between post-war Roman Catholic theology and spirituality, see for example David Tracy, 'Recent Catholic Spirituality: Unity and Diversity' in Louis Dupré and Don Saliers (eds.),

Christian Spirituality: Post-Reformation and Modern (New York: Crossroad Publishing, 1989/London: SCM Press, 1990), pp. 152–3.

2. Bernard Lonergan, *Method in Theology* (London: Darton, Longman & Todd, 1972), pp. 6–20, 101–24, 235–66.

3. Karl Rahner, *Theological Investigations*, volume 5 (London: Darton, Longman & Todd) 1966: pp. 3–22; 1971: 25–46; 1974: 68–114; also *The Practice of Faith: A Handbook of Contemporary Spirituality*, edited K. Lehmann and A. Raffelt (New York: Crossroad, 1984), passim.

4. See his multiple volume systematic theology, *The Glory of the Lord*, ET (San Francisco: Ignatius Press/Edinburgh: T & T Clark, 1982–92).

5. See *Concilium*, 9/1, 1965, pp. 5–13.

6. See Jürgen Moltmann, 'The Theology of Mystical Experience' in *Experiences of God*, ET (London: SCM Press/Philadelphia: Fortress Press, 1980), pp. 55–80. See also 'Teresa of Avila and Martin Luther: the turn to the mysticism of the cross' in the Canadian bilingual journal, *Studies in Religion/Sciences Religieuses*, 13, 1984, pp. 265–78.

7. Wolfhart Pannenberg, *Christian Spirituality and Sacramental Community* ET, (London: Darton, Longman & Todd,1983), pp. 13–17. See also his more recent essay, 'Baptism as remembered "ecstatic" identity' in David Brown and Ann Loades (eds.), *Christ: The Sacramental Word* (London: SPCK, 1996).

8. See Andrew Louth, *Denys the Areopagite* (London: Geoffrey Chapman,1989) and *The Origins of the Christian Mystical Tradition from Plato to Denys* (Oxford/New York: Oxford University Press, 1981). Also *Theology and Spirituality* (Oxford: SLG Press,1976). For John Macquarrie, see *Paths in Spirituality* (London: SCM Press,2nd Edition 1992), Chapter VI 'Theology and Spirituality'.

9. Kenneth Leech, *True God* (London: SPCK,1985, published in the USA by Harper & Row as *Experiencing God: Theology as Spirituality*).

10. See Rowan Williams, *The Wound of Knowledge: Christian Spirituality from the New Testament to St John of the Cross*, 2nd Edition (London: Darton, Longman & Todd,1990/Cambridge, Mass.: Cowley Publications,1991). Also *Teresa of Avila* (London: Chapman/Wilson Ct: Moorhouse, 1991), pp. 54–5 and Chapter 5 'Mysticism and Incarnation'.

11. Gustavo Gutiérrez, *We Drink from Our Own Wells: The Spiritual Journey of a People* (London: SCM Press, 1984), p. 1.

12. Gutiérrez, pp. 35–71.

13. Anne E. Carr, *Transforming Grace: Christian Tradition and Women's Experience* (San Francisco: Harper,1990), p. 202.

14. Carr, pp. 117–133.

15. Carr, pp. 204–14.

16. Catherine LaCugna, *God For Us: The Trinity and Christian Life* (San Francisco: HarperCollins, 1993), p. 1.

17. Karl Rahner, *The Trinity*, ET (London: Burns & Oates, 1970), p. 22.

18. For example, Colin Gunton, 'The Trinity in Modern Theology' in Peter Byrne and Leslie Houlden (eds.), *Companion Encyclopedia of Theology* (London: Routledge, 1995), p. 948.

19. There are a number of useful surveys of contemporary Trinitarian writing. See, for example, David S. Cunningham, 'Trinitarian Theology since 1990' in *Reviews in Religion and Theology*, 1995, pp. 8–16; Christoph Schwöbel, 'Introduction: The Renaissance of Trinitarian Theology: Reasons, Problems and Tasks' in Schwöbel (ed.), *Trinitarian Theology Today* (Edinburgh: T & T Clark, 1995); also Gunton, 'The Trinity in Modern Theology' in Byrne and Houlden, pp. 937–57.

20. See Robert Markus, *The End of Ancient Christianity* (Cambridge: Cambridge University Press, 1990), p. 78.

21. See especially Jürgen Moltmann, *History and the Triune God: Contributions to Trinitarian Theology*, ET (London: SCM Press/New York: Crossroad, 1992).

22. See, for example, LaCugna, *God For Us*, Chapter 8 'Persons in Communion' and Elisabeth A. Johnson, *She Who Is: The Mystery of God in Feminist Theological Discourse* (New York: Crossroad, 1996), Chapter 10 'Triune God: Mystery of Relation'.

23. Leonardo Boff, *Trinity and Society*, ET (New York: Orbis/Tunbridge Wells: Burns & Oates, 1982).

24. For example, Colin Gunton, *The Promise of Trinitarian Theology* (Edinburgh: T & T Clark, 1990) and LaCugna, *God For Us*.

25. John Zizioulas, *Being As Communion* (New York: St Vladimir's Seminary Press, 1985). Also his 'The Doctrine of the Holy Trinity: The Significance of the Cappadocian Contribution' in Schwöbel. But the medieval mystical theologian Richard of St Victor in the twelfth century also argued for the *necessity* of a community within God if God is truly to be conceived of as 'Love'. See *De Trinitate*, Book 3, Chapter 19 in Grover Zinn (ed.), *Richard of St Victor*, Classics of Western Spirituality (New York: Paulist Press, 1979).

Notes

26. See Jean-Luc Marion, *God without Being*, ET (Chicago: The University of Chicago Press), especially pp. 46–9.

27. See, for example, David Tracy, *On Naming the Present* (New York: Orbis Books, 1994), pp. 42–5. On eschatology and the Trinity, see also Gareth Jones, *Critical Theology: Questions of Truth and Method* (Cambridge: Polity Press/New York: Paragon House, 1995), pp. 183–7.

28. Nicholas Lash, *Believing Three Ways in One God: A Reading of the Apostles' Creed* (London: SCM Press, 1992), p. 13.

29. For example, LaCugna, *God For Us*, Chapter 9; Rowan Williams, 'Trinity and Revelation' in *Modern Theology* (1986), pp. 197–212; and Daniel Hardy and David Ford, *Jubilate: Theology in Praise* (London: Darton, Longman & Todd, 1984).

30. 'Theology and Spirituality: Strangers, Rivals or Partners?' in *Horizons*, 13 (1986), pp. 253–74; 'Spirituality in the Academy' in *Theological Studies*, 50 (1989), pp. 676–97; 'Spirituality as an Academic Discipline: Reflections from Experience' in *Christian Spirituality Bulletin*, 1/2 (Fall 1993), pp. 10–15; 'A Hermeneutical Approach to the Study of Christian Spirituality' in *Christian Spirituality Bulletin*, 2/1 (Spring 1994), pp. 9–14.

31. Bernard McGinn, 'The Letter and The Spirit: Spirituality as an Academic Discipline' in *Christian Spirituality Bulletin*, 1/2, Fall 1993, pp. 1–10.

32. See Bradley Hanson, 'Spirituality as Spiritual Theology' in Hanson (ed.), *Modern Christian Spirituality: Methodological and Historical Essays* (Atlanta: Scholars Press, 1990), pp. 45–51, and 'Theological Approaches to Spirituality: A Lutheran Perspective' in *Christian Spirituality Bulletin*, 2/1, Spring 1994, pp 5–8. Also Leech.

33. See the articles in *Christian Spirituality Bulletin*, 3/2, Fall 1995: Philip Endean, 'Theology out of Spirituality: The Approach of Karl Rahner', pp. 6–8; Mark McIntosh, 'Lover without a Name: Spirituality and Constructive Christology Today', pp. 9–12; J. Matthew Ashley, 'The Turn to Spirituality? The Relationship between Theology and Spirituality', pp. 13–18; Anne M. Clifford, 'Re-membering the Spiritual Core of Theology: A Response', pp. 19–21.

34. See, for example, Nicholas Lash in *The Beginning and The End of Religion* (Cambridge: Cambridge University Press, 1996), Chapter 9, 'Creation, Courtesy and Contemplation', *passim.*

215

35. David Tracy, *Blessed Rage for Order* (New York: The Seabury Press, 1975), pp. 64–71.
36. Tracy, *Blessed Rage for Order*, pp. 72–9. See also Dermot Lane, *The Experience of God* (Dublin: Veritas, 1985), p. 26, and Walter Principe, 'Pluralism in Christian Spirituality' in *The Way*, January 1992, pp. 58–60.
37. See Catherine LaCugna, 'Trinitarian Spirituality' in Michael Downey (ed.), *New Dictionary of Catholic Spirituality* (Collegeville: The Liturgical Press, 1993), pp. 968–71.
38. Andrew Louth, *Theology and Spirituality* (Fairacres Publications 55, Oxford: SLG Press, 1978), p. 4.
39. Implicitly in Alan Jones, 'Spirituality and Theology' in *Review for Religious*, 39/2, March 1980, pp. 161–76, and explicitly in Sandra Schneiders, 'Spirituality in the Academy' in *Theological Studies*, 50, 1989, pp. 676–97.

CHAPTER 4: A Practical Theology of the Trinity: Julian of Norwich

1. A number of authorities have speculated that the 'showings' or 'revelations' arose as an extension of the use of imagination in contemplative prayer. This was frequently associated with Bible meditation especially on scenes from the Gospels – a practice that grew out of the monastic tradition of *lectio divina*. See, for example, Grace Jantzen, *Julian of Norwich* (London: SPCK, 1987), Chapter 4 'Julian's Prayers' and also Denise Nowakowski Baker, *Julian of Norwich's Showings: From Vision to Book* (Princeton: Princeton University Press, 1994). Joan Nuth in *Wisdom's Daughter: The Theology of Julian of Norwich* (New York: Crossroad, 1991) refers to *lectio* in relation to Julian's theological method and overall development of her reflections, especially in her Long Text but not to such an interpretation of the visionary experience itself.
2. All citations in this chapter, unless otherwise indicated, are by chapter number from the modern English translation in The Classics of Western Spirituality series. See Edmund Colledge and James Walsh (eds.), *Julian of Norwich: Showings* (New York: Paulist Press, 1978). This work is sometimes called *Revelations of Divine Love*. Julian wrote two texts, the Short Text (ST) and the theologically more complex Long Text (LT). Internal textual evidence dates the LT to some twenty years after the original visions. Until the dating

was recently questioned it was generally assumed that the ST was written shortly after the visionary experiences and was an immediate and relatively immature response to them. For an alternative viewpoint see Nicholas Watson, 'The Composition of Julian of Norwich's *Revelations of Love*', in *Speculum* 68 (1993), pp. 637–83. The established critical edition of the Middle English texts is also edited by Colledge and Walsh as *A Book of Showings to the Anchoress Julian of Norwich*, 2 volumes (Toronto: Pontifical Institute of Medieval Studies, 1978). Some scholars prefer the edition of the LT by Marion Glasscoe, *A Revelation of Love* (Exeter: Exeter University Press, 1989). This relies on the single manuscript known as Sloane 1 because it is thought to be closer to the fourteenth-century English.

3. Brant Pelphrey, *Christ Our Mother: Julian of Norwich* (Wilmington: Michael Glazier, 1989), p. 103.

4. B. A. Windeatt (ed.), *The Book of Margery Kempe* (London: Penguin Books, 1985), Book 1, Chapter 18.

5. For helpful summaries of evidence and speculation about these matters, see Jantzen, *Julian of Norwich*, Part One and Nuth, *Wisdom's Daughter*, Chapter 1.

6. The editors of the critical edition of Julian, Edmund Colledge and James Walsh, are particularly concerned to portray her as theologically well-educated. Joan Nuth in *Wisdom's Daughter: The Theology of Julian of Norwich*, pp. 8–10, is largely convinced by their arguments. Grace Jantzen in *Julian of Norwich*, pp. 15–20, is much more cautious about the evidence for formal theological education.

7. See Ewert Cousins, 'The Humanity and Passion of Christ', especially pp. 386–9 in Jill Raitt (ed.), *Christian Spirituality: High Middle Ages and Reformation* (London: Routledge & Kegan Paul/New York: Crossroads Publishing, 1987).

8. See Ewert Cousins, 'The Humanity and the Passion of Christ' in Jill Raitt (ed.), *Christian Spirituality*, pp. 375–80; also Philip Sheldrake, *Spirituality and History: Questions of Interpretation and Method*, Chapter 6 'Context and Conflicts: The Beguines', especially pp. 152–5.

9. See for example, Peter Dinzelbacher, 'The Beginnings of Mysticism Experienced in Twelfth-Century England' in Marion Glasscoe (ed.), *The Medieval Mystical Tradition in England* (Woodbridge, Suffolk: Boydell & Brewer, 1987); also Caroline Walker Bynum, *Jesus as Mother: Studies in the Spirituality of the High Middle Ages* (Berkeley: University of California Press, 1982), Chapter 2.

Notes

10. See Caroline Walker Bynum, *Holy Feast and Holy Fast: The Religious Significance of Food to Medieval Women* (Berkeley: University of California Press, 1987), pp. 120, 199–200, 207, 209, 211–12.

11. Although the Middle English 'poynte' is translated by Colledge and Walsh as 'an instant of time' (p. 197) the chapter overall is more suggestive of a spatial image. 'By which vision I saw that he is present in all things.' 'For he is at the centre of everything.'

12. Of course it may also be the case that Julian was perfectly clear about the implications of the 'showing'. The struggle to maintain a balance with the Church's teaching may have been a rhetorical device to avoid accusations of heresy.

13. For example, Elizabeth Dreyer, 'The Trinitarian Theology of Julian of Norwich' in *Studies in Spirituality* 4 (1994), pp. 79–93.

14. See the helpful analysis in Nuth, pp. 89–94.

15. Julian uses the Middle English words 'moder' or its associated terms 'moderhede' and 'moderly' some 83 times in the Long Text. Of these, nine refer to Mary and four to 'Holy Church'. The remainder refer to Jesus Christ, God or the Trinity. See, Jennifer P. Heimmel, *'God is Our Mother': Julian of Norwich and The Medieval Image of Christian Feminine Divinity* (Salzburg: Instituut für Anglistik und Amerikanistik, 1982), pp. 50–1.

16. See, for example, Caroline Walker Bynum, *Jesus as Mother*, Chapter 4, and the listing of other sources in the critical edition of Julian, ed. Colledge and Walsh, *A Book of Showings*, pp. 151–62.

17. See Jantzen, pp. 117–18. The original references are: Anselm, Prayer to St Paul, in Benedicta Ward (ed.), *The Prayers and Meditations of St Anselm* (London: Penguin Books, 1973), pp. 153–6 and 'Ancrene Wisse' in Anne Savage and Nicholas Watson (eds.), *Anchoritic Spirituality*, The Classics of Western Spirituality (New York: Paulist Press, 1991), Part IV, p. 132 & Part VI, p. 182.

18. Ritamary Bradley, *Julian's Way: A Practical Commentary on Julian of Norwich* (London: HarperCollins, 1992), p. 146.

19. While the connection Julian makes between the lordship image and the motherhood of God is noted by several scholars, the 'feminization' of lordship and authority does not seem to have been explicitly drawn out. See, for example, Catherine Innes-Parker, 'Subversion and Conformity in Julian's *Revelation*: Authority, Vision and the Motherhood of God' in *Mystics Quarterly*, XXIII/2, March 1997, pp. 7–35 at p. 21.

20. Nuth, pp. 74–9, suggests that Julian's usage is closer to texts such as the *Ancrene Riwle* that designate 'courtaysye' as a Christian virtue of giving pleasure to others. This is perhaps to miss the point that the conventions of courtly love and of spiritual love were not unconnected!

21. For example in the Long Text, Chapter 5. Colledge and Walsh use the word 'familiar' in their modern English translation when the Middle English text uses the word 'homely'.

22. See the comments of Brant Pelphrey in *Love Was His Meaning: The Theology and Mysticism of Julian of Norwich* (Salzburg: Instituut für Anglistik und Amerikanistik, 1982), p. 106 & n. 5.

23. See for example, Jay Ruud, 'Nature and Grace in Julian of Norwich' in *Mystics Quarterly*, XIX/2, June 1993, pp. 71–81.

24. The so-called heresy of the Free Spirit was the object of a great deal of fear by Church authorities across Europe during the fourteenth century. The findings of Robert Lerner in *The Heresy of the Free Spirit in the Later Middle Ages* (Berkeley: University of California Press, 1972) have not been substantially revised by more recent scholars. Lerner convincingly demonstrates that the 'heresy' was substantially a projection of institutional fear rather than a significant reality. It was, however, one of the accusations levelled at Beguines and women mystics and perhaps known to Julian. The argument in Nuth, p. 19, that Julian's references cannot be to Wyclif and his followers is dependent on dating the Short Text to as early as *c.* 1373. As we have already seen, some scholars now argue for a much later date.

25. See Pelphrey, *Christ our Mother*, pp. 113–18.

26. They certainly do not mean 'spirit'/soul and 'matter'/body. They bear some, but not total, resemblance to the Augustinian concept of higher and lower parts of the soul. See, for example Jantzen, pp. 137–49, and Nuth, pp. 104–16.

27. See Margaret Ann Palliser, *Christ Our Mother of Mercy: Divine Mercy and Compassion in the Theology of the Showings of Julian of Norwich* (Berlin: de Gruyter, 1992), Chapter 5 (B) 'Jesus Christ: The Compassion of God and Our Compassion'.

Notes

CHAPTER 5: Spiritual Freedom in Ignatius Loyola and George Herbert

1. For general overviews of the Anglican spiritual tradition that trace its roots in *The Book of Common Prayer* see, for example, A.M. Allchin, 'Anglican Spirituality' in Stephen Sykes and John Booty (eds.), *The Study of Anglicanism* (London: SPCK/Minneapolis: Fortress Press, 1988); Paul V. Marshall, 'Anglican Spirituality' in Frank Senn (ed.), *Protestant Spiritual Traditions* (New York: Paulist Press, 1986); Gordon Wakefield, 'Anglican Spirituality' in Louis Dupré and Don Saliers (eds.), *Christian Spirituality: Post-Reformation and Modern* (New York: Crossroad/London: SCM Press, 1989). See also Gordon Mursell, 'Traditions of Spiritual Guidance: The Book of Common Prayer', in *The Way*, 31/2, April 1991, pp. 163–171.

2. See the Introduction to Jill Raitt (ed.), *Christian Spirituality: High Middle Ages and Reformation* (New York: Crossroad/London: SCM Press, 1987) and comments in Philip Sheldrake, *Spirituality and History: Questions of Interpretation and Method* (Revised Edition London: SPCK, 1995), pp. 102 and 206–13.

3. For a survey of evidence and scholarly opinion, see Philip Sheldrake, 'The Influence of the Ignatian Tradition' in *Ignatian Spirituality in Ecumenical Context, The Way Supplement*, 68, Summer 1990, pp. 74–85.

4. See Terence O'Reilly, 'The Spiritual Exercises and the Crisis of Medieval Piety' in *The Way Supplement*, no. 70, Spring 1991, pp. 101–13.

5. See Ignatius' Autobiography, or 'Reminiscences' in Joseph Munitiz and Philip Endean (eds.), *Saint Ignatius of Loyola: Personal Writings* (London: Penguin Books, 1996), pp. 22–4. For summaries of contemporary scholarship on the life of Ignatius Loyola in relationship to the main themes of his spirituality see John O'Malley, *The First Jesuits* (Cambridge, Mass.: Harvard University Press, 1993), Chapter 1 and 'Early Jesuit Spirituality: Spain and Italy' in Dupré and Saliers, pp. 3–27.

6. For a recent translation of the *Spiritual Exercises* into English see Munitiz and Endean, *Saint Ignatius of Loyola: Personal Writings*. References to the Exercises in this chapter follow the paragraph numbering (e.g. Exx 1) used in all modern editions.

7. Exx 1 describes the purpose of the Exercises as the removal of

'disordered attachments' and to 'seek and find the divine will in regard to the disposition of one's life for the good of the soul'. Implicitly seeking God's will lies behind the whole dynamic of the Rule for Discernment of Spirits (Exx 313–36).

8. From an early biography of Ignatius by Ribadeneira, quoted in Hugo Rahner, *Ignatius the Theologian*, ET (London: Chapman, 1990), p. 23.

9. Joseph Veale, 'The dynamic of the Spiritual Exercises' in *The Way Supplement*, 52, Spring 1985, p. 17.

10. Hugo Rahner, *Ignatius the Theologian* (London: Geoffrey Chapman, 1990), p. 2.

11. See Ignatius Loyola, 'Spiritual Diary' in Munitiz (ed.), *Personal Writings*, pp. 94–7 and Edmund Colledge and James Walsh (eds.), *Julian of Norwich: Showings* (New York: Paulist Press, 1978), Long Text, chapter 19.

12. See, for example, Marie-Eloise Rosenblatt, 'Women and the Exercises: Sin, Standards and New Testament Texts' in *The Way Supplement*, 70, Spring 1991, pp. 16–32.

13. See the remarks by two eminent Ignatian commentators: William Peters, *The Spiritual Exercises of St Ignatius: Exposition and Interpretation*, ET (Jersey City: Program to Adapt the Spiritual Exercises, 1968), p. 114 and David Stanley, 'Contemporary Gospel Criticism and the "Mysteries of the Life of Our Lord" in the Spiritual Exercises', in George Schner (ed.), *Ignatian Spirituality in a Secular Age* (Waterloo, Ontario: Wilfred Laurier University Press, 1984), pp. 32–4.

14. Diary, p. 84. See also p. 90.

15. *Spiritual Diary*, pp. 84–5. The reference is to a vision at La Storta outside Rome before the Jesuits were formally approved. Ignatius experienced God the Father granting his wish to live a life following Christ.

16. *Diary*, p. 85.

17. *Diary*, pp. 93–4.

18. See the comments on Ignatius' titles for God in the commentary to George Ganss' recent translation of *The Spiritual Exercises of St Ignatius*, (Chicago: Loyola University Press, 1992), pp. 144 (note 5) and 208–9.

19. Jon Sobrino, *Christology at the Crossroads*, ET (London: SCM Press, 1978), Appendix 'The Christ of the Ignatian Exercises', p. 397.

20. Juan Luis Segundo, *The Christ of the Ignatian Exercises* (New York: Orbis, 1987), pp. 41–114.
21. Rahner, *Ignatius the Theologian*, p. 17.
22. Two modern editions are: John Wall (ed.), *George Herbert: The Country Parson, The Temple* (New York: Paulist Press/London: SPCK, 1981) and Louis Martz (ed.), *George Herbert and Henry Vaughan* (Oxford/New York: Oxford University Press, 1986).
23. Allen, 'The Christian Pilgrimage in George Herbert's *The Temple*' in Bradley Hanson (ed.), *Modern Christian Spirituality: Methodological and Historical Essays* (Atlanta: Scholars Press, 1990), p. 67.
24. Isaak Walton, *Lives* (Oxford: Oxford University Press, 1927), p. 314.
25. See for example, Rosemond Tuve, *A Reading of George Herbert* (Chicago: University of Chicago Press, 1952) and Louis Martz, *The Poetry of Meditation: A Study of English Religious Literature of the Seventeenth Century* (New Haven: Yale University Press, 1954).
26. See for example, Barbara Lewalski, *Protestant Poetics and the Seventeenth-Century Religious Lyric* (Princeton: Princeton University Press, 1979) and Richard Strier, *Love Known: Theology and Experience in George Herbert's Poetry* (Chicago: University of Chicago Press, 1983).
27. See for example the introduction by Anthony Raspa to his edition of John Donne's *Devotions Upon Emergent Occasions* (New York/Oxford: Oxford University Press, 1987). Gene Veith's important study, *Reformation Spirituality: The Religion of George Herbert* (London/Toronto: Associated University Presses, 1985), understands Herbert as 'Anglican' but adopts an excessively Calvinist interpretation of the Church of England.
28. Peter Hardwick, 'The Inward Struggle of the Self with God: Gerard Manley Hopkins and George Herbert' in *The Way Supplement*, 66, Autumn 1989, *Spirituality and The Artist*, p. 33.
29. See Pat Pinsent, 'The Image of Christ in the Writings of Two Seventeenth-Century English Country Parsons: George Herbert and Thomas Traherne' in Stanley Porter, Michael Hayes and David Toombs (eds.), *Images of Christ Ancient and Modern* (Sheffield: Sheffield Academic Press, 1997), p. 235.
30. For a summary of discussions concerning this movement and Herbert's 'mysticism' in general, see Arthur Clements, *Poetry of Contemplation* (New York: State University of New York Press, 1990), pp. 81–127.

Notes

CHAPTER 6: 'Place' and Human Identity

1. Historians of culture have become increasingly interested by world views and *mentalités* and influenced by categories drawn from both anthropology and semiotics, or the theory of sign systems.
2. Walter Brueggemann, *The Land: Place as Gift, Promise and Challenge in Biblical Faith* (Philadelphia: Fortress, 1977), p. 5.
3. Arnold Berleant, *The Aesthetics of Environment* (Philadelphia: Temple University Press, 1992), p. 4. On the humanly constructed meaning of 'place' see also Simon Schama, *Landscape and Memory* (London: HarperCollins, 1995), for example pp. 6–7, 61 and 81. Schama illustrates his point particularly powerfully in Part 1 'Wood' where he discusses the different cultural and even spiritual values associated with the forest in Europe and North America.
4. On the 'spirituality' implied by landscape art, not least the contrast between English landscape painting and the art of Australia and North America, see for example Peter Fuller, *Theoria: Art and The Absence of Grace* (London, 1988), especially Chapters 14 'An Earthly Paradise?', 19 'The Art of England', 21 'The Glare of the Antipodes'.
5. Kathleen Norris, *Dakota: A Spiritual Geography* (New York: Houghton Mifflin, 1993), p. 2.
6. For reflections on landscape, the sacred and spirituality, see the work of Belden C. Lane: *Landscapes of the Sacred: Geography and Narrative in American Spirituality* (New York: Paulist Press, 1989); 'Landscape and Spirituality: A Tension between Place and Placelessness in Christian Thought' in *The Way Supplement* 73 (Spring 1992), pp. 4–13; 'Galesburg and Sinai: The Researcher as Participant in the Study of Spirituality and Sacred Place', in *Christian Spirituality Bulletin* (Spring 1994).
7. See Martin Heidegger, 'Building dwelling thinking' in *Poetry, Language, Thought* (New York: Harper & Row, 1975), pp. 145–61.
8. For some reflections on what might be called the theology of Gothic, see Christopher Wilson, *The Gothic Cathedral* (London: Thames & Hudson, 1990), especially the Introduction, pp. 64–6, 219–20, 262–3.
9. See Mircea Eliade, 'Sacred Places: Temple, Palace, "Centre of the World" ' in *Patterns in Comparative Religion* (New York: World Publishing, 1963); Victor and Edith Turner, *Image and Pilgrimage*

in Christian Culture (New York: Columbia University Press, 1978); a critique in John Eade and Michael Sallnow (eds.), *Contesting the Sacred: The Anthropology of Christian Pilgrimage* (London: Routledge, 1990), Introduction, *passim*. On conflict, see Simon Coleman and John Elsner, *Pilgrimage: Past and Present in the World Religions* (London: British Museum Press, 1995), Picture Section II The Sacred Site: Contestation and Cooperation, pp. 48–51.

10. Jürgen Moltmann, *The Crucified God: The Cross of Christ as the Foundation and Criticism of Christian Theology* (London: SCM Press, 1974).

11. Quoted in Edith Wyschogrod, *Saints and Postmodernism* (Chicago: University of Chicago Press, 1990), p. 245.

12. See Jane Hubert, 'Sacred Beliefs and Beliefs of Sacredness' in David L. Carmichael, Jane Hubert, Brian Reeves and Audhild Schanche (eds.), *Sacred Sites, Sacred Places* (London: Routledge, 1994), pp. 13–14.

13. See John Riches, *Jesus and the Transformation of Judaism* (London: Darton, Longman & Todd, 1980), p. 185; E. P. Sanders, *Paul and Palestinian Judaism* (London: SCM Press, 1977) and *Jesus and Judaism* (London: SCM Press, 1985); Marcus Braybrooke, *Time to Meet: Towards a Deeper Relationship between Jews and Christians* (London: SCM Press, 1990).

14. On different images of God and the question of forgiveness see Braybrooke, pp. 106–13. See also the Jewish theologian Marc Ellis, *Towards a Jewish Theology of Liberation* (London/New York, 1987), pp.75–8.

15. On the autobiography see 'Reminiscences' Chapter 4, no. 47, in Joseph Munitiz and Philip Endean (eds.), *St Ignatius of Loyola: Personal Writings* (London: Penguin Classics, 1996). The Spanish is from the so-called Autograph version of the text, section 47 in the standard numeration. See José Calveras and Candido Dalmases (eds.), *Exercitia Spiritualis* in *Monumenta Historica Societatis Jesu*, volume 100, new edition, Rome 1969. A modern English reading is in Munitiz and Endean.

16. See John Wilkinson (tr.), *Egeria's Travels* (London: SPCK, 1971), 20,6.

17. See Life of Daniel, 7, in E. Davies and N. Baynes, *Three Byzantine Saints* (London, 1948); and Peter Brown, *The Making of Late*

Antiquity (Cambridge, Mass: Harvard University Press, new edition 1993), pp. 13–14.

18. 2nd Epistle, especially 7–15, PG 46 1013B, cited in Coleman and Elsner, *Pilgrimage*, pp. 80–1. For Gregory's apophatic perspective on place, see Jaroslav Pelikan, *Christianity and Classical Culture* (New Haven: Yale University Press, 1993), p. 113.

19. See Benedicta Ward (ed.), *The Wisdom of the Desert Fathers* (Oxford: SLG Press, 1986), nos. 72, 70 and 68.

20. Kenneth H. Jackson, *A Celtic Miscellany* (London: Penguin Books, 1971), no. 121, p. 136.

21. Cited Aron Gurevich, *Medieval Popular Culture* (Cambridge: Cambridge University Press, 1990), pp. 40–2.

22. See, for example, Coleman and Elsner, pp. 126–8.

23. See for example the essays in the recently published David Brown and Ann Loades (eds.), *The Sense of the Sacramental: Movement and Measure, Art and Music, Place and Time* (London: SPCK, 1995), Part One 'Sacred Space'.

24. Rudolph Bultmann, *Jesus Christ and Mythology* (New York: Scribner, 1958), pp. 84–5.

25. Rowan Williams, 'Sacraments of the New Society' in David Brown and Ann Loades (eds.), *Christ: The Sacramental Word* (London: SPCK, 1996), pp. 89–90.

26. Michel de Certeau, *The Mystic Fable*, ET (Chicago: The University of Chicago Press, 1992), pp. 101–12, especially 104.

27. See the contrasting essays by Dr Susan White and Archbishop Habgood in Brown and Loades (eds.), *The Sense of the Sacramental*, pp. 31–43 and 19–30 respectively. White's ethical approach needs to be balanced by Habgood's more markedly sacramental understanding of the whole of the natural world.

28. All references to Traherne are from his *Centuries* (London: Mowbray, 1975). In this case, The First Century, no. 41.

29. Berry, 'Introduction' in Berry and Wernick (eds.), *Shadow of Spirit: Postmodernism and Religion* (London: Routledge, 1992), pp. 1–2.

30. Anne Buttimer, 'Home, Reach and the Sense of Place' in Anne Buttimer and David Seamon (eds.), *The Human Experience of Space and Place* (London: Croam Helm, 1980), p. 174.

31. See Michael Northcott, 'A Place of Our Own?' in Peter Sedgwick (ed.), *God in the City: Essays and Reflections from the Archbishop of*

Canterbury's Urban Theology Group (London, 1995), pp. 119–38, especially p. 122.

32. Berleant, pp. 86–7.

33. On the development of medieval cities see Jacques Le Goff, *Medieval Civilisation*, ET (Oxford: Blackwell, 1988), pp. 70–8. On the city as sacred, see Peter Raedts, 'The medieval city as a holy place' in Charles Caspers and Marc Schneiders (eds.), *Omnes Circumadstantes: Contributions towards a history of the role of the people in the liturgy* (Kampen: Uitgeversmaatschappij J.H.Kok, 1990), pp. 144–54.

34. Michael Novak, *The Spirit of Democratic Capitalism* (London: IEA Health and Welfare Unit, 1991). See also the devastating critique of Novak by Lash, *The Beginning and The End of Religion*, pp. 187 and 191–4.

35. John Milbank, *Theology and Social Theory: Beyond Secular Reason* (Oxford: Blackwell, 1990), pp. 380–438. For a critique see Gillian Rose, 'Diremption of Spirit' in Berry and Wernick, p. 48.

36. See John S. Dunne, *The City of the Gods: A Study in Myth and Mortality* (London: Sheldon Press, 1974), Chapter 7, 'The City of God'. For a sharp critique of the legacy of Augustine, see Richard Sennett, *The Conscience of the Eye: The Design and Social Life of Cities* (London: Faber, 1993), pp. 41–2 but also pp. xii–xiii, 5–10. Sennett is an urban historian and blames what he calls an Augustinian-Protestant 'ethic of space' for the design of much modern public space as neutral and sterile.

37. This is the emphasis of Augustine's commentary on Genesis and is cited in Robert Markus, *The End of Ancient Christianity* (Cambridge: Cambridge University Press, 1990), p. 78.

38. See Berleant, pp. 74–6 and 90–1.

39. See Donlyn Lyndon and Charles W. Moore, *Chambers for a Memory Palace* (Cambridge, Mass.: The MIT Press, 1994), p. xii. The book has many stimulating thoughts about place throughout.

Conclusion

1. A recent article by L. Gregory Jones critically analyzes the contemporary spiritual quest and compares popular spirituality unfavourably with what the Christian spiritual traditions have to offer. See 'A Thirst for God or Consumer Spirituality? Culturally-

Disciplined Practices of Being Engaged by God' in *Modern Theology*, 13/1, January 1997, pp. 3–28.

2. Phyllis Tickle, *Rediscovering the Sacred: Spirituality in America* (New York: Crossroad, 1995), p. 118.

Bibliography

Anselm of Canterbury, *The Prayers and Meditations of St* Anselm, ed. Benedicta Ward (London: Penguin Books, 1973).

Ashley, Matthew, 'The Turn to Spirituality? The Relationship Between Theology and Spirituality' in *Christian Spirituality Bulletin*, 3/2 (Fall 1995).

Astell, Ann W., *Divine Representations: Postmodernism and Spirituality* (New York: Paulist Press, 1994).
 'Postmodern Christian Spirituality: A *Coincidentia Oppositorum*?' in *Christian Spirituality Bulletin*, 4/1 (Summer 1996).

Augustine of Hippo, *De Trinitate* in *Corpus Christianorum, Series Latina*, L (Turnholt: Brepols, 1968) and English translation in Philip Schaff (ed.), *The Nicene and Post-Nicene Fathers*, First Series, vol. III (Edinburgh: T & T Clark, 1993).

Baker, Denise Nowakowski, *Julian of Norwich's Sayings: From Vision to Book* (Princeton: Princeton University Press, 1994).

von Balthasar, Hans Urs, *Word and Redemption: Essays in Theology* (New York, 1965).
 The Glory of the Lord, multiple volumes (Edinburgh: T & T Clark, 1982–92).

Barnes, Michael (ed.), *Spirituality, Imagination and Contemporary Literature, The Way Supplement*, 81 (Autumn 1994).
 Spirituality and Ethics, The Way Supplement, 88 (Spring 1997).

Barnes, Michel René, 'Augustine in Contemporary Trinitarian Theology' in *Theological Studies*, 56 (1995).

Baum, Gregory, *Essays in Critical Theology* (Kansas City: Sheed & Ward, 1994).

Benson, Robert, Constable, Giles and Lanham, Carol (eds.), *Renaissance and Renewal in the Twelfth Century* (Toronto, 1991 edition).

228

Bibliography

Berleant, Arnold, *The Aesthetics of Environment* (Philadelphia: Temple University Press, 1992).

Berry, Philippa and Wernick, Andrew (eds.), *Shadow of Spirit: Postmodernism and Religion* (London: Routledge, 1992).

Boff, Leonardo, *Trinity and Society* (New York: Orbis, 1982).

Bonsor, Jack, 'History, Dogma and Nature: Further Reflections on Postmodernism and Theology' in *Theological Studies*, 55/2 (June 1994).

Bouyer, Louis, *An Introduction to Spirituality* (New York, 1961). *A History of Christian Spirituality*, three volumes (London: Burns & Oates, 1982).

Bradley, Ritamary, *Julian's Way* (London: HarperCollins, 1992).

Brady, Veronica, 'Postmodernism and The Spiritual Life' in *The Way*, 36/3 (July 1996).

Braybrooke, Marcus, *Time to Meet: Towards a Deeper Relationship between Jews and Christians* (London: SCM Press, 1990).

Brown, David and Loades, Ann (eds.), *The Sense of the Sacramental: Movement and Measure, Art and Music, Place and Time* (London: SPCK, 1995).
Christ the Sacramental Word (London: SPCK, 1996).

Brown, Peter, *The Making of Late Antiquity* (Cambridge, Mass: Harvard University Press, 1993).

Brueggemann, Walter, *The Land: Place as Gift, Promise and Challenge in Biblical Faith* (Philadelphia: Fortress Press, 1977).

Bultmann, Rudolph, *Jesus Christ and Mythology* (New York: Scribner, 1958).

Buttimer, Anne and Seamon, David (eds.), *The Human Experience of Space and Place* (London: Croam Helm, 1980).

Bynum, Caroline Walker, *Jesus as Mother: Studies in the Spirituality of the High Middle Ages* (Berkeley: University of California Press, 1982).
Holy Feast and Holy Fast: The Religious Significance of Food to Medieval Women (Berkeley: University of California Press, 1987).

Byrne, Peter and Houlden, Leslie (eds.), *Companion Encyclopedia of Theology* (London: Routledge, 1995).

Carmichael, David L., Hubert, Jane, Reeves, Brian and Schanche, Audhild (eds.), *Sacred Sites, Sacred Places* (London: Routledge, 1994).

Carozza, Carlo, 'Mysticism and the Crisis of Religious Institutions' in *Concilium* 1994/4.

Bibliography

Carr, Anne E., *Transforming Grace: Christian Tradition and Women's Experience* (San Francisco: Harper, 1990).

Caspers, Charles and Schneiders, Marc (eds.), *Omnes Circumadstantes: Contributions towards the History of the Role of People in the Liturgy* (Kampen: Uitgeversmaatschappij J.H. Kok, 1990).

de Certeau, Michel, *Jean-Joseph Surin: Correspondence* (Paris: Desclee, 1963).

    Jean-Joseph Surin: Guide Spirituel Pour La Perfection (Paris: Desclee, 1963).

    The Mystic Fable (Chicago: University of Chicago Press, 1992).

    'Culture and Spiritual Experience' in *Concilium*, 19, 1966.

Charlesworth, Max, 'Postmodernism and Theology' in *The Way*, 36/3 (July 1996).

Clements, Arthur, *Poetry of Contemplation* (New York: State University of New York Press, 1990).

Clifford, Anne M., 'Re-membering the Spiritual Core of Theology: A Response' in *Christian Spirituality Bulletin*, 3/2 (Fall 1995).

Cloud of Unknowing, The, ed. James Walsh (New York: Paulist Press, 1981).

Coleman, Simon and Elsner, John, *Pilgrimage: Past and Present in the World Religions* (London: British Museum Press, 1995).

Cunningham, David S., 'Trinitarian Theology since 1990' in *Reviews in Religion and Theology*, 1995.

Cupitt, Don, *Taking Leave of God* (London, 1980).

Davies, E. and Bayne, N., *Three Byzantine Saints* (London, 1948).

Dionysius, *Pseudo-Dionysius: The Complete Works*, ed. Colm Luibheid and Paul Rorem (New York: Paulist Press, 1987).

Donne, John, *Devotions Upon Emergent Occasions*, ed. Anthony Raspa (Oxford: Oxford University Press, 1987).

Dreyer, Elizabeth, 'The Trinitarian Theology of Julian of Norwich' in *Studies in Spirituality*, 4 (1994).

Dunne, John S., *The City of the Gods: A Study in Myth and Mortality* (London: Sheldon Press, 1974).

Dupré, Louis and Saliers, Don (eds.), *Christian Spirituality: Post-Reformation and Modern* (New York: Crossroad/London: SCM Press, 1990).

Eade, John and Sallnow, Michael (eds.), *Contesting the Sacred: The Anthropology of Christian Pilgrimage* (London: Routledge, 1990).

Bibliography

Eckhart, Meister, *Meister Eckhart: The Essential Sermons*, ed. E. Colledge and B. McGinn (New York: Paulist Press, 1981).

Egan, Keith, 'The Divorce of Spirituality from Theology' in P. Carey and E. Muller (eds.), *Theological Education in the Catholic Tradition* (New York: Crossroad, 1997).

Eliade, Mircea, *Patterns in Comparative Religion* (New York: World Publishing, 1963).

Endean, Philip, 'Theology out of Spirituality: The Approach of Karl Rahner' in *Christian Spirituality Bulletin*, 3/2 (Fall 1995).

Fuller, Peter, *Theoria: Art and The Absence of Grace* (London, 1988).

Garrigou-Lagrange, R., *Christian Perfection and Contemplation* (St Louis: Desclee, 1937).

Gill, Robin (ed.), *Readings in Modern Theology* (London, 1995).

Glasscoe, Marion (ed.), *The Medieval Mystical Tradition in England* (Woodbridge: Boydell and Brewer, 1987).

Gregory of Nyssa, *Gregory of Nyssa; The Life of Moses*, ed. Everett Ferguson and Abraham J. Malherbe (New York: Paulist Press, 1978).

Guarino, Thomas, 'Between Foundations and Nihilism: Is *Phronesis* the *Via Media* for Theology?' in *Theological Studies*, 54/1 (March 1993).

Guigo II, *The Ladder of Monks* (Kalamazoo: Cistercian Publications, 1981).

Gunton, Colin, *The Promise of Trinitarian Theology* (Edinburgh: T & T Clark, 1990).

Gurevich, Aron, *Medieval Popular Culture* (Cambridge: Cambridge University Press, 1990).

Gutiérrez, Gustavo, *We Drink from Our Own Wells: The Spiritual Journey of a People* (London: SCM Press, 1984).

Hanson, Bradley (ed.), *Modern Christian Spirituality: Methodological and Historical Essays* (Atlanta: Scholars Press, 1990).

'Theological Approaches to Spirituality: A Lutheran Perspective' in *Christian Spirituality Bulletin*, 2/1 (Spring 1994).

Hardwick, Peter, 'The Inward Struggle of the Self with God: Gerard Manley Hopkins and George Herbert' in *The Way Supplement*, 66 (Autumn 1989).

Hardy, Daniel and Ford, David, *Jubilate: Theology in Praise* (London: Darton, Longman & Todd, 1984).

Harton, F.P., *The Elements of the Spiritual Life* (London: SPCK, 1932).

Heidegger, Martin, *Poetry, Language, Thought* (New York: Harper & Row, 1975).

231

Bibliography

Heimmel, Jennifer P., *'God is Our Mother': Julian of Norwich and The Medieval Image of Christian Feminine Divinity* (Salzburg: Instituut für Anglistik und Amerikanistik, 1982).

Herbert, George, *George Herbert: The Country Parson, The Temple*, ed. John Wall (New York: Paulist Press, 1981).

George Herbert and Henry Vaughan, ed. Louis Martz (Oxford: Oxford University Press, 1986).

Heschel, Abraham, *Man's Quest for God* (New York, 1954).

Ignatius of Loyola, *Exercitia Spiritualis*, ed. José Calveras and Candido Dalmases (Rome: Institutum Historicum Societatis Jesu, 1969).

St Ignatius of Loyola: Personal Writings, ed. Joseph Munitiz and Philip Endean (London: Penguin Classics, 1996).

The Spiritual Exercises of St Ignatius, ed. George Ganss (Chicago: Loyola University Press, 1992).

Innes-Parker, Catherine, 'Subversion and Conformity in Julian's *Revelation*: Authority, Vision and the Motherhood of God' in *Mystics Quarterly*, XXIII/2 (March 1997).

Jackson, Kenneth (ed.), *A Celtic Miscellany* (London: Penguin Books, 1971).

Jantzen, Grace, *Julian of Norwich* (London: SPCK, 1987).

John of the Cross, *The Collected Works of St John of the Cross*, ed. Kieran Kavanaugh and Otilio Rodriquez (Washington, DC: Institute of Carmelite Studies, 1979).

Johnson, Elisabeth, *She Who Is: The Mystery of God in Feminist Theological Discourse* (New York: Crossroad, 1996).

Jones, Alan, 'Spirituality and Theology' in *Review for Religious*, 39/2 (March 1980).

Jones, Gareth, *Critical Theology: Questions of Truth and Method* (Cambridge: Polity Press, 1995).

Jones, L. Gregory, 'A Thirst for God or Consumer Spirituality? Culturally-Disciplined Practices of Being Engaged by God' in *Modern Theology*, 13/1 (January 1997).

Julian of Norwich, *Julian of Norwich: Showings*, ed. E. Colledge and J. Walsh (New York: Paulist Press, 1978).

A Book of Showings to the Anchoress Julian of Norwich, 2 volumes, ed. E. Colledge and J. Walsh (Toronto: Pontifical Institute of Medieval Studies, 1978).

A Revelation of Love, ed. Marion Glasscoe (Exeter: Exeter University Press, 1989).

Kelly, Kevin, *New Directions in Moral Theology: The Challenge of Being Human* (London: Geoffrey Chapman, 1992).

Kinerk, Edward, 'Towards a Method for the Study of Spirituality' in *Review for Religious*, 40/1 (1981).

LaCugna, Catherine, *God For Us: The Trinity and Christian Life* (San Francisco: HarperCollins, 1993).

(ed.), *Freeing Theology: The Essentials of Theology in Feminist Perspective* (San Francisco: Harper, 1993).

'Trinitarian Spirituality' in Michael Downey (ed.), *New Dictionary of Catholic Spirituality* (Collegeville: The Liturgical Press, 1993).

Lakeland, Paul, *Postmodernity: Christian Identity in a Fragmented Age* (Minneapolis: Fortress Press, 1997).

Lane, Belden, *Landscapes of the Sacred: Geography and Narrative in American Spirituality* (New York: Paulist Press, 1989).

'Landscape and Spirituality: A Tension between Place and Placelessness in Christian Thought' in *The Way Supplement* 73 (Spring 1992).

'Galesburg and Sinai: The Researcher as Participant in the Study of Spirituality and Sacred Space' in *Christian Spirituality Bulletin*, 2/1 (Spring 1994).

Lane, Dermot, *The Experience of God* (Dublin: Veritas, 1985).

Lash, Nicholas, *Believing Three Ways in One God* (London: SCM Press, 1992).

The Beginning and The End of Religion (Cambridge: Cambridge University Press, 1996).

Leclercq, Jean, *The Love of Learning and Desire for God* (London: SPCK, 1978).

Leech, Kenneth, *True God* (London: SPCK, 1985).

Le Goff, Jacques, *Medieval Civilisation* (Oxford: Blackwell, 1988).

Intellectuals in the Middle Ages (Oxford: Oxford University Press, 1993).

Lerner, Robert, *The Heresy of the Free Spirit in the Later Middle Ages* (Berkeley: University of California Press, 1972).

Lewalski, Barbara, *Protestant Poetics and the Seventeenth-Century Religious Lyric* (Princeton: Princeton University Press, 1979).

Lindbeck, George, *The Nature of Doctrine: Religion and Theology in a Postliberal Age* (London: SPCK, 1984).

Lonergan, Bernard, *Method in Theology* (London: Darton, Longman and Todd, 1972).

Bibliography

Lossky, Vladimir, *The Mystical Tradition of the Eastern Church* (London, 1973).

Louth, Andrew, *Theology and Spirituality* (Oxford: SLG Press, 1976).

The Origins of the Christian Mystical Tradition from Plato to Denys (Oxford: Oxford University Press, 1981.

Discerning the Mystery: An Essay on the Nature of Theology (Oxford: Oxford University Press, 1983).

Denys the Areopagite (London: Geoffrey Chapman, 1989).

de Lubac, Henri, *Exégèse Médiévale: Les Quatres Sens de L'écriture*, four volumes (Paris: Aubier, 1959–63).

Lyndon, Donlyn and Moore, Charles W., *Chambers for a Memory Palace* (Cambridge, Mass: The MIT Press, 1994).

Lyotard, Jean-François, *The Postmodern Condition: A Report on Knowledge* (Minneapolis: University of Minnesota Press, 1984).

The Postmodern Explained (Minneapolis: University of Minnesota Press, 1993).

Macquarrie, John, *Paths in Spirituality* (London: SCM Press, Revised Edition, 1992).

Marion, Jean-Luc, *God Without Being* (Chicago: The University of Chicago Press, 1995).

Markus, Robert, *The End of Ancient Christianity* (Cambridge: Cambridge University Press, 1990).

Martz, Louis, *The Poetry of Meditation: A Study of English Religious Literature of the Seventeenth Century* (New Haven: Yale University Press, 1954).

McGinn, Bernard, 'The Letter and The Spirit: Spirituality as an Academic Discipline' in *Christian Spirituality Bulletin*, 1/2 (Fall 1993).

McGinn, Bernard, Meyendorff, John, Leclercq, Jean (eds.), *Christian Spirituality: Origins to the Twelfth Century* (New York: Crossroad, 1986).

McIntosh, Mark, 'Lover Without a Name: Spirituality and Constructive Christology Today' in *Christian Spirituality Bulletin*, 3/2 (Fall 1995).

Megyer, Eugene, 'Spiritual Theology Today' in *The Way*, 21/1 (January 1981).

Merton, Thomas, *Sign of Jonas* (New York: Doubleday, 1953).

Meyendorff, John, *Byzantine Theology* (New York: St Vladimir's Seminary Press, 1974).

Milbank, John, *Theology and Social Theory: Beyond Secular Reason* (Oxford: Blackwell, 1990).

Bibliography

Moltmann, Jürgen, *The Crucified God: The Cross of Christ as the Foundation and Criticism of Christian Theology* (London: SCM Press, 1974). *Experiences of God* (London: SCM Press, 1980). *History and the Triune God: Contributions to Trinitarian Theology* (London: SCM Press, 1992).

'Teresa of Avila and Martin Luther: the turn to the mysticism of the Cross' in *Studies in Religion*, 13, 1984.

Mursell, Gordon, 'Traditions of Spiritual Guidance: The Book of Common Prayer' in *The Way*, 31/2 (April 1991).

Nicholas of Cusa, *Nicholas of Cusa: Selected Spiritual Writings*, ed. Lawrence Bond (New York: Paulist Press, 1997).

Niebuhr, H. Richard, *Christ and Culture* (New York: Harper & Row, 1975).

Norris, Kathleen, *Dakota: A Spiritual Geography* (New York: Houghton Mifflin, 1993).

Novak, Michael, *The Spirit of Democratic Capitalism* (London: IEA Health and Welfare Unity, 1991).

Nuth, Joan, *Wisdom's Daughter: The Theology of Julian of Norwich* (New York: Crossroad, 1991).

O'Malley, John, *The First Jesuits* (Cambridge, Mass: Harvard University Press, 1993).

O'Reilly, Terence, 'The Spiritual Exercises and the Crisis of Medieval Piety' in *The Way Supplement*, 70 (Spring 1991).

Palliser, Margaret Ann, *Christ our Mother of Mercy: Divine Mercy and Compassion in the Theology of the Showings of Julian of Norwich* (Berlin: de Gruyter, 1992).

Pannenberg, Wolfhart, *Christian Spirituality and Sacramental Community* (London: Darton, Longman & Todd, 1983).

Pannikar, Raimundo, *Myth, Faith and Hermeneutics* (New York: Paulist Press, 1979).

Patrick, Anne E., *Liberating Conscience: Feminist Explorations in Catholic Moral Theology* (New York: Continuum, 1996).

'Ethics and Spirituality: The Social Justice Dimension' in *The Way Supplement*, 63 (Autumn 1988).

Pelikan, Jaroslav, *Christianity and Classical Culture* (New Haven: Yale University Press, 1993).

Pelphrey, Brant, *Christ our Mother: Julian of Norwich* (Wilmington, Michael Glazier, 1989).

Bibliography

Love was His Meaning: The Theology and Mysticism of Julian of Norwich (Salzburg: Instituut für Anglistik und Amerikanistik, 1982).

Peters, William, *The Spiritual Exercises of St Ignatius: Exposition and Interpretation* (Jersey City: PASE, 1968).

Pinsent, Pat, 'The Image of Christ in the Writings of Two Seventeenth-Century English Country Parsons: George Herbert and Thomas Traherne' in Stanley Porter, Michael Hayes and David Toombs (eds.), *Images of Christ Ancient and Modern* (Sheffield: Sheffield Academic Press, 1997).

Pourrat, Pierre, *Christian Spirituality*, volume 1 (London: Burns & Oates, 1922).

Principe, Walter, 'Towards Defining Spirituality' in *Sciences Religieuses*, 12/2 (1983).

'Pluralism in Christian Spirituality' in *The Way*, January 1992.

Rahner, Hugo, *Ignatius the Theologian* (London: Geoffrey Chapman, 1990).

Rahner, Karl, *Theological Investigations* volume 5 (London: Darton, Longman & Todd, 1966).

The Trinity (London: Burns & Oates, 1970).

The Practice of Faith: A Handbook of Contemporary Spirituality, ed. K. Lehmann and A. Raffelt (New York: Crossroad, 1984).

Raitt, Jill (ed.), *Christian Spirituality: High Middle Ages and Reformation* (London: Routledge/New York: Crossroads, 1987).

Richard of St Victor, *Richard of St Victor*, ed. Grover Zinn (New York: Paulist Press, 1979).

Riches, John, *Jesus and the Transformation of Judaism* (London: Darton, Longman & Todd, 1980).

Rosenblatt, Marie-Eloise, 'Women and the Exercises: Sin, Standards and New Testament Texts' in *The Way Supplement*, 70 (Spring 1991).

Ruud, Jay, 'Nature and Grace in Julian of Norwich' in *Mystics Quarterly*, XIX/2 (June 1993).

Ruusbroec, John, *John Ruusbroec: The Spiritual Espousals and Other Works*, ed. James Wiseman (New York: Paulist Press, 1985).

Saliba, John, 'A Christian Response to the New Age' in *The Way*, 33/3 (July 1993).

Sanders, E. P., *Paul and Palestinian Judaism* (London: SCM Press, 1977).

Jesus and Judaism (London: SCM Press, 1985).

Savage, Anne and Watson, Nicholas (eds.), *Anchoritic Spirituality* (New York: Paulist Press, 1991).

Bibliography

Schama, Simon, *Landscape and Memory* (London: HarperCollins, 1995).

Schneiders, Sandra, 'Theology and Spirituality: Strangers, Rivals or Partners?' in *Horizons*, 13 (1986).

'Spirituality in the Academy' in *Theological Studies*, 50 (1989).

'Spirituality as an Academic Discipline: Reflections from Experience' in *Christianity Spirituality Bulletin*, 1/2 (Fall 1993).

'A Hermeneutical Approach to the Study of Christian Spirituality' in *Christian Spirituality Bulletin*, 2/1 (Spring 1994).

Schner, George (ed.), *Ignatian Spirituality in a Secular Age* (Waterloo, Ontario: Wilfred Laurier University Press), 1984.

Schwöbel, Christoph (ed.), *Trinitarian Theology Today* (Edinburgh: T & T Clark, 1995).

Scott, Jamie and Simpson-Housley, Paul (eds.), *Sacred Place and Profane Spaces: Essays in the Geographics of Judaism, Christianity and Islam* (Westport CT: Greenwood, 1991).

Sedgwick, Peter (ed.), *God in the City: Essays and Reflections from the Archbishop of Canterbury's Urban Theology Group* (London: Mowbray, 1995).

Segundo, Juan Luis, *The Christ of the Ignatian Exercises* (New York: Orbis, 1987).

Senn, Frank C. (ed.), *Protestant Spiritual Traditions* (New York: Paulist Press, 1986).

Sennett, Richard, *The Conscience of the Eye: The Design and Social Life of Cities* (London: Faber, 1993).

Sheldrake, Philip, *Spirituality and History: Questions of Interpretation and Method* (London: SPCK, Revised Edition, 1996).

(ed.), *Spirituality and Psychology, The Way Supplement*, 69 (Autumn 1990).

(ed.) *The Way of Ignatius Loyola: Contemporary Approaches to the Spiritual Exercises* (London: SPCK, 1991).

'The Influence of the Ignatian Tradition' in *The Way Supplement*, 68 (Summer 1990).

Sobrino, Jon, *Christology at the Crossroads* (London: SCM Press, 1978).

Steggink, Otto, 'Study in Spirituality in Retrospect' in *Studies in Spirituality*, 1, 1991.

Stewart, Columba, 'Asceticism and Spirituality in Late Antiquity: New Vision, Impasse or Hiatus?' in *Christian Spirituality Bulletin*, 4/1 (Summer 1996).

Bibliography

Strier, Richard, *Love Known: Theology and Experience in George Herbert's Poetry* (Chicago: University of Chicago Press, 1983).

Sykes, Stephen and Booty, John (eds.), *The Study of Anglicanism* (London: SPCK, 1988).

Tanquerey, A.A., *The Spiritual Life* (Tournai: Desclee, 1930).

Tickle, Phyllis, *Rediscovering the Sacred: Spirituality in America* (New York: Crossroad, 1995).

Thomas, R.S., *Later Poems* (London: Macmillan, 1983).

Toolan, David, *Facing West from California's Shores: A Jesuit's Journey into New Age Consciousness* (New York, 1987).

Tracy, David, *Blessed Rage for Order* (New York: Seabury Press, 1975). *The Analogical Imagination: Christian Theology and The Culture of Pluralism* (New York: Crossroad, 1991).

On Naming The Present: God, Hermeneutics and Church (New York: Orbis Books, 1994).

Traherne,Thomas, *Centuries* (London: Mowbray, 1975).

Turner, Denys, *The Darkness of God: Negativity in Christian Mysticism* (Cambridge: Cambridge University Press, 1995).

Turner, Victor and Edith, *Image and Pilgrimage in Christian Culture* (New York: Columbia University Press, 1978).

Tuve, Rosemond, *A Reading of George Herbert* (Chicago: University of Chicago Press, 1952).

Van Ness, Peter, 'Spirituality and Secularity' in *The Way Supplement,* 73 (Spring 1992).

Veale, Joseph, 'The Dynamic of the Spiritual Exercises' in *The Way Supplement,* 52 (Spring 1985).

Veith, Gene, *Reformation Spirituality: The Religion of George Herbert* (London: Associated University Presses, 1985).

Waaijman, Kees, 'Toward a Phenomenological Definition of Spirituality' in *Studies in Spirituality,* 3 (1993).

Walton, Isaak, *Lives* (Oxford: Oxford University Press, 1927).

Ward, Benedicta (ed.), *The Wisdom of the Desert Fathers* (Oxford: SLG Press, 1986).

Ward, Keith, *Holding Fast to God* (London, 1982).

Watson, Nicholas, 'The Composition of Julian of Norwich's *Revelations of Love*' in *Speculum* 68 (1993).

Wilkinson, John (ed.), *Egeria's Travels* (London: SPCK, 1971).

Williams, Rowan, *Resurrection* (London: Darton, Longman & Todd, 1982).

Bibliography

The Wound of Knowledge: Christian Spirituality from the New Testament to St John of the Cross (London: Darton Longman & Todd, Revised Edition, 1990).

Teresa of Avila (London: Geoffrey Chapman, 1991).

'The Via Negativa and The Foundations of Theology: An Introduction to the Thought of V. N. Lossky' in Stephen Sykes and Derek Holmes (eds.), *New Studies in Theology* (1, London, 1980). 'Trinity and Revelation' in *Modern Theology*, 1986.

Wilson, Christopher, *The Gothic Cathedral* (London: Thames and Hudson, 1990).

Windeatt, B. A. (ed.), *The Book of Margery Kempe* (London: Penguin Books, 1985).

Woods, Richard (ed.), *Understanding Mysticism* (London: The Athlone Press, 1981).

'What is New Age Spirituality?' in *The Way*, 33/3 (July 1993).

Wyschogrod, Edith, *Spirit in Ashes: Hegel, Heidegger and Man-Made Mass Death* (New Haven: Yale University Press, 1985).

Saints and Postmodernism (Chicago: University of Chicago Press, 1990).

Zizioulas, John, *Being as Communion* (New York: St Vladimir's Seminary Press, 1985).

NAME AND SUBJECT INDEX

∞∞∞∞∞∞∞

The subject indexing is necessarily selective. Several terms referred to pervasively in the text are only indexed where there is significant direct discussion.

241

Name and Subject Index

Protestant tradition 44, 45, 46, 69ff., 87, 146, 149, 150

Rahner, Hugo 140
Rahner, Karl xiv, 30, 66, 67f., 69, 75f., 93, 95, 140f.
rationalism 4, 9, 39, 55
redemption *see* salvation
Reformation xv, 20, 40, 46, 71, 75, 129, 130, 149, 196
relationality *see* Trinity
Renaissance 196
of twelfth century 41
resurrection 134, 139
revelation 35, 49, 54, 69, 76, 81, 107, 169, 177, 186
Richard of St Victor 41, 50f., 214
Rolle, Richard 104
Roman Catholic tradition 44ff., 52, 53ff., 129, 180, 183
Roman Empire 180
Rome 150, 182
Rupert of Deutz 169
Ruusbroec, John 51f.

sacramentality 184
sacraments 183, 195
sacred-secular division 5, 12, 20, 68, 168
Salamanca 132
Sales, Francis de 44
salvation 13, 16, 46, 48, 49, 75, 76, 90f., 110f., 126, 136, 174
Schillebeeckx, Edward 134
Schneiders, Sandra 19, 84
science 7, 45, 63, 95
scripture, senses of 38
Second Vatican Council 53, 54, 55

Segundo, Juan Luis 145
Simeon Stylites 179f.
sin 50, 101, 111, 124f., 133f., 160, 174
Spain 132, 142
Spirit, Holy 4, 18, 25, 35, 50, 51, 57, 61, 83, 90, 91, 93, 110, 113f., 152
spirituality
Christocentric 91
definitions of 33ff., 58
English 63
evaluating theology xi, 15, 65, 93–5
privatization of 6
and anthropology 57, 59, 91
and buildings 165, 170, 181, 194
and context 59f., 63
and ethics 38, 43, 46, 47, 56, 57f., 184
and history 17, 33, 36–47, 54, 59, 63, 85
and literature 63
and method 33, 35
and New Age 90
and postmodernism 9, 10–14, 26f., 62, 100, 198
and psychology 33, 63f.
and science 58, 63, 95
and texts 53, 88
as academic subject 23, 33, 62, 84
as interdisciplinary 33f., 62–6, 84, 94
spiritual direction 41
spiritual theology 38, 41, 45, 46, 53ff., 60, 68, 72, 85, 87
stability, virtue of 122–3